The A–Z
of World Boxing

The A–Z
of World Boxing

An Authoritative and Entertaining Compendium of
the Fight Game from its Origins to the Present Day

Bert Blewett

with a Foreword by
Reg Gutteridge

This edition published in 2000 in Great Britain by
Greenwich Editions, 10 Blenheim Court, Brewery Road, London N7 9NT

A member of the Chrysalis Group plc

Book design by Harold King

British Library Cataloguing in Publication Data
A catalogue record for this title is available from the British Library

ISBN 0-86288-284-2

Printed in Great Britain by St Edmundsbury Press
Bury St Edmunds, Suffolk.

FOREWORD
by Reg Gutteridge

Having been reared on rubbing oils from a family always involved in boxing, which I prefer to call the fight game, I have read, or at least scanned, many tomes – but rarely have I been entranced by such an encyclopaedic book.

This is the work of a devotee who knows what he's looking at when reporting boxing and embraces the world scene. I could never attempt to produce such a soundly researched edition. I find it fascinating and easy-to-refer to with its alphabetic listing. Apart from profiles of the famous, which have been a regular feature of fistic literature, there is enlightening up-to-date information on topics ranging from age, accessories and announcers to commentators, champs, some chumps, rules, television and radio.

It's more than a reference book, it's a work of art from a respected writer and broadcaster who cares about the game.

Nice one, Bert.

Reg Gutteridge

Roy Gumbs, the former British and Commonwealth middleweight champion, with some of the essential accessories used in modern boxing.

ACCESSORIES

The most important accessory in boxing is arguably the glove. Once called mufflers, gloves have played a major role in making boxing acceptable as a sport. The development of the glove from skin-tight mitts to the state-of-the-art hand covering used today has influenced not only the style of fighting, but also the rules and regulations that govern the sport.

Other accessories, which were unheard of in the early days of fist-fighting, have since flooded the market. These include rubber-soled boxing boots, protective cups that originated in the United States in the 1930s, mouthguards that are now considered so important as a safety device that fights are often stopped if they are dislodged, and headguards that have since become mandatory in amateur boxing.

Meanwhile bag punching has literally become an art in itself. The heavy bag that John L Sullivan used before the turn of the century now looks puny in comparison with its modern counterpart. Sullivan, the last bareknuckle heavyweight champion of the world, invariably used a heavy canvas bag, filled with sand and sawdust, that was shaped like a pear.

The bag was invented by William Muldoon and was first used by Sullivan at his Purchase, New York, training camp while he was conditioning himself for his bareknuckle fight with Jake Kilrain in 1889. The bag weighed about 30 pounds.

The so-called 'bounding punch bag' came into use just before Sullivan defended his heavyweight title against Jim Corbett in 1892, but there is no record of John L having availed himself of the then comparatively new invention. Corbett, on the other hand, took to the new punch bag like a fish to water.

Bob Fitzsimmons, who succeeded Corbett as world champion in 1897, made bag punching a part of his stage act while on tour in the United States. In appearance Fitz's bag resembled that used by Corbett, except that it was much heavier. It was made of tough calf-skin and was rounder at the bottom.

In any event, when Fitzsimmons completed his stage act one night in Chicago by giving the bag a hard thump, it sped across the footlights and hit a woman spectator in the face. The woman was knocked out of her seat by the impact, and her husband threatened a lawsuit against both the owner of the theatre and the champion. The matter was settled out of court but from then on Fitzsimmons was more careful how he struck the bag in his exhibitions.

Bag manufacturers, by and large, have kept abreast of all the other advances made in the sport. In the 1980s, an American company called Sabba Incorporated developed a heavy bag that measured the impact of a punch in pounds per square foot, and a punch pad that gave the velocity of a blow in miles per hour.

In the 1990s, the Ultimate Body Bag came on the market. Manufactured in Minnesota in the United States the bag was made of tear- and water-resistant nylon cordura and 'built to last a lifetime'. Designed especially for developing the 'lost art' of body punching, the bag had twice the surface of a conventional heavy bag and two boxers could work out on it at the same time.

Later a free-standing and portable heavy bag was offered for sale that not only could be adjusted for height, but which could bend at the same point as a boxer's waist.

Such innovations have long been a part of the boxing accessory business. In the early 1940s, for example, an American company marketed boxing boots that supposedly enabled boxers to stand taller. Called 'Boxeraid Shoes', the boots were made of fine leather and, according to the money-back guarantee, increased the boxer's height by one and a quarter inches.

Ben Nadorf, the then president of the boxing equipment company, Everlast, told me in 1984 that fight fans would be surprised at some of the unusual requests his company received for equipment. Nadorf chuckled when he recalled a special request his company once received for an extra-large protective cup.

'Apparently this boy's "family jewels" must have been exceptional because his college coach pleaded with us to make an unusually large cup,' Nadorf said. 'We couldn't make it because at the time none of the moulds we were using was big enough, but I often wonder what happened to that boy.'

Requests for jumbo-size boxing gloves were more frequent and far

Bob Fitzsimmons, the first man to win three world titles, made bag punching an art.

easier to accommodate. 'I remember this guy from Texas, Cleveland Williams, who had enormous hands,' said Nadorf. 'But the biggest pair of hands I have ever seen belonged to Max Baer, the former world heavyweight champion.'

According to Nadorf, Muhammad Ali did not have large hands, but they were surprisingly soft. 'In order to protect his hands, Ali asked us to make a punch bag with a soft inner core and we obliged by manufacturing a bag stuffed with open cell foam.'

Everlast designed new headguards for use in the 1984 Olympic Games in Los Angeles and the company also pioneered the thumbless glove. 'We have never stopped doing our bit to make boxing a safer sport,' Nadorf said, 'but the best protection for a boxer is a medical check-up, both before and after a fight.'

Nadorf claimed that boxing was the tail that wagged the dog at Everlast. 'We sell more gym mats than boxing rings and more skip ropes than boxing gloves,' he said. 'But the more we tell people ours is an exercise-equipment company, the more they associate us with boxing. I guess we're stuck with the image.'

Others have tried hard to climb on to the bandwagon, including

Ben Foord, the former British Empire heavyweight champion, working out on the heavy bag in the 1930s.

an American company that designed what they called a Gyrostrike. Consisting of a high-quality durable foam body with solid wooden handles, the Gyrostrike was designed to increase speed, reflexes, eye-to-hand co-ordination, timing, accuracy, balance and concentration. Little, however, has been seen or heard of it since it was first marketed in the mid-1980s.

AGE

They called it 'One for the Ages' – and they certainly got that right. The heavyweight championship fight between World Boxing Association and International Boxing Federation champion Michael Moorer and former world champion George Foreman in Las Vegas on 5 November 1994 had more to do with age than anything else.

Making a stand for the fortysomething fighters of today, Foreman first won a benchmark decision in a Las Vegas court in August 1994 that threatened to turn the boxing world on its head.

Judge Donald Mosley ruled that Foreman was entitled to challenge Moorer for the WBA and IBF titles even though he was 45 going on 46. The WBA had threatened to strip Moorer of his title if he fought Foreman because the big fellow was not in their official ratings and had been inactive for more than a year.

The IBF were also reluctant to sanction the fight when it was first proposed at their annual convention in Reno, Nevada. Only after American promoter Bob Arum had threatened legal action if they removed Foreman from their official ratings did the IBF grudgingly grant approval on condition that Foreman passed several stringent physical examinations.

Foreman was naturally delighted when Judge Mosley ruled in his favour. 'Life, liberty, and the pursuit of happiness are alive and well and I'm living proof of it,' he said after the hearing. And under oath,

George Foreman was 45 going on 46 when he regained the heavyweight championship of the world in 1994.

he testified that he was 'in tip-top shape and able to challenge and regain the championship'.

Six weeks later the Nevada Supreme Court upheld the ruling when it declined to hear a petition brought by heavyweight contender Joe Hipp, who wanted the court to reverse the lower court order and allow him to fight Moorer instead.

Somebody once said that age is just a number but when Foreman knocked out Moorer in the tenth round with a solid right to the jaw, he became the oldest man to win a world title. And in the words of *Boxing News,* 'the most valuable antique in the world'.

'Those of us fortunate enough to have stood gaping as history books were reprinted before our very eyes will never forget the surge of energy, the paralyzing punch evoked in an arena left shellshocked and wide-eyed,' wrote Jim Fossum, sports editor of the Las Vegas *Review-Journal.* 'Foreman, as incredulous as anyone, gazed to the skies, then fell to his knees, bowed and fought back tears.'

Later the 'old man of boxing' made the most of the moment when he said, 'On this planet we will now know that the athletes in the world are between 45 and 55.'

However, the oldest champion to lose a title was Archie Moore, who was in his 48th year when he was stripped of the world light heavyweight title by the New York State Athletic Commission and the European Boxing Union in February 1962. Moore was 39 when he outboxed Joey Maxim to win the title in December 1952.

For some inexplicable reason the light heavyweight division has had more elderly champions than any other weight class with Archie Moore, Bob Fitzsimmons, Eddie Cotton and Dick Tiger among the oldest reigning champions in the history of the sport.

Boxing's youngest world champion was Wilfred Benitez, who won the junior welterweight title from Antonio Cervantes on a split decision in San Juan, Puerto Rico, in March 1976 at the age of 17 years, 5 months and 24 days. Since many countries around the world refuse to license young men under the age of 18, this was a truly remarkable achievement.

A month after Benitez had beaten Cervantes, Pipino Cuevas won the WBA welterweight title at the age of 18. At the time it seemed as though the young lions of boxing were about to take over the sport, but although Mike Tyson was later to become the youngest man to win the heavyweight title at the age of 20, experience – not youth – still proved to be the key to success in most world championship fights.

Not surprising when you consider that special permission is required for boxers 19 years of age and under to engage in ten-round bouts in the State of New York, or that New York Boxing Commission rule 216.23 stipulates that 'for all bouts over ten rounds, each boxer in such bout must be at least 21 years of age'.

A list of the youngest boxers to fight as professionals confirms that most were active in the days when boxing was loosely controlled as a sport. Baby Arizmendi of Mexico reputedly made his professional debut at the age of ten while Teddy Baldock, Al McCoy, Battling Nelson, Georges Carpentier, Kid Sullivan and John Henry Lewis all turned pro at the age of 14.

Nowadays the focus has shifted to the other end of the scale with age restriction hindering a greater number of older boxers than ever before. No wonder George Foreman has so many fans and fighters on his side.

Archie Moore, the former world light heavyweight champion, was in his 48th year when stripped of the title.

AIDS

It took the shock discovery in April 1993 that a reigning world champion was HIV-positive to convince many in the world of boxing that the time had arrived to address the problem of the AIDS epidemic, and to seriously consider measures to prevent the spread of the disease within the sport.

To its credit, the New Jersey State Athletic Commission had taken the lead in February 1987 when it insisted that all referees and cornermen wear surgical gloves in the ring. However, because AIDS was still a sensitive issue, New Jersey chairman Larry Hazzard insisted the unusual step was taken because of hygiene and not because of the dreaded disease.

Dr Ferdie Pacheco, the well-known American cornerman and boxing analyst, was among those who were critical of the New Jersey Commission's decision. Pacheco claimed the surgical gloves would remain sterile only as long as they were in a sterile environment.

'And besides, just the wearing of gloves doesn't render you incapable of getting an infection,' he said. 'It's foolish to think it's a true preventative measure. There's no medically sound basis for this.'

Despite Pacheco's reservations, the New York State Athletic Commission's Medical Advisory Board recommended both the use of surgical gloves and the adoption of mandatory HIV-testing of boxers shortly afterwards.

'I believe in human rights,' said Dr Edwin Campbell, chairman of the Board, 'but I also believe in the right to be protected from a catastrophic disease. Human rights should be for everyone. If we discover boxers who have AIDS, we'd have to exclude them. We'd have to protect the other boxers.'

The British Boxing Board of Control adopted a similar programme soon afterwards and African heavyweight Proud Kilimanjaro was among the first to be refused permission to box in Britain because of his reluctance to submit to an HIV test.

Tommy Morrison, the former WBO world heavyweight champion, who tested HIV-positive for AIDS.

'All new applicants for a licence must be HIV tested before the licence is granted and the HIV test now forms part of our annual medical,' said John Morris, general secretary of the British Boxing Board of Control.

'So far as boxers visiting this country are concerned they must be tested every time they come here unless, of course, there is only approximately one month between visits.'

And yet when the Zimbabwe Boxing Board of Control decided to start a similar programme in January 1991, the Minister of Health for Zimbabwe dismissed the HIV-testing of boxers as ludicrous. According to Dr Timothy Stamps, what he called 'bed-wrestling' was a greater health hazard.

Dr Stamps told the Harare *Herald* that boxers who had refused to be tested were completely within their rights and he referred to the World Health Organization statement which argued against screening for the virus in any sport.

'It is more likely,' said Dr Stamps, 'that boxers will get HIV infection from horizontal wrestling unprofessionally in bed, than by vertical boxing professionally in a ring.'

A year later the World Boxing Council launched an AIDS Awareness Programme at its annual convention in Cancun, Mexico, in the hope that it would enjoy the same success as its anti-drug programme in 1986. But when the alarm bells began ringing early in 1993, the International Boxing Federation became the first sanctioning body to insist on HIV-testing before all world championship fights.

Sadly, Ruben Palacios will go down in the history of boxing as the first world champion to lose his title because he tested HIV-positive. The 30-year-old Palacios had passed a similar test when he won the WBO featherweight title in London by stopping Colin McMillan in September 1992.

However, when Palacios returned to England to defend his title against John Davison in April 1993, he failed a series of six tests for the HIV virus. The World Boxing Organization had little option but to strip Palacios of the title when the British Boxing Board of Control confirmed the results.

'It is so sad,' said the then WBO Championships Committee

chairman Ed Levine. 'Palacios left Colombia to earn good money and he will be returning with a death sentence.'

When the news was flashed around the world a report appeared in the *Los Angeles Times* claiming that a Mexican preliminary boxer named Eduardo Castro had twice fought in California in 1991 even though the Nevada State Athletic Commission had already discovered he was HIV-positive and had advised all other commissions in a special bulletin.

In response, Bill Eastman, chairman of the California State Athletic Commission, confirmed that his commission was pursuing legislation that would permit the commission to demand proof that any applicant for a boxing licence was HIV-negative.

Eastman added that under current Californian law nobody in boxing is required to take an HIV test, and even if the commission knew somebody was HIV-positive, Californian law prevented it from making the information public. Such secrecy has made it difficult for boxing boards and boxing commissions to disclose information.

There was near-panic when the South African Boxing Commission disclosed in 1995 that 33 boxers had tested HIV-positive. It was the first year that the South African Commission had started to test boxers for AIDS and Hepatitis B.

Most of the controlling bodies are aware that boxers who test HIV-positive should undergo counselling by the medical profession, but how to share the information with other controlling bodies without infringing the rights of the individual remains a problem.

Former WBO heavyweight champion Tommy Morrison and former WBC super bantamweight champion Paul Banke both chose to make public disclosures themselves. Banke told *The Ring* magazine that he was dying of AIDS but claimed that he had no idea how he had contracted the virus.

Morrison went before a battery of television cameras to disclose his condition after his proposed fight with Arthur Weathers in Las Vegas in February 1996 was cancelled by the Nevada State Athletic Commission. 'I don't know if I got it from a girl or fighting,' Morrison said. 'It doesn't matter how I got it. I'm going to do everything I can to educate people. Four or five years ago I was a big, tough guy, thinking I was bulletproof. I considered myself selective. I never really thought about it.'

Once Morrison went public the Nevada State Athletic Commission was at liberty to confirm that he had tested HIV-positive. 'Nevada started testing for HIV in 1988, recording the health record of 2,150 boxers, and Tommy Morrison is only the second to test positive,' said Marc Ratner, the NSAC's executive director.

In quick succession other American boxing commissions, including Massachusetts, New York, New Jersey and California, announced that they would also start testing for the HIV virus.

According to a study conducted by the US Center for Disease Control and Prevention, there has never been a documented case of HIV transmission during an athletic competition in the 15-year history of the AIDS epidemic. CDC scientists estimate the chances of a professional athlete contracting the virus at 85 million to one.

MUHAMMAD ALI

Muhammad Ali has been calling himself the greatest for more years than most of us care to remember, but only after his last fight in December 1981 did many so-called boxing experts grudgingly admit that maybe he was right all along.

What many failed to appreciate when Ali was still in his prime was that the American brought qualities to the ring that no other champion ever had. Most of the old heavyweight champions relied almost entirely on their physical prowess to win fights, but Ali added another dimension – the mental edge.

The former three-time world heavyweight champion is no psychologist. Chances are he would have difficulty defining the word. But he did have a natural ability to browbeat his opponents with words until they literally came apart at the seams. Words, however, worked both for and against the man who once was known as Cassius Clay.

'Hitting hard don't mean nothing if you don't find nothing to hit' – Ali said about the power punchers of the heavyweight division (1963).

In many respects Ali was a product of his time – the Swinging Sixties – when all the old values were being questioned and when young people were determined to make their voices heard.

A heavyweight who claimed he could 'float like a butterfly and sting like a bee' was new to boxing and few were convinced he really belonged. After all, this was the division that had produced such hard hitters as Jack Dempsey, Joe Louis, Rocky Marciano and Sonny Liston. Ali was powder-puff by comparison.

'I said I was the greatest, not the smartest,' Ali remarked after failing the US Army intelligence test in 1964. Intelligence is one thing, common sense another. And Ali proved that you don't have to have a high IQ to become rich and famous. A pair of fast hands, remarkable reflexes, a sense of showbiz – and bingo! – even Ali could hit the jackpot.

Ali has no doubt grown wiser with age but to expect him to make sage comments on everything from pumpkins to politics was asking too much. Ali's track record shows that more often than not he merely ended up putting his foot in his mouth when he tried.

'I ain't got no quarrel with them Viet Congs,' said Ali on the Vietnam War in 1966. Talk about putting a foot in his mouth! Those few words cost Ali dearly. The world boxing organizations were quick to strip him of his world title, the politicians labelled him a 'traitor' and many who had found him amusing turned against him.

To his credit, Ali stood by his convictions – even though it cost him three of the best years of his boxing life. Some considered him stubborn, even downright foolish, but others admired him for taking a stand and have supported him ever since.

'You're an Uncle Tom nigger and you're gonna get your ass whipped,' said Ali to Ernie Terrell before their title fight in 1967.

Whether it was because of the pressure of life or through the influence of others, Ali's mouth turned nasty in the late 1960s. Terrell was only one of many to get a tongue-lashing and a vicious beating to boot.

Muhammad Ali in his prime. Ali was considered by many to be the greatest heavyweight champion of all time.

Floyd Patterson, a kind man who seemed to have difficulty in coming to terms with his own identity, was another. And the hatred Ali engendered in Joe Frazier exists to this day. 'If I pass him in the desert and he's thirsting, I drive right by,' Frazier once said. And Ali said in 1971, after the first Frazier fight, 'You get used to being hit,

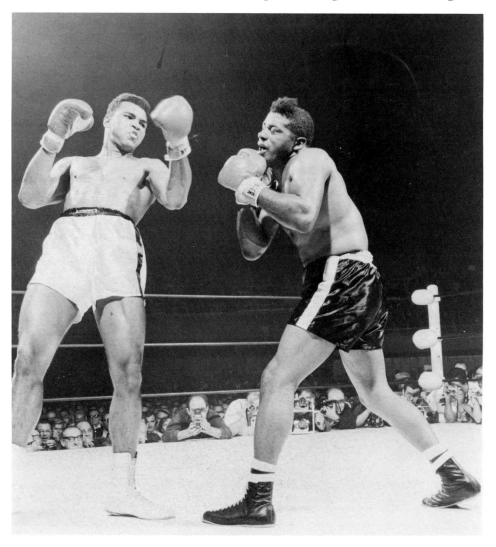

Muhammad Ali gave Floyd Patterson a brutal beating when Patterson challenged Ali for the world title in Las Vegas in 1965. Patterson fought most of the fight with an injured back and was stopped in the 12th round.

you condition yourself.'

In the beginning Ali subscribed to the view that the name of the game was to hit and not be hit. Later, as his reflexes deteriorated and he clearly outstayed his welcome as a boxer, he changed his tune. The result is the Parkinson Syndrome he now suffers.

Not only did Ali fight for too long, he fled to the Bahamas when no United States boxing commission would sanction his bout with Trevor Berbick in December 1981.

'Because he's black, the FBI figures Don King must be doing something crooked,' Ali said about the FBI's investigation of King in 1981. Few remember that it was Ali who made King the world's first great black boxing promoter. It started with the 'Rumble in the Jungle' with George Foreman in 1974. Suddenly King was a force to

Muhammad Ali in the prison cell used by president Nelson Mandela of South Africa on Robben Island.

be reckoned with in world boxing – and he has never looked back.

However, without the support of Ali the chances are King might not have made it. As King's rival Bob Arum once said of Ali: 'He's taken boxing and brought it to a new economic pitch.'

It was Ali who was largely responsible for turning professional boxing into a multi-million-dollar industry. And it was Ali who borrowed some of the tricks of show business to win support both for himself and his sport.

Long before Riddick Bowe and Lloyd Honeyghan threw their championship belts into a rubbish bin, Ali tossed his Olympic gold medal into a river because he believed it was 'tainted' by racial prejudice.

Ali, however, is no paragon. His failed marriages and failure to quit while ahead show that he is very human. Even so, he is unquestionably the world's most famous and easily recognizable sporting personality, and he gave us many years of marvellous entertainment. Nobody could ask for more.

AMATEURS

While many might describe amateurs as the junior partners in the sport, it would be unwise to deprecate their influence on the fight game or to overlook their contribution to the advancement of boxing worldwide.

Few are probably aware that the Queensberry Rules were first written with amateur boxing in mind, that the scoring of fights originated in the unpaid ranks, or that it was among the amateurs that the standing eight-count was first put into practice.

By and large, the amateurs have been surprisingly innovative in providing for change. Admittedly, computer scoring is still subject to much criticism and there are some who still question the wisdom of having made headgear mandatory in all amateur contests in 1983, but the spin-off for the sport has been a marked improvement in safety.

A two-year study on amateur boxing conducted in the United States in the early 1980s showed an injury rate of only 1.43 per cent in 6,050 bouts, while a study conducted by Johns Hopkins University in 1994 showed no relevant health damage to the 481 amateur boxers under test.

Encouraged by the success of most of the changes made in recent years, the amateur authorities introduced contests of five two-minute rounds for the first time at the World Cup competition in Bangkok in June 1994, while a women's exhibition bout between Lisa Rosen and Caryl Dennis was sanctioned for the first time in the 106-year history of the competition at the US Boxing Championships in Colorado Springs in March 1994.

In fact, so popular has boxing become as a sport among women in Finland that nearly 10,000 women are practising fitness boxing as members of the Finnish Amateur Boxing Association. Although no sparring is allowed, the word is that they work out under the direction of qualified coaches and apparently match their male counterparts in skill and technical ability.

With amateur boxing having circled the globe, it came as a terrible shock when the International Olympic Committee Programme Commission recommended that boxing be eliminated from the Olympic Games from the year 2000. Fortunately that threat no longer appears to have much support and the amateurs can now confidently prepare to meet the challenge of the twenty-first century.

By definition amateurs are, of course, unpaid but there were plans in the pipeline to compensate the world's best amateur boxers who were scheduled to compete in a tournament to be staged by the Russian Boxing Federation as part of its centenary in 1995.

International Amateur Boxing Association president Dr Anwar Choudhry welcomed the move and was so pleased at the prospect he asked the Russians to investigate ways of making it an annual event. 'The success of such a competition is assured,' he said, 'because we would be paying a lot of prize money.'

The question of prize money has been a thorn in the side of amateur boxing for years. Back in the early 1940s the New York State Athletic Commission attempted to take control of amateur boxing in the American state because it was alleged 'too much bootleg boxing was going on right under the nose of the Amateur Athletic Union'.

The Mahoney Bill, sponsoring the change, was even submitted to New York State Governor Lehman, but he vetoed it without comment after representations made by the AAU. Even today, Pro-Am tournaments are still popular in some parts of the world.

Although Africa has produced many great professional boxers, most African countries concentrate on the amateur code. However, few follow the Cuban example and bar their boxers from turning professional.

Only now is Cuba's dominance of international amateur boxing being seriously challenged. The Cubans ruled the roost for years

Teofilo Stevenson of Cuba is regarded as one of the greatest amateurs of all time. Stevenson is seen beating Solomon Ataga of Nigeria at the 1980 Moscow Olympics.

largely because they were literally unpaid professionals, working for the state. Teofilo Stevenson, who won three Olympic gold medals for Cuba and three World Amateur Championship titles (all at heavyweight), was once offered $2 million to turn professional – but decided instead to abide by his Socialist beliefs.

Cuba's rise to power in amateur boxing started in the late 1960s. One of the first to witness the change was Dr Max Novich, chief of staff of the United Hospitals Orthopedic Center in New Jersey, and a respected figure in American boxing. Novich visited Cuba for the 1974 World Amateur Boxing Championships.

'The Communist coaches are years ahead in the use of motivation for athletes,' Dr Novich admitted afterwards. 'Our coaches have only recently become interested in this phase of athletic training. When a Communist athlete loses, it is more than a loss. It is a personal disgrace almost to the point of a national shame.'

IABA president Anwar Choudhry believes that any Cuban decline would be in the interests of the sport. 'From IABA's point of view it is very good that the total supremacy of one country will end,' he said after the 1994 Goodwill Games in St Petersburg.

Amateur boxing has a long and proud history. Ever since John Sholto Douglas, the eighth Marquess of Queensberry, and John Graham Chambers founded the Amateur Athletic Club in England in 1866, the sport has prospered. And although in some countries the bond between amateur and professional has grown closer, most boxing men believe the amateurs should be allowed to do things their way.

Angelo Dundee, the famous American professional trainer, probably put it best. Speaking at a North Miami Beach gym on a winter's day in December 1990, Dundee said he had nothing but admiration for the amateurs.

'Thank God for our amateur programme which gives our young boxers plenty of foundation,' Dundee said. 'I give accolades to the amateur trainers even though they have their own way of doing things. And I believe the professionals should stay away and let them get on with it.'

ANNOUNCERS

Once their voices rang out across the arena. Nowadays, with a bit of luck, their voices ring out across the world, thanks to the wonders of satellite television.

Ring announcers can make or break a big-fight presentation. Many have developed their own individual styles. And by some strange quirk of fate, the best boxing announcers all seem to come from the United States, although there is still something special about British announcers when they intone, 'My lords, ladies and gentlemen!'

Arguably the most famous ring announcer of all time was Joe Humphreys, who invariably wore a straw hat and a bow-tie, and demanded attention by raising his right hand while calling 'Quiet, please ... quiet, please!'

'Not once during his fifty years of sports announcing did his voice falter or fail,' said Nat Fleischer, editor of *The Ring* magazine, when Humphreys died in 1936. 'Even during the days before the appearance of the microphone, his voice, with the booming range of a foghorn, carried to all parts of the arena.'

In fact, when Humphreys was invited to announce the heavyweight fight between Joe Louis and Max Baer at Yankee Stadium in New York in September 1935, he disdained the use of a microphone. He demanded and got the attention of the huge crowd by majestically raising his right hand.

As the man who stood in the centre of the ring at Boyle's Thirty Acres in Jersey City in the presence of more than 80,000 people to announce the 'Battle of the Century' between Jack Dempsey and Georges Carpentier in 1921, one would assume that Humphreys was thrilled to the bone.

And yet, when he was asked shortly before his death to name his greatest thrill as an announcer, he showed he had a feel for history. 'There are two things that stand out in my mind,' Humphreys said. 'The time I offered a prayer for Charles Lindbergh when he was crossing the Atlantic and the night that I introduced the great John L Sullivan for the first time.'

While lightweights Benny Leonard and Jack Britton square up in 1922, ring announcer Joe Humphreys rests on the ropes.

About 12 months after his death, the Boxing Writers' Association of New York unveiled a memorial to Humphreys at Madison Square Garden. The solid bronze plaque, the work of Vincenzio Miserendino, one of America's most talented sculptors, was affixed to the wall to the left of the Garden's Eighth Avenue entrance.

With Humphreys gone, it was left to Harry Balogh to fill his shoes. Frank Shain, who himself became a first-rate ring announcer, always felt that Balogh was better.

'Someone once wrote that Joe Humphreys was the dean of announcers. My feeling was that Harry Balogh was the dean,' Shain told me in New York. 'Harry was colourful, said twenty words where one would have done the trick, and was the subject of many articles. I think Harry stood head and shoulders above them all.'

Shain went on to recall the time Milton Berle had some showgirls pass the basket for donations to the US Army Relief Fund during the war years. In making the announcement that the girls would be going through the crowd, Balogh intoned: 'As the beautiful young ladies pass among you, shaking their cans, please give until it hurts.' The crowd roared with laughter.

Shain also remembered asking Balogh to teach him how to announce. 'Take a deep breath, start speaking from the diaphragm. Don't raise your voice ... ladeez and gentlemen. But don't say gentlemen fast, say it slow,' Balogh advised.

'He was great!' Shain insisted. 'We had a mutual admiration for each other.'

Shain admits that all announcers make mistakes and recalled the night in 1948 when Balogh introduced 33-year-old world light heavyweight champion Gus Lesnevich before his fight with Billy Fox. 'And now,' Balogh said, gesturing towards Lesnevich, 'a man who, like old wine, goes on for ever ...'

The United States is renowned for its great boxing announcers and, when Balogh passed from the scene, Johnny Addie was there to take his place, while out on the West Coast Jimmy Lennon was winning recognition as one of the best announcers of his time.

Lennon worked his first fight card at the Santa Monica Elks Club in 1943 before taking over as the regular announcer at the Olympic Auditorium in Los Angeles. Lennon spoke Spanish fluently and was

Former world middleweight champion Rocky Graziano playfully clips American ring announcer Frank Shain with a left hook.

meticulous about the proper pronunciation of boxers' names. 'A man is entitled to the dignity of his own name,' he would say.

Jimmy Lennon Jr, who was to follow in his father's footsteps, began announcing fights in 1982. Jimmy Jr claims he never intended to pursue a career as a ring announcer.

'My two brothers, two sisters, and I watched boxing on TV regularly,' he said. 'Sometimes, when Mom would drop a dish in the kitchen, it would sound like a bell, and we all would break into my father's announcing routine.'

When Jimmy Lennon Sr died at the age of 79 in April 1992 they played records at his funeral service that he had made himself as a singer and his nieces, the Lennon Sisters, sang too.

Indicative of how competitive announcing has become in the 1990s is the fact that Michael Buffer went to the trouble of having his famous punchline, 'Let's get ready to rumble,' copyrighted in the

United States.

Buffer, who first made a name for himself as a ring announcer on the ESPN television series *Top Rank Boxing*, admits that it took a while before he latched on to the now-famous punchline.

'I tried a couple of others, "Man your battle stations", and "Fasten your seat belts", but "Let's get ready to rumble" seemed to fit,' Buffer told Steve Farhood of *KO Magazine*.

Buffer broke into boxing as a ring announcer in 1982 and has never looked back. He has since appeared in the movies (*Harlem Nights*, *Home Boy*), on American television shows (*Grudge Match*, *The George Carlin Show*, *In Living Color*) and in TV commercials (five for the Ford Motor Company alone).

Mind you, Buffer has boxing in the blood. His grandfather, whom he never knew, was Johnny Buff, a man who held the world bantamweight title in the early 1920s.

ANTI-BOXING

Boxing men long ago learned how to live with those who wished to see the sport abolished. But while the early detractors were mostly philosophers (as in ancient Greece), the strongest opposition today comes from the medical profession.

Hardly a year goes by without a medical association somewhere in the world demanding that the sport be banned. And one of the sport's leading antagonists is Dr George Lundberg, editor of the *Journal* of the American Medical Association, who has been trying to get boxing banned for more than a decade.

'Boxing is the only sport in which a person wins by damaging his competitor's brain. That is medically and morally wrong,' Dr Lundberg declared in an editorial in June 1994.

Dr Lundberg first launched his campaign against the sport shortly after the death of Duk Koo Kim following his WBA lightweight title fight with Ray Mancini in Las Vegas in November 1982. Writing in the

Journal, Dr Lundberg claimed 'boxing is wrong at its base' and suggested that 'as a throwback to uncivilized man, should not be sanctioned by any civilized society'.

Two years later Dr Lundberg appeared on the American television programme *Sports Beat,* hosted by Howard Cosell, and expressed the opinion that amateur boxing could legally constitute child abuse.

'It is abuse,' Dr Lundberg said. 'It is predictable damage. It is children. And if adults promote, for whatever reason, such as their own pleasure, children bashing each other and hurting each other deliberately, this makes pretty good sense as a form of child abuse.'

Later, at the American Medical Association's three-day convention in Hawaii, a resolution was passed calling for the complete abolition of boxing. AMA president Dr Joseph R Boyle cited 'the dangerous effects of boxing on the health of its participants' as the reason to ban the sport. Dr Boyle added that he hoped to get 'physicians all over the country ... to participate in a public dialogue which would ultimately lead to persuading legislators and the public that boxing ought to be outlawed'.

Needless to say, the good doctor has not yet succeeded in his aim, although some American politicians were quick to jump on the bandwagon.

After a three-year probe, the New Jersey State Commission of Investigation recommended in 1987 that boxing be banned because 'no human endeavour so brutal, so susceptible to fraud and so generally degrading should be accorded any social status'. And Gene Tunney Jr, son of the famous world heavyweight champion, declared: 'It's a sport whose day has come and gone. I don't think it should be sanctioned any more.'

Britain's Loony Left picked up on the trend when Hackney, a left-wing London borough council, banned professional boxing from venues licensed by them.

'The ban is ludicrous,' said British promoter Frank Warren. 'Apart from anything else, it is an insult to the boxers of Hackney, many of whom are black and part of a community the council is trying to keep in employment.'

Next to stand up and be counted was Dr Marius Barnard, a member of South Africa's Progressive Federal Party and brother of

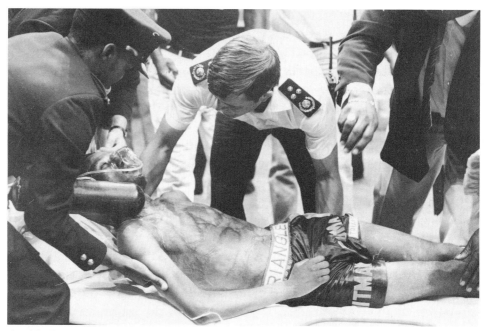

A critically injured Jacob Morake, an oxygen mask clamped over his face, is removed from the ring after being stopped in the 12th round by Brian Mitchell at Sun City. Morake died a day later of brain haemorrhage.

the famous heart surgeon Dr Chris Barnard.

Addressing the South African Parliament in 1988 during the second reading of the Boxing and Wrestling Control Amendment Bill, Dr Barnard told the House of Assembly that Parliament should support the Medical Association of South Africa in condemning the sport.

As luck would have it, during the same week that Dr Barnard tried to persuade Parliament that boxing should be banned in South Africa, M-Net Television screened an American documentary called *Is There a Doctor in the Ring?* Subject of the documentary was a young Irishman, Dr Terry Christle, who besides having won the right to practise medicine in the United States, was doing fairly well as a professional fighter.

'For me, medicine is my vocation; boxing is my sport,' Dr Christle told viewers. 'Just like other medics are attracted to different sports, I'm attracted to boxing. And as far as I'm concerned, boxing represents an expression of man's ability to fight adversity on his own. It's the last pure battle or challenge.'

Asked what he thought of those doctors who were trying to have boxing banned, Dr Christle dismissed them as being unreasonable. 'Their approach to boxing comes close to being fascist,' he said, 'because what they're saying is the people cannot engage in a certain sport.'

Dr Mortimer Shapiro, a respected psychiatrist and neurologist then serving on the New York State Athletic Commission Medical Advisory Board, took a similar line when he appeared on the American *Sports Beat* television programme in 1984.

'Should we abolish boxing?' he asked. 'That is not a medical problem. That is a moral problem. It is a sociological problem. It has nothing to do with medicine.'

There are, of course, several countries around the world where professional boxing is banned, including Cuba, Norway, Sweden and Nicaragua (while under the control of the Sandinistas).

But the first legal action to ban boxing (or prize-fighting as it was then known) was in England in 1753. Following a fight between Jack Slack and John Broughton in which he is reported to have lost £10,000 in bets, the Duke of Cumberland persuaded Parliament to enact a Bill banning participation in the sport.

The last legal interference in boxing in Britain was in 1911 when the Home Secretary banned a proposed fight between black world heavyweight champion Jack Johnson and Bombardier Billy Wells at Earls Court in London. The reason was clearly racist and much of the opposition to the proposed fight came from the clergy.

Arguably the most infamous opponent of boxing in Britain was the Right Honourable Dr Edith Summerskill, who even wrote a book in 1956 called *The Ignoble Art*. Dr Summerskill hated boxing with a passion and yet was unable to dissuade her own son from boxing for Oxford University.

Calls for boxing to be banned following the ring death of British light featherweight Bradley Stone in 1994 were quickly rejected by the British government. 'The government's line is that as long as there are proper medical safeguards anybody is entitled to pursue the sport they wish,' said Iain Sproat, the minister for Sport.

Tom Pendry, the British shadow minister for Sport, was even more positive and dismissed the calls for a ban as a kneejerk reaction. 'Where there is room for improvement, there should be improvements,' Pendry said. 'But you cannot wrap up the nation in cotton wool and say you cannot have any contact sports.'

HENRY ARMSTRONG

His life story reads like a movie script, which isn't altogether surprising when you consider that he first made a name for himself as a fighter in Tinsel Town, and with the backing of Hollywood stars Al Jolson and George Raft.

Henry Armstrong (real name Henry Jackson) even acted in a feature film himself. But *Keep Punching*, the film he made in the late 1930s, has long been forgotten. Later, after his boxing days were over, Armstrong became an ordained minister of the Church and toured the world preaching the Gospel, but it is as a fighter that he will always be remembered.

Armstrong was the first and the last boxer ever to hold three world titles simultaneously. After he had turned the trick in 1938 no boxer was ever again allowed to be champion in more than one weight division at the same time. It was a distinction that Henry wore well. Mind you, it certainly did not look that way when Armstrong turned professional in 1931 under the name of Melody Jackson.

A Mexican boxer named Baby Arizmendi was to play a major role in Armstrong's career. When they first fought in Mexico City in 1934 Armstrong lost the decision and his entire purse when the promoter ran off with the money. Two months later they met in a rematch, in a fight billed as being for the vacant Californian and Mexican world featherweight title but few took it seriously.

However, when the men met for a third time in Los Angeles in August 1936, Lady Luck, in the form of famous stage and screen star

Henry Armstrong in a scene from *Keep Punching*, a feature film he made in the 1930s.

Al Jolson, was sitting at ringside. Jolson liked what he saw, purchased Armstrong's contract for $10,000 and together with another backer, film star George Raft, appointed Eddie Mead as Henry's manager.

Armstrong lost only one of his next 29 fights before challenging Petey Sarron for the world featherweight title at Madison Square Garden, New York, in October 1937. Sarron's knockout defeat in the sixth round triggered one of the most amazing 12 months in the history of boxing.

In May 1938 Armstrong jumped two divisions to outbox Barney Ross for the welterweight title and only three months later he won the world lightweight title by beating Lou Ambers on points over 15 rounds.

A stunned Nat Fleischer, editor of *The Ring* magazine, called Armstrong 'a human dynamo, a fighter of perpetual motion'. Hype Igoe, a veteran boxing writer, compared Armstrong with Terry McGovern while George Pardy, another well-known writer of the period, described Henry as 'a blazing black comet'.

Armstrong was certainly no stylist. He believed in constant aggression, bobbing and weaving as he drove his opponents around the ring. His stamina was incredible and in his prime he was almost impossible to hurt. What's more, it seems he was also fearless.

'I can't figure this fellow out,' Mead said of Armstrong before the Sarron fight. 'If I told him he was fighting Joe Louis next week, he wouldn't say a word. He can still do 126 but wants to box in the lightweight division. I'm afraid that if he gains a few more pounds, I'll have to bring back Primo Carnera for him.'

Well, Henry did gain a few more pounds and at the end of 1938 he was obliged to relinquish the featherweight title because of weight problems. Moreover, a few months later he lost the lightweight title back to Ambers. Yet Armstrong engaged in an

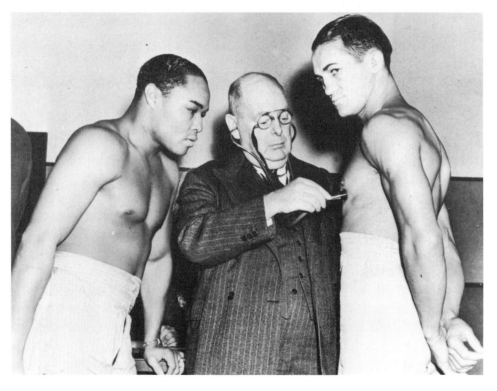

Fritzie Zivic being examined at the weigh-in before his world welterweight title fight with Henry Armstrong in 1940.

Henry Armstrong (right) on the way to beating Baby Arizmendi in 1936. Screen star Al Jolson, sitting at ringside in Los Angeles, liked what he saw and purchased Armstrong's contract for $10,000.

amazing 12 world-title fights in 1939, held Ceferino Garcia to a draw in a middleweight championship match in 1940, and then lost the welterweight title to Fritzie Zivic seven months later. The shooting star had finally begun to fizzle and fall. Even so, Armstrong kept boxing for another five years.

With his boxing career behind him, Armstrong turned to drink and was hauled before a magistrate on a charge of drunkenness. Henry was told he was letting down thousands of little boys all over the world – and the words hurt harder than any blow he had been struck in the ring.

Armstrong promptly joined the First Baptist Church and began studying for the ministry, was elected to the Boxing Hall of Fame in 1954, published an autobiography entitled *Gloves, Glory and God* in 1956, and died in Los Angeles at the age of 76 in October 1988.

ART

Boxing as an art form is as old as the sport itself. And yet, except for a few hieroglyphics and paintings found in the tombs of the pharaohs, there is no other visual record of boxing dating back to 6500 BC when it first became popular in Ethiopia and Egypt.

On the other hand, we know that boxing was a favourite subject for decorated vases and primitive friezes during the Minoan period in Crete. One of the most famous is a Minoan vase found in Cyprus which dates back to 1100 BC. And while ancient Greek boxers can be seen depicted on a vase in the British Museum, a bronze figure of Cleitomachus, who won the *pancratium* at the 141st Olympic Games, 216 BC, is on show in the National Museum in Rome.

The Romans were guilty of destroying many of the vases, friezes and statues of boxers from the Greek era, but enough remain to remind us of the first Golden Age of boxing. It was only when the sport was revived in England centuries later that artists again had an opportunity to portray its drama and excitement.

Artistic licence was widely practised. For example, Théodore Géricault's famous lithograph of the fight between Tom Molineaux and Tom Cribb in 1810 was only drawn about eight years after the event.

Among the well-known artists of the sport in the twentieth century are George Bellows, McClelland Barclay, James Chapin, James Montgomery Flagg, John Groth and LeRoy Neiman, whose best work can be seen in museums around the world.

In fact, one of the first art exhibitions devoted entirely to boxing went on show at the Museum of the City of New York late in 1947. Entitled *The Ring and the Glove*, it drew much favourable attention and later toured the United States.

Meanwhile the famous painting by George Bellows of Luis Firpo knocking Jack Dempsey out of the ring now hangs in the Whitney Museum of American Art. Museum curator Altamont Fairclough claimed in 1987 that when he looked at the painting he saw the drama of the real fight from the ringside.

'To me, this is the outstanding Bellows,' said Fairclough. 'I don't think you could have any Bellows without having this one. I have the print hanging in my home.'

The National Gallery of Art in Washington DC exhibited no fewer than 39 of the artist's works in 1982 to mark the centennial of his birth. The exhibit, entitled *Bellows: The Boxing Pictures*, was the first exhibition to focus solely on the boxing paintings of this American artist.

Perhaps the most popular print or postcard, however, is that of the mural by James Montgomery Flagg of Dempsey fighting Jess Willard. Dempsey himself commissioned Flagg to paint the huge mural in the early 1950s for his Broadway restaurant.

When the 55-foot by 24-foot work was unveiled, it received critical acclaim and quickly became a major attraction. When Dempsey was forced to close the restaurant because the landlord refused to renew his lease, the mural was shipped to the Smithsonian Institution in Washington DC.

A surprising number of ex-boxers have turned their hand to

painting pictures. Who would have thought that a tough guy like American middleweight Rocky Graziano was a painter? Graziano explained how it happened at an Athlete Art exhibition in New York a few years before his death.

'When I was a kid, I couldn't get adjusted to grade school so they sent me to art class because the teacher there was also a gym teacher,' Rocky said. 'When I first became a fighter I didn't tell anyone I was a painter because it felt funny saying it in those days.'

Graziano admitted he couldn't afford to buy a Picasso so he copied Picasso's paintings instead. 'I like this one [Rocky pointed to a copy of a Cubist work by Picasso] because it looks like some of the guys I beat up.'

Former world welterweight and middleweight champion Mickey Walker was another fighter who became relatively famous as an artist.

As a boy, Walker wanted to be an architect, so maybe the old urge to draw returned when he quit the ring. Whatever the reason – and some say it happened after Mickey saw the movie *The Moon and Sixpence*, which was based on the life of Paul Gauguin – the ex-boxer turned to painting pictures. Like Gauguin's work, they were full of colour, moving an American art critic to place Walker among the Primitives.

French culture sprang a surprise in 1926 when a talented sculptor decided to become a professional boxer. Emile 'Spider' Pladner was a successful sculptor in Paris when he turned pro after winning the European amateur flyweight title in 1925. Pladner went on to become the NBA world champion when he knocked out Frankie Genaro in one round in Paris in 1929.

With a bold, distinctive style, America's LeRoy Neiman has become 'Mister Boxing' of the art world in the 1990s. Neiman admits boxing has fascinated him ever since he was a young boy growing up in St Paul, Minnesota. 'When I wasn't boxing, I was sketching fighters in the gym,' he says. Today Neiman's works are considered major treasures and can be found in many private art collections and museums.

For some inexplicable reason, boxing sculpture has become the in-thing in the 1990s. In 1991 *The Art of Sport* produced an exquisitely crafted piece of Muhammad Ali standing over the fallen Sonny Liston in their second fight for the heavyweight championship of the world.

The one-eighth scale tableau was the work of Ken Fallon and each

Few artists have been able to capture the drama and excitement of a big fight as faithfully as Leroy Neiman. Here Mike Tyson is depicted in action against Razor Ruddock in March 1991.

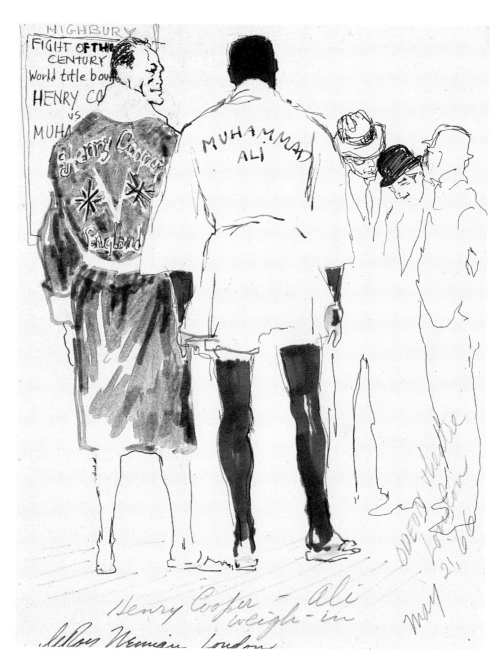

There is more to boxing than the fights, as Leroy Neiman discovered when he captured this scene of Muhammad Ali and Henry Cooper weighing-in at the Odeon in London for their world heavyweight title fight in May 1966.

numbered piece in a limited edition of 7,500 was hand-produced in the Staffordshire Potteries in England.

A year later British sculptor Neale Andrew, working in bronze, completed a bust and a figure of former world heavyweight champion Mike Tyson that were later exhibited in the art galleries of London.

And in 1994 Diablo Art of California produced two limited edition works by Niels Andersen of boxers in action. Simply called *KO*, Andersen's work in bronze stood on a solid walnut base.

ATTENDANCES

At first they claimed that 136,000 fans had packed the Aztec Stadium in Mexico City for Don King's 'Grand Slam of Boxing'. Later the official count was recorded as 132,274. Either way, it was a new world record for paid attendance at a boxing match, and this despite live television coverage around the world.

King had offered Mexican great Julio Cesar Chavez a chance to showcase his talents in front of his own people in a WBC super lightweight title fight against Greg Haugen – and the local fans filled the huge stadium to capacity.

With the cheapest seats costing 5,000 pesos (about £1), those up in the gods could do little more than savour the atmosphere rather than closely follow the fight. Even so, they booed thunderously as Haugen came to the ring to the strains of 'Born in the USA'.

'And the roar they produced when Chavez made his way to the roped square is one of those memories that will stay with you for a lifetime,' Daniel Herbert reported in *Boxing News*. 'Imagine 136,000 people chanting your name, uniting in their desire for you to do well. It's more powerful than any drug.'

It all happened on 20 February 1993 with five world title fights on the bill. Chavez retained his WBC super lightweight title by stopping

Haugen in five rounds; Azumah Nelson retained his WBC super featherweight title with a 12-round points victory over Gabriel Ruelas; Terry Norris knocked out Maurice Blocker in two rounds to retain his WBC super welterweight title; and Michael Nunn knocked out Danny Morgan in one round in defence of his WBA super middleweight crown.

Only twice since the sport of boxing entered the television age in the late 1940s has crowd attendance exceeded 80,000. First, when David Kotey defended his WBC featherweight title against Danny Lopez in Accra, Ghana, on 5 November 1976 and an estimated 100,000 people packed the local Sports Stadium, and then when

Julio Cesar Chavez, the Mexican Marvel, who was largely responsible for setting a new world attendance record in Mexico City in February 1993.

John Tate and Gerrie Coetzee fought for the vacant WBA heavyweight title on 20 October 1979 in Pretoria, South Africa. An estimated 82,000 fans crammed into Loftus Versveld, the local rugby stadium.

American promoter Mike Jacobs had predicted in the early 1940s that television would be the medium that would kill large gates at boxing tournaments and, with only a few exceptions, Jacobs has been proved right.

Almost all the big fight crowds were recorded in the pre-television age of the sport. The largest-ever attendance at a boxing match was recorded on 16 August 1941 when 135,132 people poured into Juneau Park, Milwaukee, Wisconsin, for a middleweight bout between Tony Zale and Billy Pryor. The non-title fight was promoted by the Fraternal Order of the Eagles and no admission was charged.

Until Chavez and Haugen broke the record, the previous highest-paid attendance at a fight was at the Sesquicentennial Stadium in Philadelphia on 23 September 1926 when Jack Dempsey defended his world heavyweight title against Gene Tunney. Ironically, the only reason promoter Tex Rickard had chosen Philadelphia for the fight was because the New York State Athletic Commission had revoked Dempsey's boxing licence following his refusal to fight Harry Wills.

The cream of American society attended the fight, including James M Cox, Democratic nominee for US president; three cabinet members, six US governors, members of the diplomatic corps, captains of industry and personalities such as golf king Bobby Jones, horse-racing tycoon Joseph E Widener and George H Walker, the man who donated the Walker Cup to golf. Almost everyone got soaked to the skin in the driving rain that fell throughout the fight.

Only scheduled for ten rounds, the fight was decided on points when Tunney easily outboxed the ageing champion. Asked later by his actress wife Estelle Taylor what went wrong, Dempsey replied: 'Honey, I just forgot to duck.'

The rematch in Soldiers Field, Chicago, on 22 September 1927 drew fewer people – the crowd was recorded as 104,943 – but produced greater drama when Dempsey dropped Tunney in the seventh round for the famous 'Long Count'. A left hook did the damage but when Dempsey refused to return to a neutral corner, referee Dave Barry delayed the count.

'My God!' Battling Nelson exclaimed from the press section, where he held a stopwatch on the fallen fighter. 'He was down for 16 seconds!' Others insisted it was 14 seconds. In any event, Tunney got up to retain his title on points over ten rounds.

Other fights that drew large crowds included the heavyweight bout between Joe Louis and Max Baer on 24 September 1935 at Yankee Stadium, New York (88,150); the world heavyweight title fight between Jack Dempsey and Luis Firpo on 24 September 1923 at the Polo Grounds, New York (82,000); the fight for the British version of the world light heavyweight title between Len Harvey and Jock McAvoy on 10 July 1939 at White City, London (82,000); and the world heavyweight title fight between Jack Dempsey and Georges Carpentier on 2 July 1921 at Boyle's Thirty Acres, Jersey City, New Jersey (80,183).

The highest indoor attendance for a world heavyweight championship fight was recorded at the Superdome, New Orleans, on 15 September 1978 when 63,350 people watched Muhammad Ali regain the title by outboxing Leon Spinks over 15 rounds.

The highest attendance at a non-heavyweight world championship fight was recorded at the Polo Grounds, New York, on 12 September 1951 when 61,437 fans witnessed Sugar Ray Robinson regain the world middleweight title by knocking out Randolph Turpin in the tenth round.

One of the smallest attendances at a world heavyweight championship fight was recorded at St Dominic's Hall, Lewiston, Maine, on 25 May 1965, when only 2,434 people paid to see Muhammad Ali knock out Sonny Liston in one round.

ATTIRE

In the beginning boys boxed naked. Not surprising considering that the 'athletic uniform' at the ancient Olympics was complete nudity. Later, when the Games spread to Crete and Rome, special protectors were worn. Several have been found in the ruins of the Knossos amphitheatre.

When boxing as a sport was revived in England in the seventeenth century, the bareknuckle bruisers invariably wore breeches or long tights, often with a sash tied around the waist. Broughton's Rules of 1743 made it mandatory for boxers to be stripped to the waist and declared that no person be permitted to seize his opponent by the breeches.

While the London Prize Ring Rules of 1838 made similar stipulations in relation to dress, Rule 5 went even further: 'On the men being stripped it shall be the duty of the seconds to examine their drawers, and if any objection arises as to the insertion of improper substances therein, they shall appeal to their umpires, who, with the concurrence of the referee, shall direct what alterations shall be made.'

The revised London Prize Ring Rules of 1853 even described the kind of footwear permissible: 'The spikes in the fighting boots shall be confined to three in number, which shall not exceed three-eighths of an inch from the sole of the boot, and shall not be less than one-eighth of an inch broad at the point; two to be placed in the broadest part of the sole and one in the heel ...'

The Marquess of Queensberry Rules, which were published in 1867, were less specific about ring attire although Rule 11 clearly stated that 'no shoes or boots with springs' would be allowed.

The apparent lack of guidance in the rules led many to believe that they could wear what they pleased when they entered the ring. Bob Fitzsimmons and Jim Corbett both boxed in what appeared to be bathing costumes when they fought for the world heavyweight title in Carson City, Nevada, in March 1897.

Billy Papke, who was world middleweight champion for two-and-a-half months after he had beaten Stanley Ketchel in September 1908, often boxed in what can only be described as brief skants – long before skants became popular as underwear. Other contemporaries of Papke seemed to prefer baggy, three-quarter-length shorts.

It was only in the early 1930s that boxing trunks became standardized. And later, when fights were televised on a regular basis in the late 1940s, the TV networks insisted on boxers wearing either black or white trunks for easy identification by viewers.

The custom of wearing trunks carrying advertising started in Europe in the early 1970s and gradually spread across the world when sports sponsorship became a major financial factor. Mexican great Julio Cesar Chavez, a former triple world champion, now often comes to the ring with so much advertising on his trunks that he could easily be mistaken for a walking billboard.

Of course, some boxers still prefer to carry their own messages. For example, when Roger Mayweather successfully defended his WBC super lightweight title against Harold Brazier in Las Vegas in June 1988, Brazier had the words 'I love you, Mom' embroidered on his trunks.

And when Sugar Ray Leonard defended the WBC super middleweight title against Thomas Hearns in Las Vegas in June 1989, he wore the word 'Amandla' on the waistband of his trunks and 'Free South Africa' on his T-shirt.

'Leonard's political convictions are strictly his own business and he had no right to try and shove them down the throats of millions of people around the world. And besides, the last thing boxing fans want is for the ring to become a platform for political sloganeering,' the South African magazine *Boxing World* declared in an editorial.

The dress code, however, already lay in tatters in many parts of the world – and this despite US rules that stipulate that 'each boxer on a program must provide himself with the ring costume selected and approved by the commission'.

Soon boxers in the United States began appearing in the ring in the most outlandish costumes. Chief offenders were men like former WBO junior welterweight champion Hector Camacho, the self-styled 'Macho Man' of boxing; former WBA welterweight champion

Hector Camacho, the former WBC lightweight champion, on his way to the ring in an Indian headdress.

Meldrick Taylor, who on occasions wore what appeared to be a tiger-skin loincloth; and former WBO and IBF featherweight champion Jorge Paez, who once wore a pair of trunks embroidered with sequins that looked to be almost as heavy as he was.

To their credit, the British Boxing Board of Control stuck to tradition and insisted that boxers in Britain 'box in Regulation boots without heels or spikes, with Regulation shorts' until the late nineties.

South African rules are even more specific. The South African Boxing control Act not only outlaws the wearing of tight-fitting trunks but Rule 21 1b categorically states that 'the trunks shall be secured at the hips of the boxer, but no metal or other buckles or straps shall be worn, and the bottom hems of the trunks shall reach to at least halfway between the groin and the knees'.

And yet, while boxing in the second half of the twentieth century may well have become more like cabaret (as British boxing historian

Peter McInnes has claimed), there is evidence that many in the fight game would secretly like to turn back the clock.

This probably explains why Game Promotions of London were able to successfully market nineteenth-century replica boxing shorts in 1994. Described as Old Victorian in style, the black shorts had traditional tie-up knee-length bottoms, classic, extra large belt loops and were supplied with an authentic white waist scarf.

AWARDS

In few other sports have participants been more generously rewarded for their achievements than in boxing. The practice of awarding trophies to boxers can be traced back to 800 BC and the chances are boxers were being rewarded for their efforts long before that.

But whereas most modern recipients are awarded belts, medals or cups in recognition of their services to the sport, victors in the ancient Olympic Games were given laurel wreaths and the Emperor Caligula of Rome is reputed to have rewarded his victorious African boxers with young virgins during AD 100.

The custom of naming a Boxer of the Year was first started by *The Ring* magazine in 1928 and this practice has become so widespread that no self-respecting boxing publication now misses the opportunity to name its own award winners. The method of finding a winner varies from publication to publication but *Boxing World,* the South African monthly, is one of the few magazines to organize a ballot among the national media.

Nor are the awards restricted to boxing publications. The Boxing Writers' Association of America has been honouring boxers since 1938, the World Boxing Council started naming a Boxer of the Year in 1977, and the British Boxing Board of Control inaugurated its own awards in 1984.

A variety of people connected with the sport are now honoured in one way or another. In the United States, for example, there are

World champions Willie Pep, Joe Louis, Gus Lesnevich and Rocky Graziano attend the 1948 awards dinner of the New York Boxing Writers' Association.

awards for Excellence in Boxing Journalism and Broadcasting while the British Boxing Board even has an award for Sportsmanship. And in 1994 the Professional Boxers Association held their first 'celebration dinner and awards ceremony to boxers by boxers' in London.

The then WBO super middleweight champion Chris Eubank startled the 500 strong gathering when he made an unsolicited speech urging his fellow professionals to 'take charge of their own careers before it's too late'. Even allowing for the fact that the PBA is a boxer's union, Eubank's speech did not sit well with many of those present.

'Boxers must remember that they are the employers, and behave accordingly,' Eubank said. 'We engage managers to negotiate on our behalf and to get us the best available deal, but the contracts belong to us.

'We are the employers. We pay them 25 per cent to handle negotiations, so that we are freed from that worry and responsibility, but too often we are made to feel like the employee. If boxers don't ensure that every detail of every deal is reported back to them, they risk ending up bitter, twisted and resentful.'

Others have also used award ceremonies to make a statement of their own. When Gerrie Coetzee, who was later to become the WBA heavyweight champion, was acclaimed South Africa's Boxer of the Year for 1979 by a landslide 80 per cent of the vote in a nationwide poll, he gave the organizers a difficult time and a kingsize headache.

Right up until the last minute, Coetzee was in two minds whether or not to attend the awards banquet. After having agreed to come, Coetzee changed his mind on the day of the event and only the considerable influence of Stan Christodoulou saved the situation.

'I would rather fight John Tate ten times than come to this sort of thing,' Coetzee said when he finally got in front of the microphones.

Muhammad Ali turned the 1974 Boxing Writers' Association dinner in New York into turmoil when, after hurling insults at George Foreman all night long, he and the then world heavyweight champion almost came to blows in front of the distinguished audience.

It happened when Ali made a violent grab at Foreman's championship belt. When Big George slapped his arm away the two men were suddenly locked together, muscles taut and eyes blazing.

'It was no longer a publicity stunt,' said boxing historian Chris Greyvenstein, who attended the banquet. 'Ali was wrestling wildly as bystanders jumped in to pull them apart. I was looking directly at Foreman and, while outwardly calm, he was obviously angry. He glanced down at his shirt which had been torn and suddenly grabbed the bottom of Ali's smart blue coat at the back, and without any ceremony, ripped it all the way up to the collar.'

Making sure he was being firmly held by his minders, Ali continued to scream insults at the top of his voice and to throw glasses against the draped wall behind the dais. Foreman looked at him with contempt on his face and then allowed himself to be led from the hall.

Ali had meanwhile become quite hysterical. 'I'll beat your Christian ass for you!' he screamed at Foreman, who was scheduled to defend the world title against Ali in their famous 'Rumble in the Jungle'. 'You white-flag-waving nigger you! Where's that nigger staying? I'll kill him!'

Besides boxing people honouring their own, the trend today is for the state to also make awards. Hardly a year passes without a boxing personality being included in the British honours list and, on 11 May 1984, the United States Congress posthumously honoured Joe Louis, the former world heavyweight champion.

The ceremony was held at the White House with US President Ronald Reagan presenting Joe's widow, Martha, with a Congressional Gold Medal. Public law 97-246, which was promulgated on 26 August 1982, authorized the presentation of the gold medal in honour of Louis for his accomplishments, which did much to bolster the spirit of the American people during one of the most crucial times in US history.

Three days later, the Hon Charles A Hayes, Congressman of the 1st District of Illinois, presented Mrs Louis with a certificate of special congressional recognition in honour of her late husband for his outstanding and invaluable contribution in the world of sports.

BAREKNUCKLE

If you think all boxing prior to the introduction of the Queensberry Rules was conducted with bare fists, think again. Fist-fighting is probably as old as the human race but although archaeological findings place the birth of boxing as a sport between 6500 and 8000 BC, the first available visual evidence only appears in Egyptian hieroglyphics around 5000 BC.

Even so, a bas-relief in Baghdad dating back to 3000 BC and a mosaic in the Bardo museum in Tunisia both show that many men of the period preferred to fight with some sort of covering over their hands. And a bronze statue of an ancient Greek gladiator in the National Museum in Rome has both hands bound with leather thongs.

Moreover, when Homer described an epic battle between Epeius and Euryalus in Book XXIII of the *Iliad*, he mentioned how both men used 'well-cut thongs of the hide of an ox of the field' to cover their hands.

By the time the Olympics were taken to Rome, soft hand coverings had been replaced by the *cestus*, complete with pointed metal studs. The gladiators who wore these deadly hand-wrappings literally fought for their lives. Fortunately, when boxing died in the Dark Ages, these hideous 'accessories' died with it.

It was not until the seventeenth century that boxing again emerged as a sport in England. Samuel Pepys described a fairground fight in his diary for 1662 and a report of a prize-fight between the Duke of Albemarle's footman and a butcher appeared in the *Protestant Mercury* in January 1681.

By 1716 James Figg had issued his famous calling card, engraved by his friend, the celebrated William Hogarth, announcing that he 'teached fencing, singlestick and boxing'. Figg also claimed he was an expert at boxing and in 1719 became the first man to be recognized as champion of England.

John Broughton, described by many as the Father of Boxing, followed Figg's example and in 1747 a notice appeared in a London newspaper inviting those 'willing to be instructed in the mystery of boxing' to attend Broughton's academy at Tottenham Court Road.

A one-time yeoman of the guard of King George II, Broughton was responsible for devising the first Rules of Boxing in 1743. Although he also invented the muffler, these padded gloves were strictly for sparring, and were not intended for use in the prize ring.

Bareknuckle boxing did not achieve real recognition in the United States until the nineteenth century, by which time the London Prize Ring Rules were accepted everywhere the sport was practised. The first American to make a name for himself in the prize ring was Tom Molineaux, a black man and former slave.

Bareknuckle boxing survived as a sport for roughly two hundred years. The 'prize ring' (named after the original circular enclosure in which the men fought) projected a certain spirit of chivalry that was sadly lacking when boxing died in the Dark Ages. Among the great bareknuckle champions were men like Tom Cribb, Daniel Mendoza, Tom Sayers, John C Heenan, Tom Molineaux and John L Sullivan.

Mind you, there were times when bareknuckle fights seemed

It took John L Sullivan (left) 75 rounds to knock out Jake Kilrain in the last bareknuckle fight for the heavyweight championship of the world in July 1889.

interminable. The longest – a bout between Jonathan Smith and James Kelly outside Melbourne, Australia, in 1855 – lasted for six hours and 15 minutes.

Other notably long bareknuckle battles were those between William Sheriff and Jimmy Welch at Philadelphia in April 1884 (five hours, three minutes and 45 seconds), Barney Malone and Jan Silberbauer at Kimberley, South Africa, in 1890 (five hours and two minutes), and Con Orem and Hugh O'Neil at Virginia City, Montana, in 1865 (five hours and 30 minutes).

The last major bareknuckle fight took place in a wooden arena outside Richburg, Mississippi, on the estate of Charles Rich on 8 July 1889. John L Sullivan retained his heavyweight championship of the world by stopping Jake Kilrain in the 75th round after two hours and

15 minutes of fighting.

Neither man was greatly injured by his opponent, but both were exhausted by the long struggle under a blazing, midday sun. At the end of the 75th round, a doctor at ringside remarked to Kilrain's seconds: 'If you keep sending that man of yours out there, he will surely drop dead of exhaustion.' Mike Donovan then reluctantly tossed in the sponge.

Sullivan was later arrested by eight Tennessee policemen for breaking the anti-prize-fight law of the state of Mississippi. John L was handcuffed and taken to a Nashville gaol but was released the following day.

However, Sullivan's troubles did not end there. He was later tried and convicted in New York and was sentenced to a year in prison. He got off with a thousand-dollar fine on appeal. Kilrain was also put on trial in Mississippi and was sentenced to two months in jail.

In the event, Kilrain spent the two months at the home of Charles Rich, where he was treated as an honoured guest.

BELL

The assumption that the expression 'saved by the bell' is as old as boxing itself is not only false, it is now technically incorrect. Almost without exception, most boxing rules now stipulate that a boxer can only be saved by the bell in the last round, and even in many championship contests that rule no longer applies.

Moreover, the start and end of a round was not always signalled by the sound of a bell. Under London Prize Ring Rules, the call of 'Time' signalled the start of a round, and the round only ended when there was a knockdown.

Many boxers had been saved by the bell following the publication of the Queensberry Rules in 1867, but in 1963 the World Boxing Association and the New York State Athletic Commission modified the rules to allow the referee to continue counting even though the bell had sounded ending the round.

In terms of the amendment, the count would continue until either the boxer got up or was counted out. Only in the final round could the boxer still be saved by the bell.

The use of a bell or gong to signify the start or finish of a round can be traced back to the nineteenth century, but the first time a gong was used in a heavyweight championship fight was when James J Corbett challenged John L Sullivan for the world title at the Olympic Club in New Orleans on 7 September 1892.

At least two contemporary reports of the fight mention the bell being rung at the end of the 17th round, although in his autobiography *The Roar of the Crowd*, Corbett claims 'Time' was called to start the fight and fails to mention the use of a gong.

An automatic timekeeper that not only timed the rounds but triggered the sound of the gong was first installed by the California Athletic Club in 1891. The first fight in which it was used was the historic heavyweight contest between James J Corbett and Peter Jackson on 21 May 1891.

The unique timing mechanism was introduced primarily to stop unscrupulous seconds and timekeepers from cutting a round short, or lengthening a bout in order to favour one fighter over another. Other boxing clubs on the American West Coast were quick to follow the CAC example – but not so the rest of the world.

By a strange quirk of fate, 90 years later, a major heavyweight fight in Nassau in the Bahamas was controlled by the timekeeper striking a cowbell with a hammer. As luck would have it, this also happened to be the fight in which Trevor Berbick beat Muhammad Ali on 11 December 1981.

'Ali deserved better – a clash of cymbals or the vibrations of a native gong. Actually he deserved a symphony orchestra. But the last round of his career ended with a cowbell tinkling,' Dave Anderson wrote in the *New York Times*.

More understandable perhaps was the use of a pair of spanners to signify the start and end of a round during a professional boxing tournament at the MDC Stadium in Chilomoni, Malawi, in 1994. Saidi Yazidu of Tanzania, who lost to Ali Faki in the main event, was clearly upset by the primitive arrangements.

Adamson Kambwiri, secretary of the Malawi Boxing Board of Control, later told the *Daily Times* of Malawi that the Board had been obliged to improvise in the absence of a bell and claimed that no official complaint had been received.

BELTS

Boxing and belts go hand in glove – and that is the way it has been for nearly two hundred years.

George III of England started the practice when he presented a belt to the British bareknuckle bruiser Tom Cribb after Cribb had beaten the black American Tom Molineaux at Copthall Common on 18 December 1810.

Fifty years later, when Tom Sayers fought John C Heenan of the United States at Farnborough, the winner was to receive a silver belt that had been presented to Sayers by his friends after he had beaten Billy Percy. However, when the crowd cut the ropes after 42 rounds, the fight was declared a draw and it was decided to award each man with a special silver belt to commemorate the occasion.

One of boxing's more infamous belts was that presented to Jake Kilrain in 1886 by the *Police Gazette*, an American publication that covered prize-fighting. John L Sullivan was widely recognized as the heavyweight champion of the world at the time but Richard K Fox, publisher of the *Police Gazette*, gave the belt to Kilrain when Sullivan refused to accept Jake's challenge.

Angered by Fox's actions, Boston boxing fans collected $10,000, bought a gold belt with 397 diamonds and presented it to Sullivan. John L was delighted and dismissed Kilrain's belt with contempt. 'I wouldn't put it around the neck of a goddamn dog,' he said.

Belts have always seemed the most appropriate way in which to reward a boxing champion for his achievements. And arguably the

Jim Watt proudly poses with the European Boxing Union and Lonsdale belts.

most famous of all are the Lonsdale Belts. The first of these was presented to Freddie Welsh by the 5th Earl of Lonsdale after Welsh had beaten Johnny Summers at the National Sporting Club for the British lightweight title in November 1909.

By presenting the belts, the National Sporting Club wanted to ensure that all championship fights would take place at the club. The original Lonsdale Belts had gold content and at one time holders of the belts were guaranteed a pension of £1 per week for life after they had reached the age of 50.

The belts were awarded to any boxer who won the British title three times at the same weight. Until the 1940s Lonsdale Belts were made of 9-carat gold but subsequent belts were gold plated because of the costs.

Floral emblems of the British Isles serve as solid gold links in the belt's design – the shamrock of Ireland, the thistle of Scotland, the rose of England and the daffodil of Wales. Porcelain medallions portraying the early days of boxing further embellish the links, as does the truly fine porcelain inset of Lord Lonsdale.

Twenty-two Lonsdale Belts were issued by the National Sporting Club and 19 were won outright. When the National Sporting Club went out of business, the British Boxing Board of Control carried on the tradition.

Henry Cooper, the former British heavyweight champion, is the only man ever to win three Lonsdale Belts outright. Moreover, no one can break Cooper's record because the rules were changed in 1987, restricting a boxer to only one belt in each weight division.

A Lonsdale Belt was also presented to Joe Louis after the great American boxer successfully defended his world heavyweight title against British challenger Tommy Farr in New York in 1937.

And in a splendid gesture, the British Boxing Board of Control decided to honour ex-world champion Charlie Magri in 1987 for his outstanding contribution to British boxing by presenting him with a Lonsdale Belt in perpetuity. Magri never made a single defence of the British flyweight title but through no fault of his own (there was never a suitable challenger).

In keeping with boxing tradition, *The Ring* magazine began awarding belts to world champions in 1922. World heavyweight champion Jack Dempsey was the first recipient and, in 1923, editor-publisher Nat Fleischer induced promoter Tex Rickard to make a presentation of a diamond-studded gold belt to each new champion. Rickard discontinued the practice in 1927 but *The Ring* has kept the tradition alive to the present day.

Almost without exception, all the so-called world sanctioning bodies now also present their titleholders with championship belts. The World Boxing Council started the practice in 1975 and also offered a championship ring as a symbol of the champion's greatness.

Back in 1910 black Americans contributed towards a diamond-studded belt for Jack Johnson, the first black man to win the

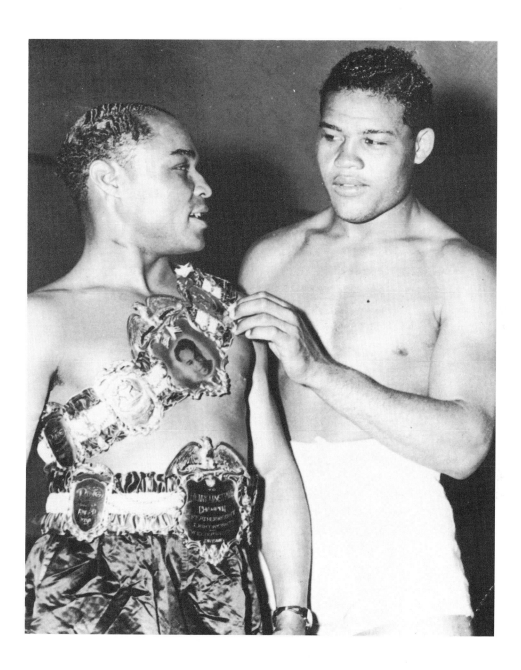

Joe Louis admires *The Ring* magazine championship belts awarded to Henry Armstrong, the only man to hold three world titles simultaneously.

heavyweight championship of the world. A contemporary newspaper report claimed that the belt was made of solid gold, studded with 200 diamonds and worth approximately $25,000.

The belt was inscribed: 'Presented to Jack A Johnson, champion of champions, by popular subscription from his friends and admirers as a token of their esteem', and was awarded to Johnson at a time when the black boxer had few friends in the white American boxing community.

A brewery started the practice of awarding belts to South African champions in 1977. The Old Buck Belts were redesigned three years later but the practice has continued uninterrupted for nearly 20 years. The first man to win an Old Buck Belt was Tsietsie Maretloane, who then also went on to become the first outright

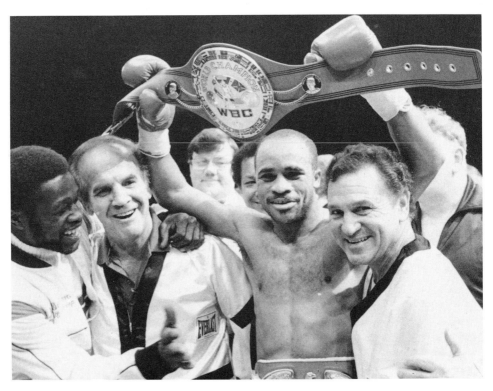

Lloyd Honeyghan is all smiles after winning the WBC welterweight title.

owner of an Old Buck Belt by successfully defending his South African featherweight title three times. In addition, Old Buck has presented belts to the winners of every world championship fight held in South Africa since 1978.

BETTING

The relationship between boxing and betting has always been uneasy but thanks largely to the growth of casino boxing in the United States, the two have finally come to terms.

The Las Vegas casinos are involved in few other sports besides boxing and for many years the casinos concentrated almost exclusively on heavyweight bouts. 'Lighter weight fights bring the fans, but the heavyweights bring everyone,' said Bob Halloran, the then president of sports at the Mirage Hotel casino, in July 1992.

Between puffs on his cigar, Halloran explained what made boxing tick in the gambling resort town. 'If the casinos ever get out of boxing the purse moneys will be cut by 80 per cent or more,' he said. 'Sixty per cent of the people who attend casino fights are fight fans. The other 40 per cent are customers or gamblers who need to have a reason to justify their trip.'

Halloran admitted that the casinos use boxing to attract people: 'When we get ticket requests from the celebrities we know we've got a winner,' he said and added, 'You can't put a number on the potential value of a big fight to the casino. Basically, we use boxing as a marketing tool to improve business.'

Huge electronic betting boards quote the odds on everything from the round the fight will end to the result. 'The betting odds are a reflection of public perception,' said George Luckman, a respected Las Vegas boxing expert who runs the Gamblers Book Club on South 11th Street.

Sadly, it wasn't always that way. Gambling has often hurt the sport more than it has helped. In the eighteenth century boxing was banned by legislation in England because of a gambling loss suffered by the Duke of Cumberland, and the sport was outlawed in Chicago, Illinois, shortly after the turn of the century following a 'fixed' fight between Joe Gans and Terry McGovern. Corruption in the sport also resulted in the repeal of the Horton Law, which permitted fights to a decision and the posting of forfeits and side bets, in New York State in 1900.

The first of many among the British nobility to sponsor and bet heavily on fighters, the Duke of Cumberland was the patron of John Broughton until Jack Slack beat the fat and fortysomething Father of Boxing in 14 minutes in April 1750.

Slack blinded Broughton with heavy blows to the eyes and when a hard right to the jaw sent Broughton to the boards, the duke was horrified. 'What are you about, Broughton?' he asked the fighter.

'I cannot see, my lord,' Broughton answered. 'Stand me before my opponent and I will fight on.'

The fight, however, was already over and having lost £10,000 in bets, the duke accused Broughton of bribery. Livid with rage, he stormed off and later arranged to have legislation passed in Parliament to ban boxing in England. In the event, only Broughton's boxing establishment was closed.

The Gans–McGovern fight in Chicago in December 1900 was plagued by rumours of a fix from the day it was first announced. The word was that Gans would go down in an early round in order to collect wagers that his backers had placed on the fight. And when the Old Master was knocked out in the second round, all hell broke loose. Huge sums of money, both in Chicago and elsewhere, had been wagered on the fight and the result stank to high heaven.

'I do not wish to accuse any fighter of faking, but if Gans was trying last night I don't know much about the game,' referee George Siler declared in the *Chicago Tribune*.

The public's outrage was picked up by the politicians and the clergy and except for established members-only clubs like the Chicago Athletic Association, boxing was outlawed within city limits. It took many years for the ban to be lifted.

Betting on boxing is almost as old as the sport itself and no law is ever likely to stop the practice. In fact, odds have been quoted on heavyweight championship fights and others since the nineteenth century. Only once have bookmakers declined to offer official odds on a heavyweight championship fight.

It happened on 22 August 1957 when Floyd Patterson defended the world heavyweight title against Olympic champion Pete Rademacher in Seattle, Washington. American bookmakers considered Patterson such an overwhelming favourite no odds were offered.

Following the success of casino boxing in Las Vegas and elsewhere, oddsmakers now have an important role to play in the sport. Almost every casino has one. And Herb Lambeck, regarded by many as one of the most knowledgeable, certainly got it right when he analysed the 3–1 odds on Michael Moorer beating George Foreman in 1994 for *Flash*, the American trade paper.

'Since the demise of Mike Tyson upsets in heavyweight championships have become the norm rather than the exception,' Lambeck told *Flash*. 'Moorer ballooned to 245 after winning the title. Looks ripe to be taken. Throw out Big George's uninspired effort against Tommy Morrison, simply a giveaway. Moorer doesn't have the best beard in the world, and I can see Foreman clocking him. New champion.'

BOARDS

The British call them boards, the Americans call them commissions, but both were established with the same purpose in mind – to control the sport of boxing.

American control of the sport tends to be a touch more political than that of the British, largely because many of the appointments to the state athletic commissions are based on political affiliations. But between them, the boards in Britain and the Commonwealth, the commissions in the United States, the Americas and the East, and the unions and federations in Europe have given boxing the legitimacy it needed to survive as a sport in the twentieth century.

The irony is that the British Boxing Board of Control has no legal standing in the United Kingdom – unlike the majority of commissions in the United States, several of the boxing boards in the Commonwealth, and some of the unions and federations in Europe, many of which are the creatures of statute. In fact, the British Board was obliged to become a limited company in the early 1990s largely in order to protect its members from possible lawsuits.

The British Board, which has served as a model for so many others in the Commonwealth, is actually an extension of the old National Sporting Club, which was formed in London in March 1891 to control the sport under the Marquess of Queensberry Rules.

The first suggestion that a boxing board be formed to control the sport in Britain came from *Sporting Life* in 1909 and a move to have boxing legalized in Britain was made at a meeting in July 1925, when a Commander Kenworthy proposed a Boxing Bill be submitted to the Home Office. However, after much discussion it was considered unnecessary on the grounds that the legality of boxing had already been established in several court cases, the mitigating factor being that the sport was properly conducted under Rules.

Marshall Hall, QC, Recorder, set the seal of approval on the sport when he declared in November 1898: 'There is absolutely nothing illegal in boxing itself. It is a noble and manly art, which I hope will never die out in this country.' Fortunately for boxing others in the British legal profession have invariably shared this sentiment.

Following two preliminary meetings in 1914, the National Sporting Club attempted to establish a British Boxing Board of Control in February 1918, but the Board received no official recognition and was lightly regarded by both the boxing community and the press, largely because the Club's influence on the sport was still clearly evident.

It was not until 1 January 1929 that the present British Boxing Board of Control was formed, following a meeting the previous year at which it was accepted that the Board and the National Sporting Club were, in effect, one and the same body.

Charles Donmall was appointed the first general secretary of the Board and the National Sporting Club had a permanent seat on the Board until it ceased to operate as a club in 1937. The Board subsequently took over administration and control of the Lonsdale Belts, established a Benevolent Fund for boxers, and took the initiative in establishing a World Boxing Committee that led to the formation of the World Boxing Council in February 1963.

There is a mistaken belief that the World Boxing Council, World Boxing Association, International Boxing Federation, World Boxing Organization and other such bodies control world boxing. In fact, they do nothing of the sort. Their function is virtually limited to sanctioning title fights, for which they demand a sizeable fee, both from the promoter and the boxers. True, they have altered the rules for championship boxing from time to time and they also insist on nominating the officials, but that is where their responsibility ends.

The actual control of boxing still rests in the hands of local boards or commissions, who may or may not choose to be affiliated to the world bodies.

BOOKS

Few sports can boast of a written history as rich in detail and as fascinating in content as boxing. And whether it was Homer describing a fight between Euryalus and Epeius in the *Iliad* more than 3,000 years ago, or the Roman poet Virgil writing about boxing in Greece, or Lord Byron noting in his diary of 20 March 1814 that he had again sparred with John Jackson, or William Hazlitt describing the fight between Thomas Hickman and Bill Neate, the focus has always been on the fighters.

Boxing's appeal among men worldwide even lured some writers into donning the gloves themselves. And so it was that Paul Gallico, the prize-winning American author, saved his job at the New York *Daily News* by putting on the gloves with world heavyweight

American baseball star Babe Ruth and world heavyweight champion Jack Dempsey compare fists in 1926.

champion Jack Dempsey in 1921.

'After one minute and 27 seconds I was flat on my back with a cut lip and a prize headache. But I also had a story,' Gallico recalled years later.

George Plimpton, yet another renowned American author, took out an instructional book dated 1807 from the local library and taught himself how to shadow-box, before writing a book on the subject.

Plimpton even went as far as to write to Archie Moore, asking the then world light heavyweight champion 'if in the cause of literature' a phrase he underlined twice – Ole Archie would be willing to box a three-round exhibition with him in New York. Moore, who fancied himself as a man of letters, promptly replied and confirmed that he would be 'delighted to participate'.

The men met in a well-publicized exhibition in Stillman's Gym –

and Plimpton got a much admired bloody nose.

In more recent times Randy Gordon, a staff writer for *The Ring* who was destined to become the magazine's editor and later chairman of the New York State Athletic Commission, took out a professional licence and engaged in at least one pro fight to find out firsthand what it was really like to punch for pay.

Captain John Godfrey, who is credited with writing the first book on boxing in 1747, also acquired some practical experience of the sport before including two chapters on boxing in his book *A Treatise Upon the Useful Science of Defence*. 'I have purchased my knowledge with many a broken head and bruises in every part of me,' Godfrey informed his readers.

The book, two copies of which are held in the British Museum, was largely instructional but Godfrey did devote some space to the characters of boxing, including John Broughton, whom he described as 'none so fit, so able to lead up the van'. Others who caught his fancy were Pipes ('the neatest boxer I remember'), Whitaker ('a very strong fellow, but a clumsy boxer'), and James ('he is delicate in his blows, and has a wrist as delightful to those who see him fight, as it is sickly to those who fight against him').

An important contribution to the history of the sport came in 1789 when Daniel Mendoza, who was the champion of England at the end of the eighteenth century, published a little book entitled *The Art of Boxing*. Again the book was largely instructional. Mendoza later published his handwritten memoirs in 1816, a copy of which (complete with marble boards and leather spine) is included in the personal collection of British journalist Peter McInnes.

Pierce Egan, a printer's compositor, song writer and freelance journalist, became boxing's first historian of note when he produced the first volume of *Boxiana* in 1812. Printed and published by his employer George Smeeton, in St Martin's Lane, London, it offered a fascinating history of the prize ring.

This first volume of *Boxiana* reappeared in 1818 together with a second one under the banner of publishers Sherwood, Neely and Jones. A third volume followed in 1821 but Egan then fell into dispute with his publishers, who sought an injunction to prevent him from having further editions of *Boxiana* published elsewhere.

Sherwood's published a fourth volume of *Boxiana* anonymously in 1824, and when the injunction against Egan was declined in the High Court by Lord Eldon, the Lord High Chancellor, Egan wrote two further volumes entitled *New Series Boxiana*. These were published by George Virtue of Paternoster Row in 1828 and 1829 respectively.

Nearly a century and a half later, A J Liebling, the renowned American author whose book *The Sweet Science* is now considered a classic on boxing, described Egan as 'the greatest writer about the ring who ever lived'.

'He belonged to London, and no man has ever presented a more enthusiastic picture of all aspects of its life except the genteel. He was a hack journalist, a song writer, a conductor of puff-sheets and, I am inclined to suspect, a shakedown man,' Liebling declared.

This opinion was not shared by Henry Downes Miles, who published five volumes on the London Prize Ring between 1880 and 1906, and who invariably referred to Egan as an 'illiterate'. Miles openly despised Egan and accused him of slapdash journalism. His own *Pugilistica* series is more authentic and detailed than *Boxiana* and he can rightly claim to be the first to have produced a biographical book on a boxer – his *Sometime Champion of England*, the story of Tom Sayers, which was published in 1866.

Thousands of books on boxing have been published since Captain Godfrey's first couple of chapters on the sport in 1747, but two men stand head and shoulders above the rest as the best of the modern historians: Nat Fleischer and Gilbert Odd.

Fleischer, the New York *Evening Telegram* sports editor who conceived the idea of a monthly illustrated boxing magazine in 1922 which he aptly called *The Ring*, was a prolific writer of books on boxing and together with Sam André produced the first illustrated history of the sport in 1959.

Odd, a British journalist who eventually became editor of *Boxing News*, had most of his work published after the Second World War. His books on boxing were both innovative and informative and between them these two writers had a profound influence on the sport in the twentieth century.

Odd was also among the first to write a book on the contribution that women have made to boxing. His book *The Women in the Corner*, published in 1978, related how women had influenced no fewer than 25 top fighters, including great champions like Jack Dempsey, Stanley Ketchel, Jack Johnson, Jimmy Wilde, Rocky Graziano and Joe Louis.

Since then women have started to produce boxing books of their own and so remarkably good has been the quality that even the chauvinists have felt the urge to stand up and cheer. Two works in particular are worth mentioning: Joyce Carol Oates *On Boxing* (1987) and *The Prizefighters: An Intimate Look at Champions and Contenders* by Arlene Schulman (1994).

Both books offer new insights into the sport with *The Prizefighters* being marketed mostly on the strength of its mood photography, while *On Boxing* provides a female perspective that was sadly lacking in the past.

BOOTS

Almost without exception every set of rules written for boxing makes the wearing of shoes or boots mandatory.

The London Prize Ring Rules described the footwear permissible in detail: 'The spikes in the fighting boots shall be confined to three in number, which shall not exceed three-eighths of an inch from the sole of the boot, and shall not be less than one-eighth of an inch broad at the point; two to be placed in the broadest part of the sole and one in the heel; and that in the event of a man wearing any other spikes either in the toes or elsewhere, he shall be compelled either to remove them or provide other boots properly spiked, the penalty for refusal to be a loss of the stakes.'

The Marquess of Queensberry Rules, which were drafted in 1865 and widely adopted in 1892, outlawed the use of spikes altogether. 'No shoes or boots with springs allowed,' read Rule 11.

A conversation recorded by Pierce Egan, boxing's first great historian, after a fight in December 1800 between Jem Belcher and Andrew Gamble, clearly confirms that boots were an important part of a boxer's footwear at the time.

Belcher: 'Dan Mendoza!'
Mendoza: 'Well, what do you want?'
Belcher: 'I say, these were the shoes I bought to give you a thrashing in Scotland.'
Mendoza: 'Well, the time may come.'
Belcher: 'I wish you'd do it now.'

The boxer's backers had enough good sense not to allow that to happen. Unfortunately, Belcher lost the sight of an eye when he was struck in the face while playing rackets. Belcher made a comeback to the ring a couple of years later but the fight with Mendoza never materialized.

As one would expect, boxing boots have changed in style over the years, with rubber soles now more popular than leather. But back in the 1940s an American company miscalculated when they attempted to market boxing boots that supposedly enabled boxers to stand

The advertisement for Boxeraid boxing boots that appeared in American magazines in the early 1940s.

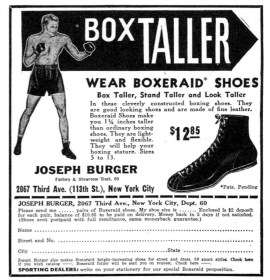

taller. Such gimmicks have little appeal in a conservative sport like boxing.

Due to circumstances, many men have been obliged to box barefoot from time to time. However, the first world championship fight in which both contestants were granted permission to remove their boots took place in Bangkok on 2 May 1954, when Jimmy Carruthers defended his bantamweight title against Chamrem Songkitrat.

The fight was held in a raging typhoon that not only drenched the spectators, but made a lake out of the ring. According to Nat Fleischer, who was at ringside as the official representative of both the National Boxing Association and the European Boxing Union, 'bulbs from the overhead lighting system crashed to the canvas every now and then forcing temporary halts while the broom brigade rushed into the ring to sweep it clean'.

Fleischer gave permission for the boxers to fight barefoot when a request was made at the weigh-in, first by Carruthers and then by Songkitrat. Carruthers, who retained his title on points, stepped on glass in the 11th round and cut his foot, but it would have been impossible to proceed with the fight had the men been required to wear shoes.

Fleischer later claimed it was the most dramatic fight he had ever seen. 'Even more dramatic, because of the circumstances, than Dempsey–Firpo,' he said.

BOXEROBICS

It's the buzzword of the 1990s in health clubs around the world. What Jane Fonda started with her workout videotapes, others have aimed to better with boxerobics – working out to a boxing theme in order to take the boredom out of aerobics.

Videotapes have flooded the market. In *Boxerobics*, a 60-minute videotape produced in the United States, American ring announcer Jimmy Lennon Jr introduces four boxing instructors who demonstrate the twelve basics. 'From beginner to advanced athlete – you will benefit from this thorough workout!' the producers promise.

Nor does the choice end there. Kenny Weldon, described as 'America's No 1 Boxing Teacher and Trainer', offers a complete videotape training series conveniently divided into ten 'rounds' of workouts. Included are 'phase exercises, strength exercises, stance and rhythm, line exercises, jumps and step-ups', etc. There are also instructions on how to workout on the heavy bag, double end bag, jump rope, speed bag and the hand pads.

Working under the supervision of Dr Daniel Hamner, an American specialist in sports medicine, former middleweight contender Michael Olajide developed an exercise programme called 'boxaerobics' that combined both boxing training methods and aerobics.

'Fitness is the harmony between the physical and the mental. Men can do simple aerobics, but don't feel comfortable. The addition of boxing makes it an acceptable form of exercise,' Olajide claimed.

And according to the ex-boxer, women will also find the programme to their liking. 'They can get in there and beat on the pads and relieve all their built-up tension, as well as getting in their daily aerobic workout,' he explained.

If this all sounds new, it isn't. As long ago as 1814 Lord Byron noted in his journal, 'I have been boxing, for exercise, with Jackson for this last month daily' and added: 'I feel all the better for it, in spirits, though my arms and shoulders are very stiff.'

An illustrated article in the 27 February 1905 edition of the New York *Evening World* claimed, 'The Modern Maid Will Help Her Health by Boxing,' while a subheading promised, 'A Half Hour a Day with the Gloves Will Give a Girl Self-Control, Buoyancy and Grace.'

But just as boxerobics is not designed to turn people into pugilists, it was not the intention of the *Evening World* to make the modern maid a boxer. Even so, the urge to fight has sometimes become irrepressible.

James Toney, the former IBF super middleweight champion, sparred with the celebrated American defence attorney Robert Shapiro in Los Angeles

A case in point was that of the famous American defence lawyer Robert Shapiro, who took time off from defending O J Simpson in Los Angeles in 1994, to spar a couple of rounds with the then IBF super middleweight champion James Toney. Evidently Shapiro had been working with a private boxing trainer and wanted to test his skills against a real world champion.

Shapiro picked a real toughie in Toney. 'Who's that old, bald man coming in here?' Toney yelled when Shapiro entered the Outlaw Gym in LA. 'You're a lawyer? I hate lawyers. You want to get into the ring with me? I'll knock you cold.'

In the event, Toney fended off the lawyer's wild aggression with obvious amusement while only throwing a few light punches in return. 'He was such a great sport,' Toney's vivacious manager, Jackie Kallen, said of Shapiro. 'I've had fighters in to spar with Toney and they've shown more fear than Shapiro did.'

Kallen was later to experience some degree of fear herself when Toney allegedly threatened to shoot her after losing his world title to Roy Jones.

BRIBES

Bribery has long been the bane of boxing. But while fixed fights were prevalent in the days of the London Prize Ring, stricter control of the sport has virtually eliminated the practice today.

This was confirmed when the Manhattan District Attorney's office brought a charge of bribery against Ray Mercer following his heavyweight fight with Jesse Ferguson at Madison Square Garden in New York on 6 February 1993.

The prosecution relied heavily upon evidence provided by the electronic media (the fight had been videotaped by Home Box Office) but even though Ferguson told the jury that 'during the match I was offered $100,000 to go down', Mercer was eventually acquitted of the charge.

'This is just another sad story in society. They have people running around killing other people and they want me in court for fighting. That's crazy,' Mercer said after the case had dragged on for nine days.

New York State Athletic Commission chairman Randy Gordon dismissed the whole thing as 'ridiculous' and so too did Jake LaMotta, the former world middleweight champion, who years earlier had admitted before the Kefauver Anti-Crime Committee to taking a dive in a fight with Billy Fox. 'How can you talk about throwing a fight when you're fighting? That's not the way it's done,' said LaMotta.

The Manhattan District Attorney's office thought otherwise and replayed a videotape of the fight in court to substantiate its claim. The trouble was, hardly anyone could hear what the fighters were saying through their mouthguards and when referee Wayne Kelly testified that he did not hear Mercer offer Ferguson any money, the case for the prosecution looked lost.

Mercer's alleged motive for making the bribe was to preserve a multi-million-dollar payday in a championship fight with Riddick Bowe. Ferguson got the Bowe fight instead.

Proving bribery in a boxing match is no easy task, as the Manhattan District Attorney's office discovered to its cost. No one was ever able to prove that Joe Gans took a dive in his Chicago fight with Terry McGovern in December 1900, but the suspicion exists to this day. And Gans, who died in August 1910, was unwelcome in the Windy City for the rest of his life.

The only reason we know middleweight champions Rocky Graziano and Jake LaMotta were offered bribes is because they saw fit to admit it. Sugar Ray Robinson also claimed in his autobiography *Sugar Ray* that he was offered, but refused, a bribe before his fight with Graziano in Chicago in 1952. According to Robinson, the Big Man who controlled the Mafia in Chicago at the time offered him a million dollars to take a dive.

'I'm sorry,' Robinson said he replied. 'I guess I'm too stupid to be anything but a winner. But it was nice of you to ask me. Not many people get a chance to turn down a million dollars.'

Graziano had his boxing licence revoked by the New York State Athletic Commission in 1947 for not reporting an alleged bribe at the time it was made. The Mob allegedly offered Graziano $100,000 to take a dive against Ruben 'Cowboy' Shank. Rather than go through with the fight and too frightened to refuse, Graziano suddenly developed back trouble and the fight never came off.

LaMotta admits that he was twice approached to throw fights. The first time, in June 1947, he refused. Jake was offered $100,000 to take a dive against Tony Janiro. 'If they had threatened me it wouldn't have made any difference,' he said. 'I was too stupid to be scared.'

In November of the same year, 'they' came back with another offer of $100,000 for LaMotta to lose to Billy Fox. LaMotta hesitated but

Joe Gans, the former world lightweight champion, allegedly 'took a dive' in his Chicago fight with Terry McGovern in December 1900.

Rocky Graziano drives a right to the face of Tony Janiro in their 1950 fight. Graziano had his licence revoked in 1947 for not reporting an alleged bribe.

eventually said yes to the fix, no to the money, but on condition that he was to be given a shot at the world middleweight title.

Fox only learned about LaMotta's alleged dive before his second fight with Gus Lesnevich. 'I read about it in the papers. And I heard people talking about it, too,' he recalled years later. After LaMotta admitted to taking a dive in evidence he gave to the Kefauver Anti-Crime Committee, Fox felt emotionally upset. 'I was disgusted,' he said. 'Not with myself, but with what my manager was trying to do.'

Officials have also been the target for bribes. Lou Tabat of Las Vegas – a boxing judge for 25 years – claims he was offered bribes of $2,000, then $5,000 and finally $10,000 to favour WBA featherweight champion Yung Park in his scoring of Park's title defence against Eloy Rojas in Seoul, South Korea, in December 1993.

Money was forced into his suit coat pocket against his will and twice he tossed the money back. 'I was stunned,' Tabat said. 'It was the first time in my life anyone had tried something like that. My first thought was to protect boxing, to protect the sport.'

Rojas won the championship on a split decision.

BROTHERS

Arguably the most successful brothers in boxing were probably Leon and Michael Spinks, if only because they both won the heavyweight championship of the world. However, the Spinks brothers were by no means the first set of siblings to win world titles.

That honour belongs to the Attell brothers, a couple of Jewish-American boys who boxed around the turn of the century. Abe claimed the featherweight title after beating George Dixon on points over 15 rounds in October 1901 and Monte won the California version of the world bantamweight title when he knocked out Frankie Nell in 18 rounds in June 1909.

Ten sets of brothers have turned the trick since the Attell boys both laid claim to world championships, but only five siblings have held world titles simultaneously. They include the Attell brothers, Donald and Bruce Curry, Khaosai and Kaokor Galaxy, Terry and Orlin Norris and Rafael and Gabriel Ruelas.

Few of the brothers experienced such abject poverty as the Ruelas boys. Growing up with 11 brothers and sisters on a cattle ranch in Yerba Buena, Mexico, they lacked all the amenities most young people take for granted.

'Where we come from is like going back a hundred years in time,' Gabriel recalled after becoming the WBC super featherweight champion of the world. 'We were lucky to have a radio. We had no socks, no shoes, no TV, no electricity. Our light at night was the moon. We lived like Indians.'

Leon Spinks and his brother Michael are the only brothers to have won the world heavyweight title.

Donald Curry, the former WBA welterweight champion, whose brother Bruce won the WBC super lightweight title.

Even after they legally moved to Southern California to live with an older sister when Gabriel was ten and Rafael nine, the brothers didn't have it easy. They slept on the living-room floor for seven years.

The Spinks boys also had it tough. The product of one of the poorest ghettos in St Louis, Missouri, they are the only brothers to have won the world heavyweight title (Leon in 1978 and Michael in 1985) and Olympic gold medals in the same year (1976). But the brothers are remembered as much for their mother (little Mrs Kay Spinks) as they are for their achievements in the ring.

Mrs Spinks, an ebullient lady with tremendous faith in her Maker, was there in Las Vegas when Leon shocked the world by beating Muhammad Ali for the heavyweight title in only his eighth professional fight. 'Didn't I tell you he would do it?' Mrs Spinks asked the press in Leon's dressing room afterwards, a Bible still clutched firmly in her gloved hand.

However, when Leon was knocked out in one round by Gerrie Coetzee in Monte Carlo in June 1979, the little lady was less

The five fighting Zivic brothers of Pittsburgh, USA. Only Fritzie went on to become a world champion.

forgiving. 'You were off guard,' Mrs Spinks yelled at her son as he left the ring. 'You shouldn't fight off guard.'

'Don't holler at me, Momma,' Leon cried. 'I just lost the fight, that's all.'

In retrospect the Spinks brothers were lucky: Michael is the only man to have won both the world light heavyweight and heavyweight titles, and no one has won the world heavyweight title in fewer fights than Leon.

Many boxing families have produced a world champion without the other brothers making it to the top. The Weaver triplets – Floyd, Lloyd and Troy – were never able to match the achievements of older brother Mike, who won the world heavyweight title in 1980 by knocking out John Tate.

Many of the most famous champions of all time had brothers who also boxed: men who are all but forgotten today. There was Rudy Clay, who sometimes fought on the same bill as his more famous brother Muhammad Ali (aka Cassius Clay); and Bernhard Dempsey, whose brother Jack was the toast of the United States in the Roaring Twenties.

Fritzie, Jack, Pete, Joe and Eddie Zivic were all useful fighters from the American steel town of Pittsburgh, but only Fritzie became a world champion at welterweight in 1940. Willie Toweel of South Africa nearly emulated his elder brother Vic by winning the world bantamweight title in 1955 (his fight with Robert Cohen was declared a draw), but brothers Alan, Frazer and Jimmy were little more than average in boxing ability.

The best-known heavyweight brothers besides Leon and Michael Spinks were the Baer brothers. Max won the world heavyweight title in 1934 when he dropped Primo Carnera 11 times en route to scoring an 11th-round knockout, while younger brother Buddy twice challenged Joe Louis unsuccessfully for the title in the 1940s.

Back in August 1938 the Finazzo brothers – all six of them – set a record that still stands today when they fought on the same show in Baltimore. From Sam (the oldest at 27) to John (the youngest at 14), all six brothers – the others were Joe, Victor, Eddie and Jack – took turns climbing into the Carlin Arena ring. Victor (19) fought Buddy Taylor over ten rounds in the main event.

George, Danny and Nick Acevedo made New York Golden Gloves history when they became the first trio of brothers to win titles in the same tournament in 1992. Previously at least five two-brother combinations had won titles, but no family had ever completed the hat-trick.

George (19) easily won the 112-pound Open title; Danny (17) beat former Gloves champion Radames Torres to win the 125-pound Open championship and Nick (17) completed the family sweep by taking the 132-pound crown.

An even more notable event in Scottish amateur boxing occurred in 1930 when the brothers J and R Whiteford both reached the final of the heavyweight division – but refused to fight each other.

CAMPS

Three thousand years ago the Greek philosopher Plato recognized the need of training for a fight when he declared: 'Surely, if we were boxers, we should have been learning to fight many days before and exercising ourselves in imitating all those blows and wards which we were intending to use in the hour of conflict.'

And yet, despite Plato's sound observation it was not until after 600 BC that boxers enjoyed the benefit of training in special gymnasiums. Even so, when the sport of boxing was restarted in England in the seventeenth century, training was again neglected until the eighteenth century.

It took the near defeat of English champion Tom Cribb by Tom Molineaux of the United States in 1810 to convince the British that a man had to be fit to fight. And by the time Cribb and Molineaux met in a rematch a year later, Captain Barclay Allardyce had come to the fore as the first scientific trainer of prize-fighters in modern history.

Barclay believed in long walks between bouts of running and

made Cribb walk 60 miles on his second day of training in order to get something to eat. The British boxer was so changed in appearance by the time he again shaped up to Molineaux that the black fighter exclaimed: 'This is not Master Cribb. This is a strange man whom I do not know.'

Training camps were still unknown at the time but after Professor Mike Donovan, a former middleweight champion who twice held his own in fights with John L Sullivan, wrote in 1893 that 'it is a good plan to train at a long distance from centers of business and pleasure', the idea quickly caught on.

Donovan was the boxing instructor of the New York Athletic Club and when he advised boxers to 'choose your training quarters in a mountainous or hilly part of the country, where you can be sure of pure air and be free from dust', few were prepared to argue.

Mind you, the early training camps were hardly places of pleasure. When Nellie Bly, a woman reporter for the New York *World*, visited John L Sullivan at his camp in Belfast, New York, in 1889, the heavyweight champion made no attempt to hide his feelings. 'It's the worst thing going,' he said when asked whether training was pleasant. 'A fellow would rather fight twelve dozen times than train once, but it's got to be done.'

American heavyweight King Levinsky echoed these sentiments nearly 50 years later when he went to England to fight Jack Doyle. Levinsky trained at the Dumbbell Inn, a rural hostelry not far from Slough. Asked by a visiting reporter how he, a Chicago city boy, was settling down amid the charms of the peaceful English countryside, Levinsky gave the reporter a long, searching look before answering. 'I gotta,' he said.

It didn't take promoters long to realize that training camps could also be good for publicity. When Tom Heeney established his training camp at Lakeside, New Jersey, while preparing for his heavyweight title fight with Gene Tunney in 1928, promoter Tex Rickard invited a group of bankers to the camp to watch Heeney train.

Rickard, who believed in doing everything in style, made use of a luxury yacht for the trip. Unfortunately, the journey took a little longer than Rickard had anticipated and the bored boxer decided to

The legendary greats, Jack Dempsey and Max Baer, sparring during the days when Baer was heavyweight champion of the world.

take out his frustration on Phil Messurio, his sparring partner.

When Rickard and his VIP group arrived, he was greeted by a spectator. 'Hiya, Tex. Why didn't you get here in time to see your man almost get knocked out?'

'What do you mean?' Rickard asked.

'Why, the training is all over. His sparring partner just battered him all over the ring.'

The story quickly spread, the fight drew poorly at the gate, and Rickard lost a small fortune in money.

At the urging of his manager Joe Jacobs, former world heavyweight champion Max Schmeling also went looking for publicity when he visited Pompton Lakes, New Jersey, before his first fight with Joe Louis in 1936.

Asked why he was there, Schmeling told Bill Miller, the so-called camp director: 'To watch Joe work out.' Horrified, Miller fetched Louis's co-manager, Julian Black, who explained that he didn't think it was a very good idea.

Max Mahon, Schmeling's trainer, suggested that they should at least let the boxers pose together. Black hesitated but finally agreed 'as long as it wasn't in public view'. And then after 40 minutes Louis, his hands taped and wearing boxing boots, a vest and underwear, arrived in the room for the picture to be taken.

Louis loved to do his training at Pompton Lakes but in later years Rocky Marciano preferred Grossinger's. Barney Ross, the former world welterweight champion, had first sparred in an outdoor ring at Grossinger's in 1934 and, like Marciano, he did not enjoy the full facilities of the resort hotel.

Marciano spent most of his time in a tiny wooden farmhouse near the airstrip for private planes and did his sparring in the ski lodge. Ingemar Johansson changed all that when he arrived at Grossinger's in 1959 to train for his first fight with Floyd Patterson in New York. Johansson chose to live in a fancy cottage near the swimming pool, installed his fiancée Birgit, and went about his business as though he was on vacation.

Besides the usual training routines, Johansson added his own series of Swedish callisthenics and spent at least six minutes a day punching a strange contraption called a *slungboll*. Suspended from

Muhammad Ali in a pensive mood at his Deer Lake training camp.

a board by its 18-inch strap handle, it was harder to hit consistently than the ordinary speedball.

Afterwards Johansson claimed that his preparation for the fight had been better than that of Patterson. 'He was put in a closed-in unhealthy gymnasium under artificially ascetic conditions. He slept in a cubicle-type room in the training barn, far from his wife and children ...'

Johansson knocked out Patterson in the third round and ever since most champions have lived like kings in their training camps, unlike the hotel Max Schmeling chose as his base for his title defence against Young Stribling in Cleveland, Ohio, in 1931.

It was an hotel that also had among its guests a whole raft of undertakers – morticians, as the Americans call them – on hand for their annual convention. Every time the boxer walked through the foyer to the improvised gym where he sparred, he had to pass rows of coffins and grisly wax figures displayed to boost brands of embalming fluid.

An equally weird set-up was the training camp promoter Mike Jacobs established at Long Beach, New Jersey, for Tommy Farr when the British heavyweight went over to America in 1937 to challenge Joe Louis for the world heavyweight title.

The Farr camp occupied a large 14-room house on the sea front, about a mile from the stadium where Tommy did his training. The house never knew a dull moment. Farr was at loggerheads with his manager Ted Broadribb at the time and any conversation that became necessary between them generally had to be conducted through third parties, often with exciting results.

Farr not only was in frequent arguments with the other members of his entourage but at times he carried his embattled moods into interviews he had with visiting writers, threatening to punch this one on the nose or throw that one out on his ear.

One afternoon the camp's chef, a chubby gent named Barker, was discovered belting away lustily at a ham he had hung from the lighting fixtures on the kitchen ceiling.

'What's the idea?' asked a surprised caller.

'Just punching the bag,' Barker replied. 'Everybody in this joint is fighting, so I may as well get into shape myself.'

CARDS

A practice that was fashionable at the turn of the century returned in the 1990s when several American companies again started to offer boxing cards for sale. The big difference, of course, is that at the turn of the century the cards were given away free by cigarette companies, whereas today they have to be purchased in sets.

A W Sports of California re-created the collecting craze in 1990 by first choosing Muhammad Ali as their company spokesman and then using the former world heavyweight champion to market the cards throughout the world. While the face of the cards carried a colour picture of a fighter, the reverse side offered statistical and historical information.

Brown's Boxing Cards had issued their first set in 1985 but in black and white only, whereas A W Sports Inc launched their cards with a 150-card colour set. Kayo Cards followed soon after with a 220-colour-card set and since then Ringlords has also entered the market.

Boxing cards have a long history and can be traced back to the early 1880s, about the time that John L Sullivan won the heavyweight title from Paddy Ryan. Cigarette manufacturers Goodwin & Goodwin began to give away pictures of various American personalities of the time, including prize-fighters.

Other cigarette companies joined in the competition, with Allen & Ginter in particular putting out beautiful cards, all intended to increase the sale of cigarette brands now long gone and forgotten.

From the makers of Mecca cigarettes came a series of attractive cards, featuring such renowned fighters as John L Sullivan, James J Jeffries, Jack Johnson, Kid McCoy and James J Corbett, among others. Fifty-six full-colour reproductions were issued in booklet form by General Publishing Company of Canada in 1988, with an introduction by Bert Randolph Sugar.

'Classic Boxing Cards is a celebration of the time when the two worlds of boxing and cigarette cards were both at their zenith, giving colour to the American landscape back in that first decade and a half of the twentieth century. It was a time that, unfortunately, was never to be duplicated in either world,' Sugar wrote in his introduction.

Sadly, the quality of the cards fell sharply at the outbreak of the First World War because German-made printing-ink pigments were no longer available to American manufacturers.

Using state-of-the-art equipment, today's printers are capable of producing superb cards, and advance copies of the Muhammad Ali card created a heavy demand among collectors in the United States.

JULIO CESAR CHAVEZ

A polite ripple of applause greeted Julio Cesar Chavez as he entered the ring at the Convention Center in Atlantic City to defend his WBC and IBF junior welterweight titles against Kyung-Duk Ahn in December 1990. Compared with the roar from the crowd that welcomed Mike Tyson two bouts later, it was very nearly a snub – and there lay the rub.

Once considered the best boxer, pound for pound, in the world, Chavez was often obliged to play second fiddle to men like Tyson, Sugar Ray Leonard and Thomas Hearns. And although the Mexican boxer smiled readily, deep down it hurt.

The frustration finally got the better of the boxer at a press conference in Las Vegas before his rematch with Meldrick Taylor in September 1994. 'Why am I so criticized?' Chavez asked. 'Is it because I am Mexican?'

Even at the peak of his brilliant boxing career, Chavez appeared to have three strikes against him. One, he was Mexican; two, he spoke only Spanish; and three, he had long been associated with two of the most controversial men in boxing – WBC president José Sulaiman and American promoter Don King.

The records show that only a handful of Latin fighters have ever succeeded in capturing the imagination of the greater American public, but Chavez still suspects that there is an American media conspiracy against him.

Flashback to the days when Julio Cesar Chavez ruled the junior lightweight division. Above: Chavez vs Giovanni Parisi. Below: watching while the referee counts out Ruben Castillo in the sixth round.

To his credit, King tried to overcome the problem and turn Chavez into a popular folk hero when he got Francesco Scavullo of *Cosmopolitan* magazine to photograph Chavez in his New York studio; arranged for the fighter to make an anti-drug commercial for Mexican TV, and persuaded the organizers to let Julio judge the Miss Mexico Pageant.

But the only result of King's marketing campaign was a bit part for Chavez in Orion Pictures' feature film *The Honoured Society* and little else.

'Chavez is very, very popular, but not the most loved,' explained Fernando Paramo, sports editor for the Los Angeles based *La Opinion*, the largest-selling Spanish daily newspaper in the United States. 'I would say his biggest triumph as an idol was that about 8,000 people drove 450 kilometres from Los Angeles to see him fight Meldrick Taylor in Las Vegas.'

A year earlier, in 1989, Chavez was getting bad press in his native Mexico. Fernando Gutierrez Perez asked aloud in the *Mexican City Excelsior* whether Chavez had a drink problem and claimed that the boxer was 'overweight and confused by fame, money, vanity and bad friends'. It's true that Julio got drunk – well, sort of – after the Taylor fight, but only by sipping champagne with hotel owner Steve Wynn of the Las Vegas Mirage.

'In boxing, one measure of greatness is how a champion rebounds from his first defeat,' *The Ring* magazine declared after the first Taylor fight, and added, 'Chavez rebounded before being defeated. This is not to suggest that he'll win for as long as he chooses to fight ... but his future battles aside, Chavez left an indelible mark on the fight game with his thrilling victory.'

Nobody disputes that JC Superstar's last-gasp victory over Taylor in that first fight was anything less than magnificent (referee Richard Steele stopped the fight with only two seconds remaining in the last round). However, there are those who suggest that Taylor was not given the smartest advice by his corner coming up for the 12th and final round.

'You need this round,' trainer George Benton told Taylor. 'This fight is hanging on this round, Mel,' said Lou Duva, who was assisting Benton.

Chavez has been boxing as a professional since the age of 17.

In fact, all three judges had Taylor comfortably ahead at that stage of the fight by margins of two, five and seven points and as Bob Raissman wrote in the New York *Daily News*, 'What the cornermen told Taylor may have explained why he was defeated.'

And yet, while it would be unfair to play down the Mexican's dramatic victory, the fact that an early loss in his career was later changed to a win in order to clean up his record does not sit well with the rank and file of the fight game. Chavez was evidently disqualified in the first round of his 12th professional fight against Miguel Ruiz when the referee accused him of striking Ruiz after the bell.

For several years the fight appeared as a loss for Chavez in both the *Ring Record Book* and *Pugilato* but the local boxing commission in Culiacan officially changed the result the next day. The fight is now recorded as a one-round knockout win for Chavez.

There was a time when Chavez was hoping to score 100 victories without defeat, but Pernell Whitaker spoiled his fun by holding him to a draw in 1993, and then Frankie Randall unexpectedly beat him on points in January 1994. Chavez beat Randall on a technical decision in their rematch. However, the victory was unconvincing and many insist Randall was robbed.

Chavez has been boxing as a professional since the age of 17 and the wear and tear of 90-odd fights has started to take its toll. Moreover, JC Superstar was never a spectacular fighter. He works mostly on the inside, throwing hooks to the head or digging blows to the body, and this style does not always come across well on television.

On the other hand, he has been remarkably durable. Larry Merchant, Home Box Office's renowned television commentator, marvelled after watching Chavez emerge unscathed from a clash of heads with José Luis Ramirez: 'I don't know what Chavez has got for a skin, but you sure could make a helluva sofa from it.'

CLUBS

Arguably the most famous club in the history of boxing was the National Sporting Club of London, which first opened its doors at 43 King Street, Covent Garden, on 5 March 1891.

The NSC was by no means boxing's first club – founded by John Fleming and A F 'Peggy' Bettinson, it actually rose from the ashes of the infamous Pelican Club – but it was destined to become the most influential in the history of the sport.

Over the years the club built up a great tradition for sportsmanship and fair play and did much to make boxing more acceptable as a sport. Bouts were held after dinner and members and their guests were expected to wear evening dress. The fights were fought in complete silence as no talking or cheering was permitted during the rounds.

The club began to lose some of its influence in the 1920s and in October 1928 the NSC opened its doors to the general public for the first time. The original NSC finally went into voluntary liquidation in 1940 but the club's contribution to boxing – and especially British boxing – should never be underestimated.

The success of the NSC inspired the formation of similar clubs both in Paris and New York but they did not last long. Club fights were popular in the United States before the turn of the century and Mechanics Pavilion in California was as widely known in its day as was the old Madison Square Garden of New York and the NSC of London.

Nor should it be forgotten that it was the Olympic Club that hosted the famous Carnival of Champions in New Orleans in 1892, during which John L Sullivan and Jim Corbett became the first men to fight with gloves for the heavyweight championship of the world.

When the Horton Law, which governed boxing in the state of New York, was repealed in 1900, club membership became a lifeline for the sport until 1911 when the Frawley Law brought boxing back to the state.

However, it was only after the Walker Law came into effect on 24 May 1920 that the need for club membership finally fell away. Two years earlier, the anti-boxing law had been upheld by Supreme Court Justice Peter A Henrick, who ruled in the case of The People *vs* Packey O'Gatty that the repeal of the Frawley Law in November 1917 automatically outlawed club-membership boxing in New York.

Little wonder that in order for the sport to survive, American boxing became famous for its clubs. New York, which had become the mecca of boxing, had a bunch of them ranging from the Fairmont Athletic Club on 137th Street and Third Avenue to the Sharkey Athletic Club on 66th Street and Columbus Avenue. The Fairmont, which was owned by Billy Gibson (the man destined to pilot both Benny Leonard and Gene Tunney to world titles) was arguably the most successful.

Under the club-membership system boxing fans had no real protection and whenever a boxer in a top-of-the-bill bout failed to turn up, as was frequently the case, any old bout was put on in its place. Nobody got his money back.

Many great fights were staged at the Fairmont AC. Jack Dempsey's first two fights in New York were fought at the club, and the legendary Benny Leonard developed there as a young boxer. A number of foreign boxers also fought at the club including Jem Driscoll, Owen Moran, Charles Ledoux and Marcel Moreau.

Driscoll, a thin, scrawny, anaemic-looking individual, beat Leach Cross in a great fight at the club. Afterwards the men happened to meet in a Turkish bath. Leach looked at the skinny little British boxing master and exclaimed: 'Well, I'll be jiggered! Are you the fellow that just handed me a fine pasting at the Fairmont Club?'

The boxing-club tradition in the United States lasted until well after the end of the Second World War, though membership was no longer a necessity. St Nicholas Arena on West 66th Street was a boxing club for 66 years until it was demolished in 1962 to make way for a 40-storey building for ABC Television.

'St Nick's was the best of all the clubs,' said Al Braverman, a former manager and trainer and now the director of boxing for Don King Productions. 'The Broadway Arena rates second. But St Nick's had an overhanging balcony. You could see from anywhere up there. Looking down at the ring was sensational. Those seats were better than ringside.'

Benny Leonard died at St Nick's while refereeing a fight there on 18 April 1947.

Among the few genuine fight clubs still being used in the United States is the Blue Horizon in Philadelphia. Built as a Frat House for Temple University in 1864, the Horizon believes in giving fans value for money and in February 1995 staged a 17-bout card with Rodney Moore and Joe Alexander topping the bill.

One of the few countries where boxing is still run on a club basis is Japan, where club owners are often former professionals who are also allowed both to manage and promote.

First-year Japanese professional boxers are eligible to enter Japan's unique Shinjin-O or rookie competition, which is run on a regional basis with the finals being held in Tokyo each year. The competition invariably produces at least one future national champion.

COLLECTORS

They value the past more than the present. Some collect as a hobby, but for many it has become an obsession. And while some specialize, others collect everything they can lay their hands on.

'Only a collector is able to understand the joy experienced in adding another item to his collection,' explained Ron Jackson, a South African-based collector whose collection of boxing memorabilia is one of the finest in the world.

'The real collector, the one driven by some strange impulse, finds there is nothing that cannot become the object of his obsession. He always has a craving for some item which he inwardly knows is unattainable.'

Jerry Fitch, who describes the collection he houses in Cleveland, USA, as modest, insists that collectors of boxing memorabilia are unique. 'Those of us who collect soon realize that we are strictly a minority,' he said. 'And yet collectors are among the fight game's most avid fans. They spend countless hours searching, writing and seeking out fellow collectors so they can fulfil their dreams.'

To assist them in their quest, at least two publications were launched in the United States to cater specifically for boxing collectors. *Fistic Fever*, which was published in California by Ronald Marshall, evidently has an uncertain future. But under the editorship of Don Scott, *Boxing Collectors' News* has been published monthly since 1988 and offers articles on boxing cards, programmes, tickets, autographs, equipment, books, photographs, etc in each issue. In addition, it also lists hundreds of items for sale and auction by collectors and dealers.

Prices offered are often surprisingly good. At a public auction in San Francisco in 1992 the original boxing glove, patented in 1879, was sold for $38,500. The gloves worn by James J Corbett in his 1892 world heavyweight title fight with John L Sullivan fetched $41,250. And the robe worn by world heavyweight champion Rocky Marciano for his 1955 title defence against Don Cockell was sold for $29,700.

The death of former world heavyweight champion Joe Louis in 1981 caused a tremendous demand among boxing collectors for memorabilia connected with the legendary Brown Bomber. No other fighter had so many books and souvenir items issued that were related directly to him.

Among the rarest of the collectables were Joe Louis posters; the Joe Louis medallions issued by the International Numismatic Society to commemorate his 1938 victory over Max Schmeling; the 29 September 1941 issue of *Time* magazine that featured Louis on the cover; the 40-odd 16mm films of Louis fights; the painting by B Peak of the Louis–Schmeling fight that was issued as a limited edition by *Sports Illustrated* in 1972; the Joe Louis Thermometer; the Radiola

Joe Louis made yet another break-through against the colour bar when Chesterfield cigarettes decided to use him in an advertising campaign.

Company record album of the Louis–Sharkey fight; and the Louis–Conn and Louis–Walcott unofficial programmes marketed by black businessmen.

Some collectors have even created their own collectables. Back in the 1930s, Dr Walter H Jacobs, a New York dentist, started to make casts of famous fighting fists. His collection ranged from the huge fist of Primo Carnera to the much smaller hands of Jack Dempsey and Jack Johnson.

The method used to make the casts was simple. First Jacobs made a mould of the hand, poured plaster into it, and then allowed it to harden. The mould was opened and the cast, an accurate reproduction of the hand, was then bronzed.

'One of the smallest hands in the whole collection, including those of bantamweights and flyweights, is that of Tony Canzoneri,' Jacobs wrote in the April 1939 issue of *The Ring* magazine. 'It is a chubby, round hand, with a narrow wrist and short fingers. Yes, almost feminine!'

Another outstanding hand in the collection was that of Henry Armstrong, the only man ever to hold three world titles simultaneously. 'Armstrong's hand is symmetrical,' Jacobs wrote. 'It is cleanly built. The fingers and wrist are wiry and at the present time there are no indications of any breaks or strains.'

Where to house such valuable collections has been the concern of many in boxing. Several recent donations of printed materials have prompted the International Boxing Hall of Fame in Canastota, New York, to begin planning an enlarged research and library facility connected with the museum.

With donations from such famous collectors as Jack Fiske, the doyen of American boxing writers, and lifelong boxing fan and historian Charles F Parker, the Hall of Fame collection has grown rapidly. Included are 500 newspapers from the US west and east coasts covering many title fights from the 1890s to the present, championship fight programmes, press releases from Madison Square Garden during the 1960s and 1970s, photo files of champions and non-champions, and a host of books and boxing magazines.

'With these recent additions to our library we think we may now have the most extensive and complete library on boxing in the world,' Edward Brophy, the Boxing Hall of Fame executive director, said in 1994. But the chances are Brophy hasn't yet visited former Fleet Street journalist Peter McInnes, whose huge collection of boxing memorabilia has virtually taken over his entire house in Bournemouth.

'No one has yet been able to define this so-called madness of collecting,' says Ron Jackson. 'But this much I know from personal experience: collectors get enormous pleasure from their strange pursuit.'

COMEBACKS

Somebody once said that boxers never really quit. And judging by the number of fighters who have decided to return to the ring – especially in the last decade – the fellow obviously knew what he was talking about.

Mind you, boxers have been making comebacks ever since records of fist-fights were first kept around 6000 BC. Trouble is, only a handful have made a success of it. The old boxing adage that 'they never come back' held good for half a century or more after the adoption of the Queensberry Rules.

Then Floyd Patterson regained the world heavyweight title from Ingemar Johansson in 1960 and suddenly the old bogy had lost its sting. But the man who really buried it – good and proper – was Muhammad Ali. Unlike Patterson, Ali had been away from the ring for more than three years when he launched his comeback against Jerry Quarry in October 1970. Moreover, Ali went on to regain the heavyweight title not once, but twice.

In fact, if they ever decide to crown anyone King of the Comeback, Muhammad Ali is likely to be the first choice. Yet even Ali made one comeback too many. Larry Holmes humiliated him in

Floyd Patterson became the first man to regain the world heavyweight title when he knocked out Ingemar Johansson in five rounds in June 1960.

their 1980 title fight, and a year later there was the sad sight of Trevor Berbick beating him in the Bahamas.

Of course, the greatest comeback of all time must surely belong to George Foreman. His first attempt to regain the world heavyweight title in April 1991 ended in defeat when Evander Holyfield outboxed him over 12 rounds in Atlantic City. And when Tommy Morrison beat him on points in a WBO title fight in June 1993, most thought they had seen the last of the big fellow in a boxing ring.

Not only did Foreman prove them wrong, he astonished the world by bouncing back with a sensational tenth-round knockout of Michael Moorer in November 1994 to become the oldest man to win a world championship. 'On this planet we will now know that the athletes in the world are between 45 and 55,' said the nearly 46-year-old punching preacher.

Few boxers ever quit at the peak of their careers unless they are forced to: Sugar Ray Leonard had no choice. A detached retina in his left eye cut his career short in 1982. 'I will not come back and that's it ... the feeling is gone,' Leonard said when he announced his retirement from the ring.

Two years later Leonard was back, only to retire once more after an unimpressive ninth-round stoppage of Kevin Howard. And then, roughly three years later, he was back again, outboxing Marvin Hagler to win the world middleweight title. Leonard added both the world super middleweight title and the world light heavyweight title to his collection before he finally retired for good at the age of 34 in 1991.

Almost without exception, every boxer finds a reason to justify making a comeback. 'I'm coming back for the challenge, not for the money, not the adulation,' Leonard said when he first decided to return to the ring.

'When I first retired, a lot of people said, "I'm so proud of you," or "You're so intelligent to retire." But no one was asking me how I truly felt. They just accepted the fact that I retired. Just because I'm established financially doesn't mean I still don't have goals to accomplish and things to shoot for.'

On the night Leonard first announced he would never box again, his eventual return was predicted by Dave Jacobs, his original trainer, who had fallen out of favour and was no longer a member of Sugar Ray's entourage.

'He's a fighter,' Jacobs said at the time. 'I think I know him as well as anyone. He'll be out a few months, then he'll change his mind. It happens to fighters – not the mediocre ones, but the great ones.'

Jacobs certainly got that right. Almost all the great ones, except perhaps Rocky Marciano and Gene Tunney, have changed their minds – Muhammad Ali and Joe Frazier in the 1970s, Joe Louis and Sugar Ray Robinson in the 1950s and Jack Dempsey and Jim Jeffries in an earlier age.

COMICS

Asked by a reader in the February 1995 issue of *Boxing Illustrated* magazine to name the man who best typified the old-time boxing manager, American boxing historian Herb Goldman replied: 'Knobby Walsh of Joe Palooka fame.'

Never mind that Knobby Walsh was a fictitious character in a comic strip; as far as Goldman was concerned the hundreds of millions of readers of the Joe Palooka comic strip would surely know what he meant.

And besides, there came a time when Ham Fisher, the man who first started drawing the Joe Palooka strip on 19 April 1930, often spoke of Joe as a real person and sometimes seemed to think that he himself was Knobby Walsh.

And yet, while Joe Palooka was unquestionably the most famous boxing comic strip of all time, there were others before it that were also good but not nearly as successful. These included Rube Goldberg's Mike & Ike and Vic Forsythe's Dynamite Dunn, which often used real personalities like the then world heavyweight champion Jack Dempsey among its characters.

In fact, boxing cartoons can be traced back to the eighteenth century and among the great sports cartoonists who have included boxing in their portfolio are Willard Mullin, Thaddeus Aloysius Dorgan 'TAD', Bob Edgren, Rube Goldberg, Robert Ripley, Bill Gallo, Hype Igoe and Ted Carroll.

But the king of the comic strip was undeniably Fisher, the one-time cartoonist-reporter-writer and part-time advertising salesman for the *Wilkes-Barre Herald*. Fisher first conceived the idea of a boxing comic strip in 1921 but it was not until 1930 that the strip got off the ground. After modest success, the strip really caught on when the New York *Mirror* began running it on 1 January 1931.

One of the reasons it took so long for Fisher to sell his idea was because the early Joe Palooka was arguably one of the worst-drawn comic strips ever seen. It was only after Fisher got Phil Boyle to redraw the strip that he managed to sell the concept.

'There was no secret to the appeal of Fisher's heavyweight champ; Palooka himself had pretty much spelled it out when he declared he would fight only "crooks and bullies". Each episode, daily and Sunday, was a morality play with Palooka taking the part of the forces of light and his opponents – in the ring or out – representing evil in varying degrees,' Charles Singer wrote in the December 1983 issue of *The Ring* magazine.

Palooka was one of the first cartoon characters to join the Armed Forces in the Second World War, giving up his title to enlist in the army in 1941. From Pearl Harbor to VJ Day, Joe worked ceaselessly for the American war effort, not only in newspapers, but also in countless posters and pamphlets for the US Defense Department.

Fisher himself was never considered a very good artist and except for the faces of Joe and Knobby, it was Alfred Caplin who drew virtually the entire strip. Later Caplin started his own comic strips and then launched a vendetta which included an article in *The Atlantic* about his years with Fisher entitled 'I Remember Monster'.

The feud came to a head when Fisher accused Caplin of public obscenity at an FCC hearing. His failure to prove the charge resulted in Fisher being expelled by the National Cartoonists Society, and two days after Christmas 1955, he committed suicide.

The Joe Palooka comic strip was read worldwide and became the basis for several Hollywood movies.

What they say often influences what you see. Sometimes they say too much; seldom do they say too little. And yet without them, watching fights on television would not be half the fun it is today.

Few will have forgotten how commentator Reg Gutteridge set the scene before the start of the WBO super middleweight title fight between Chris Eubank and Nigel Benn in Manchester in October 1993 with only four words. As Eubank strode arrogantly to the ring and brashly hopped over the ropes, Gutteridge told ITV viewers: 'The ego has landed!'

American commentator Howard Cosell, who always prided himself on 'telling it like it is', also caught the mood of the middleweight match between Hugo Corro and Vito Antuofermo in 1979 with a few well-chosen words. As the ABC network crossed to ringside after a commercial break, Cosell intoned with all the gravity of a High Court judge: 'We're back live in Monte Carlo; which is more than we can say for the fight.'

Boring bouts often try the patience of even the most committed commentators. Describing a lacklustre heavyweight fight for SABC television between Stanley Ross and Johnny du Plooy in Johannesburg in 1986, I could not resist a stinging retort. At one point, after Ross had been scolded by his corner, viewers heard the American exclaim: 'I'm fighting like hell.' At which I interjected: 'If you believe that, you'll believe anything.'

Striking a balance between bias and objectivity can often be difficult for some commentators. Harry Carpenter of the BBC admitted after the world heavyweight title fight between Mike Tyson and Frank Bruno in Las Vegas in 1989 that he had become 'over-emotional' during the telecast.

Carpenter, an otherwise competent commentator and much admired in Britain, made no attempt to hide his feelings as he rooted openly for the British boxer. 'Get in there, Frank!' he called out during one of the rounds. Carpenter's commentary was so slanted,

Above: Chris Eubank strutting his stuff on the way to the ring for his fight with Graciano Rocchigiani in Berlin.

Left: commentator Reg Gutteridge used only four words to describe Eubank's entry into the ring for his fight with Nigel Benn: 'The ego has landed.'

one TV critic even accused him of working from the deck of the *Titanic*.

By and large the quality of boxing broadcasts has improved immeasurably since the early days of television and this despite the fact that Don Dunphy, the doyen of American commentators, told *KO Magazine* in 1990 that he did not think some of the new fellows worked hard enough at improving their standard. 'I can tell by listening to them that they don't do anything about getting better from week to week,' he said.

Dunphy had been broadcasting fights on radio since June 1941 when he switched to television in 1960. And in the style of Bob Stanton and Jimmy Powers, who were the notable American TV commentators in the 1950s, Dunphy only intruded on the visuals to evaluate the effect of a punch and offer analysis.

'TV and radio announcing require different styles, so it was fortunate for me that there was a lapse of almost four months between the end of radio and the beginning of TV. If I had done radio one week and started TV the next I'm sure it would have been hard,' Dunphy wrote in his autobiography *Don Dunphy at Ringside*.

Dunphy, whose first radio broadcast was of the famous fight between Joe Louis and Billy Conn in 1941, realized that his old blow-by-blow descriptions would be out of place on television and deliberately developed a new style for the electronic medium. Dunphy did most of his work at a time when Friday Night Fights had almost become an institution on American television and he insists that 24 March 1962 was the beginning of the end.

That was the night Emile Griffith stopped Benny 'Kid' Paret in the 12th round at Madison Square Garden to regain the world welterweight title. Paret died ten days later from injuries he sustained in the fight. There was a national outcry in the US for boxing to be banned and when Davey Moore died after losing his world featherweight title to Sugar Ramos in 1963, the ABC network decided it was time to drop the fight series.

The rise of Muhammad Ali (aka Cassius Clay) to heavyweight stardom saved the day for TV boxing in the United States and also led to Howard Cosell making a name for himself as a boxing commentator. Cosell is the only commentator ever to be featured on

Don Dunphy (seen here, seated, with American heavyweight Lou Nova) was regarded as one of the best radio and television boxing commentators in the United States.

the cover of *The Ring* magazine (January 1980) and has been the subject of more discussion than any other boxing commentator in the history of television.

Many claim, perhaps unfairly, that Cosell rode to fame on the back of Ali but few can deny that he was unique as a commentator. At ringside he always appeared to be larger than life and who else would have had the nerve to recite the lyrics of Bob Dylan's 'Forever Young' as Ali regained the heavyweight title for the third time?

Yet Cosell's TV show, *Sports Beat*, failed miserably and his attempt at hosting a variety show was an even bigger disaster. 'For boxing at least, Cosell introduced an element of openness,' said José Torres, the former world light heavyweight champion and one-time president of the World Boxing Organization.

Cosell also made a grandstand exit from the sport he professed to love after calling the heavyweight fight between Larry Holmes and Tex Cobb in 1982. 'I was one of those people waving goodbye with both hands – and both feet,' Jeff Ryan admitted in the January 1992 issue of *The Ring*.

'Though hardly an apologist for the fight game's ills, I none the less got acid indigestion listening to the ravings of a man who seemingly discovered boxing's ills as suddenly as Jed Clampett discovered oil. And in the years that immediately followed Cosell's dismount from the TV boxing throne, I concluded that his leaving cost boxing nothing.'

As managing editor of *The Ring* magazine, Ryan has since done a rethink and has come to the conclusion that Cosell was not so bad for boxing after all.

A new trend that started in the 1980s and accelerated in the 1990s was the introduction of boxers and ex-boxers as colour commentators or analysts for TV broadcasts. Some, like former WBA lightweight champion Sean O'Grady, have even made a career of it. Mind you, O'Grady prepared himself well for the assignment. He majored in broadcasting at Central Oklahoma University.

Even so, he paid heavily for his first mistake on air. While calling a Ray 'Boom Boom' Mancini fight for CBS television, O'Grady said that Mancini, 'like so many Italian fighters takes a great punch'. The comment was interpreted as biased and politically incorrect for a sports broadcast, and after fulfilling his CBS contract he was not invited back.

O'Grady now does most of his work for USA Network but has also done the odd broadcast from such faraway places as South Africa. 'His observations are succinct, introspective and relevant,' says New York boxing writer Robert Mladinich.

On this side of the Atlantic, former WBC lightweight champion Jim Watt fills the role admirably for ITV. Ironically, Watt also beat O'Grady in a title defence in Glasgow in November 1980, so they really do have much in common.

'Some bitch about his accent, but we all have one,' says Reg Gutteridge, the Grand Old Man of British television and a colleague of Watt. 'Jim has become very aware of the production needs of TV. He's a real pro – and a wealthy one, too.'

Gutteridge, whose grandfather, Arthur, boxed on the opening of London's crusty National Sporting Club in 1891 and whose father and uncle became big-time trainers and seconds, was awarded an OBE at Buckingham Palace. A year earlier, Gutteridge was the first Briton to be awarded the American Boxing Writers' Association's

'Excellence in Boxing Broadcast Journalism' award.

He has been lead commentator with Marvin Hagler, Floyd Patterson (radio in South Africa), Don Curry, Henry Cooper and others, but the tie-up with Jim Watt brought touches of humour mixed with authority. When Johnny Nelson fought a title bore with Carlos DeLeon, they said, 'This fight is being sponsored by the British Medical Association' and 'It's as repetitious as chewing gum'. When Naseem Hamed first displayed his ring antics, they registered their disapproval with, 'Don't ring us, we'll ring you.'

While interviewing him for *Boxing Monthly* in 1991, Scottish boxing writer Brian Donald asked Jim Watt, former WBC champion about his own philosophy on TV boxing.

'The last thing someone watching a fight on television wants to hear, particularly if he is a boxing fan, is "Tom Smith has just thrown a left hook." The fan has eyes. He can see that for himself,' Watt said.

'What I try to do is give an insider's analysis of what the fighter's game plan might or ought to be, how he is probably feeling at a particular point in the contest, fight tactics. The fan can see the hook

Sean O'Grady, the former WBA lightweight champion, has become a successful television boxing commentator.

or uppercut, but does he appreciate that these punches may be part of a wider game plan? Does he know how the boxer might be feeling when things go wrong? On television I try to analyse the action and the actions of the fighters but even I don't get things right all the time.'

Of course, some fighters can be too terse in what they say. Commenting between rounds on the action in the fight between Muhammad Ali and George Foreman in Kinshasa, Zaire, in 1974, Joe Frazier pulled no punches.

'George is fighting foolish,' Frazier said after the seventh round. It was the understatement of the evening. Foreman was knocked out in the eighth.

COMMISSIONS

Although they can now be found in countries throughout the world, boxing commissions – as opposed to boxing boards – originated in the United States. But while both the boards and the commissions were established with the express purpose of controlling the sport, in practice their style of administration often reflects the laws and social values of the countries in which they are based.

A typical example was that of the Japan Boxing Commission, which stripped eight Japanese boxers and trainers of their right to apply for JBC licences after competing in bouts sanctioned by the International Boxing Federation in 1983. And a more recent example was the decision of the South African Boxing Commission to withdraw recognition of the World Boxing Federation in 1994 until such time as the WBF had convinced the commission that it was a fully democratic and bona fide world-sanctioning body.

For many years the most powerful and influential boxing commission in the world was the New York State Athletic Commission, which first took up its duties on 1 September 1920 after the Walker Law had been enacted in the state three months earlier. Nowadays the Nevada State Athletic Commission and, to a lesser extent, the New Jersey and California State Athletic Commissions, have assumed that role – largely because New York is no longer the mecca of boxing.

And yet the irony is that it was an Englishman, William Gavin, who drafted the rules upon which New York State Senator James J Walker based his Walker Boxing Bill in order to legalize professional boxing in the state. Gavin had gone to the States in 1918 with the intention of starting a similar organization to the National Sporting Club of London. The club, which was to be located at 41st Street and Sixth Avenue, had Major Anthony Drexel Biddle and other top New York financiers as supporters, while Tex Rickard had agreed to become its matchmaker.

However, when it seemed certain that the Walker Bill would pass, Rickard withdrew from Gavin's proposed International Sporting Club and obtained a lease to promote boxing at Madison Square Garden. As a result, when boxing was legalized in the state of New York, it was Rickard, not Gavin, who became the main beneficiary.

Worse still, when those who had bought membership in the International Sporting Club demanded to know what had become of their money and requested an accounting of the huge sum collected, Gavin told them the money had been spent in 'entertaining' state legislators. Pressed for an explanation, Gavin claimed that the 'entertainment' was 'just common graft to have the bill passed'. He then left on the first boat back to England.

Although the International Sporting Club never got off the ground, boxing in New York was an instant success under the Walker Bill and soon other states followed the New York example. Even so, there are still some states in America today without a boxing commission and the plan to introduce federal control of the sport has been pursued for many years without success.

The National Boxing Association of America was established in 1921 with federal control in mind, but when New York, Pennsylvania, California and Massachusetts all refused to join, the NBA became little more than a lame duck. Later, in 1963, it was to change its name to the World Boxing Association.

Less than a year after it was established, the Simpson–Brundage Bill altered the status of the New York State Athletic Commission by also giving it control of professional wrestling. However, an attempt by the commission to take control of amateur boxing in the state failed when Governor Lehman vetoed the Mahoney Bill in 1941.

Other notable changes made by the New York State Athletic Commission over the years include the adoption of the no-foul rule in 1930, a four-point scoring system in 1948, compulsory insurance for boxers in 1949, the mandatory eight-count in 1951, the three-knockdown rule in 1957, a ring with four ropes in 1963 and the thumbless glove in 1982.

On the downside there have been some major setbacks. Twice the New York State Supreme Court ordered the commission to reverse decisions. First, on 11 April 1921, when Justice John MacCrate ruled that the referee's original decision in the bantamweight bout between Packey O'Gatty and Roy Moore should stand and then, on 17 February 1955, when Justice Bernard Botein reversed the decision in the fight between Joey Giardello and Billy Graham.

Far more embarrassing, however, was the silly sight of Max Schmeling weighing-in for his phoney heavyweight fight with James J Braddock in 1937 while the world champion was hundreds of miles away in Chicago. Ten years later the commission was obliged to do an egg dance of sorts after it had sanctioned the first fight between Joe Louis and Jersey Joe Walcott as a ten-round exhibition.

The New York Commission also backtracked on the compulsory use of the thumbless glove after a number of boxers went on strike and caused a tournament to be cancelled in the 1980s.

Yet there was a time when both the New York and Californian commissions were so powerful they crowned their own 'world' champions. Joe Frazier was among the last of the heavyweight champions to be given such recognition by New York when he beat Buster Mathis in 1968.

COMPUTERS

Millions saw the fight around the world. Photographs were taken and a full-length movie was produced. But although you may recall sitting in a cinema 25 years ago and watching Rocky Marciano beat Muhammad Ali, it was just an illusion. It was the fight that was but wasn't.

The thought of a fight between Marciano and Ali had fascinated boxing fans for years and with Ali forced into exile by the world boxing bodies because of his refusal to serve in the US Armed Forces in the late 1960s, a clever businessman grasped the opportunity. He produced what was commonly called a 'computer fight'.

Not only did Ali and Marciano train for the fight, they actually got into the ring to exchange blows. But unknown to many, their movements were programmed by a computer.

The film had Marciano winning on a technical knockout late in the fight. (Ali responded to the result by suggesting that the computer was probably made in Alabama.) It was only later that it emerged that the movie-makers had produced two endings. One with Marciano winning, the other with the decision going to Ali.

Public sentiment at the time was almost entirely behind Marciano, so it came as no surprise that the former undefeated world heavy-weight champion was made the winner. Marciano, who wore a hairpiece for the making of the fake fight, died before the film was released to the theatres and never knew which version of the fight the movie-makers would choose.

Years later when Larry Holmes closed in on Marciano's unbeaten record, the *New York Post* decided to ask an IBM–AT (supposedly the most sophisticated computer in the world at the time) to forecast the result of a fight between Marciano and Holmes. The computer came up with a tenth-round knockout victory for Marciano and the newspaper gave the result a splash spread. Holmes was unimpressed. 'How can you beat a white man at a white man's game?' he asked.

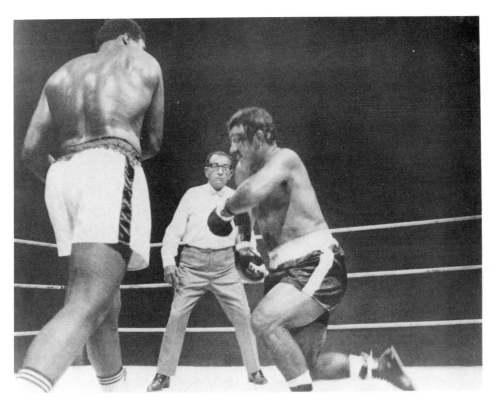

Muhammad Ali and Rocky Marciano in their famous 'computer fight'. The referee is Chris Dundee.

Others questioned the wisdom of making use of computers for the scoring of bouts in amateur boxing. It was the Russians who took the initiative. A device was developed by graduates at the Moscow Institute for Design Engineers in the early 1970s and was tested in the 1974 USSR national championships.

The computer's international debut was originally scheduled for the 1977 European championships but after protests by top amateur officials, who claimed the device still needed further development, it was put on hold.

In this age of automation, when computers perform more and more jobs to perfection, it would seem only logical to use them in boxing at its weakest and most haphazard point – the judging of fights – but so far nobody has come up with a fail-safe system that

Larry Holmes chats with trainer Richie Giachetti. 'How can you beat a white man at a white man's game?' Holmes asked when a computer predicted Rocky Marciano would have knocked him out.

eliminates the human element.

Judges must still push the buttons to score points and after some of the diabolical decisions delivered at the 1992 Barcelona Olympics, it is obvious that much work still needs to be done to perfect the system.

On a more positive note, computers have been invaluable in providing the kind of statistics for boxing that were simply unobtainable ten or more years ago. The CompuBox Punchstats has clearly added to the enjoyment of television viewers, especially in the United States where it is frequently used on cable and pay-per-view networks like ESPN, HBO and TVKO.

The brainchild of Logan Hobson and Bob Canobbio, the Punchstats provides a feast of information both while a fight is in progress and after a decision has been rendered. At the touch of a key Messrs Hobson and Canobbio can tell you who threw the most punches in a fight, who connected with the most blows, who threw the fewest number of blows, etc.

According to CompuBox the most punches thrown in a fight were those they recorded in the battle between Zack Padilla and Ray Oliveira in December 1993. Between them, Padilla and Oliveira threw 3,020 punches in 12 rounds of fighting; an average of 252 blows per round, or a punch every 1.40 seconds.

At the other end of the scale, Trevor Berbick threw only four blows in the first round of his heavyweight fight with Carl Williams in June 1988. To nobody's great surprise, Berbick was beaten on points over 12 rounds.

CONTESTS

So you thought a 'contest' only applied to boxing? Well, think again because this is how the California State Athletic Commission defines the word in clause 18625 of its rules and regulations:

> Contest or match are synonymous, may be used interchangeably, and include boxing, kickboxing, martial arts exhibitions, wrestling matches, and means a fight, prize-fight, boxing contest, pugilistic contest, kickboxing contest, martial arts contest, sparring match, between two or more persons, where full or partial contact is used or intended which may result or be intended to result in physical harm to the opponent. In any exhibition or sparring match, the opponents are not required to use their best efforts.

Yet, however boxing is defined, a contest is what boxing is all about. Some may object to the words 'result in physical harm to the opponent', but in the final analysis men fight to prove their physical superiority.

Admittedly, they do not fight as often as they once did, and several have had relatively short careers, but that is largely because the promotion of boxing has changed radically in recent years. The chances are we will never see another boxer like Abe the Newsboy (Abraham Hollandersky) who took part in 1,309 contests (many of them exhibitions on naval vessels) between 1905 and 1918, or even a fighter like the famous Welsh flyweight Jimmy Wilde, who claimed a total of 864 contests (many of which took place in fairground boxing booths).

And since rematches are frowned upon by modern boxing boards and sanctioning bodies, it is unlikely that we will ever see a series of fights like those that took place between Ted 'Kid' Lewis and Jack Britton (20 contests), Sam Langford and Harry Wills (22), Langford and Sam McVey (15) and Langford and Joe Jeannette (14).

A number of boxers have engaged in three or more contests on the same day or night but seldom against first-class opposition. South African heavyweight François Botha was one of the more recent to turn the trick when he knocked out Artie Hooks, Russell Rierson and Mickey Jones in one round apiece in Oklahoma City on 19 November 1992.

George Foreman, who was then a former world heavyweight champion, took on five men in exhibition bouts on 26 April 1975 and in earlier years former world lightweight champion Jack McAuliffe, American light heavyweight Battling Levinsky, American welterweight Kid McCoy, former world lightweight champion Freddy Welsh and American heavyweight Tony Galento all beat three opponents in a single day.

CUTMEN

There is a temptation to describe them as the surgeons of the sport, but while they may be called upon to widen a cut in order to clean and repair it on the odd occasion, their prime objective is to patch up the wound – and all in 60 seconds or less.

Although cutmen are now accepted as specialists in the sport, many trainers are of the mistaken belief that it is a job they can safely do themselves. And to be perfectly honest, few fighters can afford the luxury of a specialist cutman except in a major fight. On the other hand, the days of trainers using their 'secret' solutions, and especially coagulants such as Monsel's solution, are long gone.

Having seen many of their outstanding boxers like Katsyua Onizuka, Leonard Tamakuma and Kenju Lizumi forced into retirement in the prime of their careers because of eye problems, the Japan Boxing Commission hosted a medical seminar early in 1995 to

Cornermen have a mere 60 seconds in which to work between rounds. Here Piet Crous, the former WBA cruiserweight champion, gets the attention of his cornermen during his fight with Ossie Ocasio.

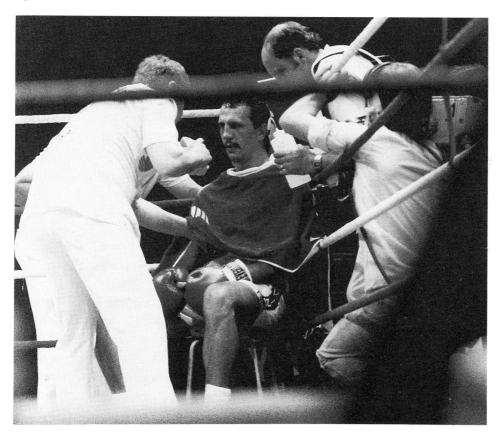

enable ophthalmologists to instruct Japanese managers and trainers on the treatment and care of eye injuries. Such seminars are strongly recommended and the wonder is that they are not held more often.

Almost without exception, all the world-sanctioning bodies now restrict what may or may not be used between rounds in a corner during a championship fight.

'Only vaseline, used under the discretion of the referee, and nothing else, will be allowed on the face, arms, or any part of the body of a boxer during a fight,' says the World Boxing Council in Article XIII rule 15 of their world championship rules and regulations. 'No smelling salts, ammonia or other substances may be administered to revive a boxer or for any other reason during a fight. In case of a cut, only a solution of adrenalin 1/1000 shall be used in the corner to attend to the cut.'

The World Boxing Association also clearly specifies what may or may not be used:

> 'The discretional use of coagulants, like a solution of adrenalin (1/1000) as approved by the ringside physician, may be allowed between rounds to stop bleeding of minor cuts and lacerations sustained by a contestant. The use of "iron type" coagulants such as Monsel's solution are absolutely prohibited and the use of such coagulants to or by any contestant shall be considered a violation and shall be cause for immediate disqualification.'

With only 60 seconds or less available between rounds, speed is essential when working on cuts and lacerations. Henry Cooper, the former British heavyweight champion, explained in his autobiography how Danny Holland would prepare beforehand in the corner for any emergency.

'Danny had developed the cut business to a fine art,' Cooper recalled. 'He would get the adrenalin out and opened as soon as he saw a cut, and he had the cotton swab stick out and in the bottle with his thumb over the top. He made the swab stick beforehand in the dressing room, so he was all ready to jump straight up in the ring and, without wasting time unscrewing bottle lids, to get to work.'

With blood gushing from his left eye, Henry Cooper attacks Muhammad Ali in the sixth round of their world title fight in London in 1966. Seconds later the referee stopped the fight.

Cooper, who pointed out that it was his twin brother George and not himself who was the bleeder in the family, added that Holland was always the first to enter the ring between rounds.

The average boxing fan is unlikely to remember the names of famous cutmen, whose skill is of a very specialized nature. Ralph Citro, for example, is more likely to be remembered for his *Computer Boxing Update* record book than for the sterling work he did between rounds as a cutman.

Dr Rosetta Garries, on the other hand, will probably be remembered as the only woman to take on the job so far. Garries, a trauma surgeon and plastic surgeon in private practice in New York City, worked with a couple of American fighters – super middleweight Steve Little and middleweight Bernard Hopkins – in the early 1990s. Like the doctor she is, Garries wore her green scrub uniform in the corner and refused to carry the traditional cotton swabs in her mouth.

Cutmen, by and large, are an unobtrusive lot. Men like Dennie Mancini, Angelo Dundee, Paddy Byrne, Alan Toweel, Ace Marotta, Al Gavin, Freddie King and Ralph Citro have carved a special niche for themselves in the history of boxing.

A writer once asked Alan Toweel, a member of the famous South African fighting family, whether he had his own 'secret' solution for attending to eye cuts. 'Yes, I've got certain stuff but I wouldn't say it was secret,' he said. 'If your fighter has a cut eye you've got to know how to close the wound. And believe me, with all due respect to doctors, I don't believe in stitches.'

And nor, it seems, do any of the other famous cutmen (and women).

DEATHS

Speaking to the media in London after his brutal battle with Gerald

McClellan in February 1995, WBC super middleweight champion Nigel Benn called boxing the 'hurt business' and claimed that everyone knew the risks. Well, yes, they do. Boxing is undeniably a dangerous sport and frankly there is no room for the faint-hearted in the fight game. But while most boxers are aware of the high risks involved, few are unduly concerned because nowadays they can look with confidence to the boxing boards and commissions to provide a safety net.

Of course, there is a limit to the precautions that can realistically be taken and ring fatalities, although considerably reduced in number in the 1990s, are unlikely to be completely eliminated from the sport. Frank Warren, who co-promoted the Benn–McClellan world title fight with Don King, implied as much afterwards. 'The measures we had were the best you could get,' he said, 'short of having an operating theatre at ringside.'

Such self-examination comes easy to a sport that is constantly under attack.

'Boxing, because of its nefarious history and its blatant brutality, is an easy target. And when a fighter dies, everyone is quick to point an accusing finger at the system and say the reason a fighter is dead was because not enough was done to protect him,' the *Las Vegas Sun* commented after the death of Wangila Napunyi in July 1994.

'Fact is, Nevada has been the leader in boxing reform and safety. For years, it has led the way in trying to provide uniform rules and protect the fighters. We'll never know if Wangila Napunyi would be alive today had he used 10-ounce gloves instead of 8-ouncers or if someone had performed a CAT scan on him prior to his entering the ring. But to indict an entire sport based on one tragedy is wrong.'

British newspapers, by and large, adopted a similar sensible stance following the ring death of Bradley Stone in April 1994. 'The urge to regulate and restrain, whether or not reinforced by a predictable misfortune, is very powerful in certain sectors of the community. The key test of whether to accede to it is whether damage is done to those who are not willing participants. In this case it has not. The urge should be resolutely resisted,' declared the *Independent* in an editorial.

It is pointless to deny that boxing is a dangerous sport, sometimes brutal and often violent. But having made that admission we should be able to claim that at least it is *controlled* violence. Unfortunately, the lack of uniformity in control is one of boxing's biggest weaknesses. The United States, for example, has almost as many boxing commissions as states – but with little co-operation between them.

The New York State Athletic Commission, once the trendsetter for the sport, has lost much of its influence now that New York is no longer the mecca of boxing. And the tragedy is that the New York Commission was by far the most innovative in the States.

The on-going squabble between the so-called sanctioning bodies has done little to help the sport. But to their credit, many lesser-known boxing administrators have been trying for years to reduce the risk of serious injury in the ring. Of course there are those who claim they are not trying hard enough.

Ray Mancini exchanges left hands with Duk Koo Kim in the 12th round of their WBA lightweight title fight in Las Vegas. Kim suffered severe brain damage after being knocked out in the 14th round and died five days later.

That, however, is patently unfair. Hardly a year goes by without the introduction of some rule to safeguard the boxer. Sadly, many of these rules are often resisted by the very people they have been designed to protect.

Most boxing administrators long ago learned never to tempt fate. A case in point was that of Leon Rains of the Pennsylvania State Athletic Commission, who made the mistake of boldly claiming in 1945 that, as a direct result of pre-fight medical examinations, only three ring deaths had been recorded in the state in 14 years. Less than 12 months later three ring deaths were recorded in the state in one year.

Boxing men are the first to admit that even one death is one too many, but history shows that almost without exception after every ring death an attempt has been made to improve safety. For example, when George Stevenson died following a bareknuckle fight with John Broughton in London in 1741, Broughton was so emotionally upset he wrote a set of Rules for the Prize Ring that remained in force for nearly a hundred years.

The first fatality in a world championship fight was also recorded in London. Walter Croot was well ahead on points going into the 20th and final round of his bantamweight title fight with Jimmy Barry in December 1897 when, with less than a minute left in the round, Barry caught Croot with a hard right to the jaw. Croot struck his head on the ring floor as he fell and died of his injuries a few days later.

Barry and the top officials of the National Sporting Club were charged with manslaughter but after a long and sensational trial, all were acquitted. The tragedy, however, left its mark on the American boxer. Barry, who retired undefeated in 1899, never won another fight on a knockout. In fact, his last seven fights all ended in drawn decisions.

The first death as a result of a prize-fight in the United States occurred on 13 September 1842 when Tom McCoy died following a bareknuckle contest with Chris Lilly on an open field somewhere between Yonkers and Hastings, New York. The fight, which lasted 120 rounds or 2 hours and 40 minutes, ended when McCoy was knocked out and died. The tragedy gave American legislators an excuse to outlaw boxing throughout the United States, forcing the sport underground or out to sea, where fights were often held on barges.

Even more unjust was the treatment meted out to Yankee Sullivan, an early claimant of the American championship. Sullivan was arrested, found guilty and sentenced to two years in a state prison – and all because he had acted as an adviser to Lilly.

Seventy years were to pass before another boxing fatality again stirred the American nation and largely because Luther McCarty's moment of death was captured on film by a photographer at the ringside. It happened on a dull, gloomy day in May 1913 in a wooden barn in Calgary, Canada.

Many Americans had pinned their hopes on McCarty, a handsome young heavyweight from Wild Horse Canyon in Nebraska, to regain the world title from the hated black champion Jack Johnson. Few believed that Arthur Pelkey would be much of a match for McCarty.

But unbeknown to many, McCarty had injured himself in a fall from a horse and when Pelkey caught him with a right uppercut and then peppered his face with a barrage of right hands, the strapping heavyweight looked to be in desperate trouble. As McCarty fell to the floor, flat on his face, and referee Ed Smith walked across the ring to count him out, a ray of sunshine broke through the gloom and bathed the boxer's body in light.

The moment Smith had completed his count the sunlight disappeared and Luther McCarty lay dead on the ring canvas. It was this chilling, surreal image that was captured by the photographer.

At least four other heavyweight hopefuls had their boxing careers tarnished by tragedy. Bull Young died after a fight with Jess Willard (1913), Frankie Campbell after a fight with Max Baer (1930), Ernie Schaaf after a fight with Primo Carnera (1933) and Sam Baroudi after a fight with Ezzard Charles (1948). Willard, Baer, Carnera and Charles all went on to win the heavyweight championship of the world.

An autopsy showed that Schaaf had suffered a blood clot on the brain following an earlier fight with Max Baer in August 1932, but Carnera's unscrupulous handlers quickly seized upon the tragedy and turned it into publicity for the 'Ambling Alp'. In unbelievably bad taste, they pointed to Schaaf's death as proof of the Italian's 'murderous' fists.

In truth, it was Baer who possessed the lethal punch. The

Californian heavyweight had scored over a dozen knockouts and was only in his second year as a professional when he was matched against Frankie Campbell on 25 August 1930.

In the second round a Campbell punch caused Baer to slip to the canvas. Thinking he had scored a knockdown, Campbell turned his back on Baer and headed for a neutral corner. Enraged, Baer leapt to his feet and tore after him, striking him with a savage right to the jaw as he turned his head.

Badly hurt, Campbell managed to defend himself for two more rounds but collapsed in the fifth. Six hours later he died in hospital. Many blamed Baer for the tragedy but Max was later exonerated by a court of law. Even so, he remained emotionally unstable for a long time afterwards and some boxing experts suspect he never again punched with full force.

Max Baer, then a young California heavyweight, in the coroner's court following the death of Frankie Campbell in 1930.

Millions of American TV viewers saw Benny Paret horribly beaten by Emile Griffith in their world welterweight title fight in 1962. Paret later died of his injuries following his 12th round knockout.

The first ring death seen on national television in the United States very nearly brought boxing to its knees. With millions watching across the nation, Emile Griffith regained the world welterweight title when he knocked out Benny 'Kid' Paret in 12 rounds at Madison Square Garden, New York, on 24 March 1962. As Paret fell to the canvas, horribly beaten, he slipped into a coma and died ten days later.

The reaction worldwide was predictable but no less disturbing, and according to TV commentator Don Dunphy, the tragedy caused television executives to do a rethink about the then popular *Friday Night Fights* programme.

Based loosely on the rumour that Paret had accused Griffith of being gay at the weigh-in for the fight, a stage play called *Blade to the Heat* attempted (unsuccessfully) to recapture the drama when it ran briefly at the Public Theater in New York late in 1994.

Boxing in the US suffered an even greater blow when almost

Sumito Urayama's was one of four ring deaths recorded in 1981. Knocked out in his first pro fight, his ring career lasted only 73 seconds. He died six days later in a Tokyo hospital.

exactly one year later Davey Moore died following a televised world featherweight title fight with Sugar Ramos in Los Angeles. Moore died of a whiplash to his brain stem after his neck struck the bottom rope of a three-rope ring.

Between 1946 and 1964 the annual number of ring deaths worldwide hardly ever dropped below double digits. According to the *Ring Record Book* the highest number of ring deaths (22) was recorded in 1953. Thankfully, stricter control of the sport and the introduction of stringent safety measures had the effect of drastically reducing the number of ring deaths recorded in the 1980s and the 1990s.

However, while statistics show that many other sports are more dangerous than boxing, the day that boxing men become complacent and decide to rest on their laurels is the day boxing as a sport will die. It is to be hoped that day will never come.

DECISIONS

Once, all fights were fought to a finish. In fact, it was only after the introduction of the Queensberry Rules, late in the nineteenth century, that the notion that fights be restricted to a scheduled number of rounds and a decision be rendered gained acceptance. At first, scoring was by rounds only and the referee was the sole arbiter (referees still are for domestic boxing in Britain). Later, points systems were devised and judges were appointed to assist in reaching a decision.

Boxing historians are unable to agree on which fight was the first to be decided by decision. Some claim it was the bout between Charlie Mitchell and Jack Knifton for the heavyweight championship of England in December 1882.

Others insist that the first championship fight to be decided by decision was the lightweight contest between Jack McAuliffe and Jack Hopper in New York on 27 February 1886 (McAuliffe won on points over 17 rounds). The first British championship fight to be decided on points was the heavyweight bout between Jem Smith and Jack Wannop in London on 30 September 1889 (Smith was declared the winner after ten rounds).

In the United States, the Horton Law became the instrument that paved the way for fights to a decision. When the law was enacted in November 1896 it not only lifted the then ban on boxing in the state of New York, it also abolished the restriction on the number of rounds permissible. The Lewis Law repealed the Horton Law in 1900 and for the next 11 years boxing in the state of New York was conducted on a club-membership basis only.

The Frawley Law brought the sport in New York back to the public in 1911 but on condition that all contests be exhibition bouts and that no decisions were rendered. As a result, no man could win a fight except by knockout and until the Walker Law came into effect in 1920, both the fans and the fighters had to rely on what commonly became known as 'newspaper decisions'.

'Newspaper decisions, while extremely interesting and elucidating much discussion with respect to certain bouts, are at the same time extremely valuable in evaluating the careers of many of the old-timers,' Herb Goldman, the then editor of *The Ring Record Book*, wrote in the Foreword to the 1987 edition. Goldman added that the majority of newspaper decisions were incontrovertible and were 'at least as accurate as any official decision would have been'.

In fact, some of the early official decisions were highly suspect, for example, the ten-round welterweight bout between the then undefeated lightweight champion Jack McAuliffe and Tommy Ryan in Scranton, Pennsylvania, on 30 September 1897.

It had been agreed beforehand that the decision would be a draw and that McAuliffe would not try to knock Ryan out. McAuliffe breached the agreement when he floored Ryan in the second round but then gave him an opportunity to recover.

Under the impression that Ryan was to be the winner if he was still on his feet at the end of the tenth round, referee Pat Murphy promptly awarded the decision to the Philadelphian. But when he became aware of the agreement, Murphy changed the result and gave the decision to McAuliffe.

That the referee's decision is final was confirmed by the New York State Supreme Court on 11 April 1921 when Justice John MacCrate ruled that referee Ed Pollack's original decision in the fight between Packey O'Gatty and Roy Moore should stand. Pollack had disqualified Moore for a foul in the third round but the New York State Athletic Commission had later changed the result to 'no contest'.

Referee Harry Ertle gave two decisions after Mike McTigue and Young Stribling had fought for the world light heavyweight title in Columbus, Georgia, on 4 October 1923. First he declared the fight a draw, then proclaimed Stribling the winner and new champion while under threat by an infuriated partisan mob, and finally nullified the verdict in favour of Stribling when he advised the media that the original draw decision would stand.

Arguably one of the most controversial reversals of a decision followed the welterweight fight in New York's Madison Square Garden between Joey Giardello and Billy Graham in December 1952. Giardello won the ten-round bout on a split decision but New York commissioners Robert Christenberry and C B Powell altered the scorecard of judge Joe Agnello at the ringside, making Graham the winner.

Giardello was flabbergasted. 'If they're going to reverse judges and referees like that, what's the use of paying officials? Why don't those commissioners just go in there and do the refereeing and judging themselves?' he asked.

Giardello sued in the New York State Supreme Court and on 17 February 1953, Justice Bernard Botein reversed the reversal with the comment that the boxing commission's reasoning 'was so vague as to be meaningless'. The judge also noted that 'the scoring of a prize fight is not a routine process, like the scoring of a tennis match ... a boxing official's judgment reflects not only his perceptiveness and experience, but is inevitably coloured by his own sense of prize-fighting values'.

If, on the other hand, the officials misinterpret the rules a reversal of the decision by the commission is justified. In fact, this has happened in a number of fights throughout the world.

Among the more notable were the fights between Joe Dundee and Charlie O'Connell in New York in February 1925, between Sugar Ray Robinson and Gerhard Hecht in Berlin in June 1951, and between Joey Giardello and Willie Vaughan in Kansas City, Missouri, in March 1957. In each case there had been an error in the scorecards or the rules had been incorrectly applied.

This was certainly the case when referee Jesus Celis awarded a technical knockout victory to Benedicto Villablanca after his WBA junior lightweight title fight with Sam Serrano in Santiago, Chile, had been stopped at the start of the 11th round in June 1982.

Serrano had been cut over the eye early in the fight but then proceeded to outbox Villablanca. At the start of the 11th round the cut began bleeding profusely and Celis called the ringside doctor to examine it. The doctor declared the cut 'too deep and wide' for the fight to continue and Celis awarded the decision to Villablanca.

The suggestion was that the cut had been caused by a punch, but 20 days later the WBA Championships Committee ruled that the cut had been caused by a butt, declared the fight void and reinstated Serrano as champion. Later the decision was changed to a 'technical win' for Serrano.

Something similar happened six years later when New Jersey State Athletic Commission chairman Larry Hazzard voided the decision in the controversial WBA welterweight title fight in which Marlon Starling was knocked out by Tomas Molinares with an after-the-bell blow in Atlantic City.

Referee Joe Cortez counted out Starling when the champion was dropped by a right-hander that the referee thought was in motion as the bell sounded to end the sixth round. However, Hazzard claimed that careful study of the video recording showed that Molinares started throwing the right a split second after the bell had sounded. The New Jersey Commission therefore changed the result to 'no decision'.

Managers, of course, are always looking for a way in which to give their boxers an edge. Sid Flaherty did it by hiring all his own officials when his featherweight Gil Cadilli fought Willie Pep in San Francisco in March 1955.

Flaherty was able to turn the trick because the fight was held on

Marlon Starling was unlucky to be knocked out by a punch after the bell in his fight with Tomas Molinares.

United States government land, where the California State Athletic Commission had no jurisdiction. Cadilli was awarded a highly controversial points decision after ten rounds. Two months later Pep reversed the result by beating Cadilli on points over ten rounds in Detroit.

JACK DEMPSEY

Chris Greyvenstein, the renowned South African sportswriter and author of *The Fighters*, a history of South African boxing, had the good fortune twice to meet Jack Dempsey in person. This is the tribute he wrote for *Boxing World* magazine after Dempsey's death in 1983:

Muhammad Ali was holding court as usual, but he lost his audience as the VIP guests in one of the luxurious lounges of New

Legendary heavyweight champion Jack Dempsey.

York's Waldorf Hotel turned to watch an elderly man in a dress-suit limp into the room, leaning on his walking-stick, a handsome, middle-aged woman gently guiding him to his table. At the age of 80, Jack Dempsey could still dominate any gathering simply by being there.

I met him twice, once in the restaurant which carried his name and served as a Broadway landmark for several generations and then again on this particular evening when he was one of the guests of honour at the annual banquet of the New York Boxing Writers' Association. Hardly a basis on which to lay claim that I knew the man who took professional boxing from dingy backstreet halls to vast stadiums and multi-million-dollar purses, but enough to remember him as more than just another old champion whose fame is gathering dust in the record books.

The meeting in the restaurant was arranged by a mutual friend who knew exactly what time Dempsey would leave the nearby apartment where he and his third, much-younger wife, Deanna, had lived for many years, to pay his nightly visit to the restaurant. He apparently always sat at the same table, the wall with the life-sized mural by James Montgomery Flagg, showing the young, lean challenger winning the world championship by savagely destroying Jess Willard under a blazing sun in Toledo, Ohio, more than a half-a-century before. Before Dempsey and his companions had a chance to settle down there was a queue of tourists waiting to shake hands and collect autographs in front of us and it was some time before my friend, a veteran newspaperman who had covered Dempsey's championship fights in his day, could make the introduction.

A handshake, a 'Hiya, pal, Cape Town, South Africa? That's a long way to come' and then an offer of a slice of 'Jack Dempsey's Cheesecake', said to be such a sought-after delicacy that supplies were airmailed daily to addicts in London and Paris, and coffee.

There is not much that remains to be asked of a man about whom millions of words have been written, including more than a dozen books, and you are tempted, no matter how hard you try to resist, to simply sit and stare at one of the few people in the world of whom it could truthfully be said that he was a legend in his own lifetime.

The king-sized menu, with every dish or drink carrying a name somehow connected with either Dempsey or one of the opponents with whom he engaged in million-dollar contests during the era of the Charleston, Prohibition, silent movies and no income tax, is duly signed. So, also, a fistful of post card pictures brought on cue by a waiter and a photographer, who for many years had been making a good living taking photographs of the old fighter, smiling benevolently, his massive arm around the shoulder of someone he has just met and is likely never to meet again, pops up to do his stuff. This was Dempsey, the former champion, at work, but somehow, probably through many years of practice or just because he genuinely liked people, he managed to project total sincerity.

Dempsey had a remarkably magnetic personality and he could never walk down a street without being followed by a gawking throng of celebrity watchers. I was told that crowds used to gather outside his favourite barbershop whenever he went for his daily shave, and until failing health forced him to withdraw from public life, was paid large sums of money to make appearances at functions in support of projects ranging from charity to the strictly commercial. Even during the Depression years of the early 1930s Dempsey earned up to 10,000 dollars a night by refereeing fights or wrestling matches; often his fee dwarfed the purses paid to the actual contestants. Long after his retirement he continued to be paid what were astronomical sums for those days to engage in exhibition bouts and his lifetime earnings have been estimated at 10 million dollars.

Even people who actively dislike boxing could not resist his charm. There was, for instance, the South African who very reluctantly agreed to visit Dempsey's restaurant some years ago. A lay preacher and a committed pacifist, he held strong views against violent sports and he regarded professional boxers in particular as mindless brutes. Dempsey's quiet charm completely captivated him, however, and he ended up by filching the old champion's half-smoked cigar from the ash tray as a souvenir, ruefully discovering later that it had burned a hole in his pocket.

But Dempsey was not always sophisticated, popular and rich. Born William Harrison Dempsey in Manassa, Colorado, in 1895 of Scottish-Irish-Red Indian descent, he was the ninth child and fifth son of poverty-stricken Mormon parents. His formal education was sketchy and he was doing odd jobs to augment the family income by the time he was 11 years old. An older brother, Bernie, was a professional boxer of sorts and he gave him his first basic lessons with the gloves but his main contribution to the future champion's success was to force him to chew gum stripped from pine trees in the firm belief that this would give him a jaw so tough that it would be virtually impregnable to any punch.

At the age of 16 Dempsey was tall, painfully skinny, but quite able to look after himself in the ring, and he decided to leave home with a vague dream that fame and fortune was waiting for him somewhere. For three years he wandered around the mining towns of the American West. Underfed, hardly training and hopelessly lost when it came to guarding his financial interests, Dempsey fought some of the hardest contests of his career during those years, usually against much bigger and older opponents and with the promise of a square meal frequently the only purse. His strict Mormon upbringing (in later life he was a 'Jack' Mormon, a term for someone who had defected from the sect) kept him from crime but he was little more than an itinerant tramp.

'I went hungry for days rather than steal,' he was later to tell one of his dozen or so biographers. 'I begged, humbly, for any kind of job to earn a flop [a bed] and a meal. I was a starving kid, wandering in search of food, sometimes almost like an animal, living as best I could with the weapons of survival God gave me. My fists. And I guess my chin.'

The managers he acquired were either incompetent or crudely intent on exploiting him. His first trip to New York was a disaster. Broke, with three fractured ribs following a bout against a hardened professional, and sadly disillusioned, he made his way back to the West by 'riding the rods'. This is an American description for hitching an illegal ride on a train by lying on the narrow steel beams underneath a carriage – a lethal thing to do. It requires that the 'passenger' stays awake and alert throughout the journey; or otherwise he will slip off and die a horrible death under the wheels.

But about this time he came to the notice of one of boxing's legendary characters, Jack 'Doc' Kearns, an unscrupulous but shrewd manager who made and squandered several fortunes in a career which would take more than one book to recount in detail. Dempsey was the one to bring him his first fortune and, in many ways, he was the man who made Dempsey a world champion. An out-and-out gambler and confidence trickster, he rushed Dempsey through a series of fights which established his reputation. For all his faults, Kearns knew his business and he gave his protégé the support he had always lacked outside the ring. This included good food and expert training; and, of course, Dempsey no longer had to cope with cheating promoters. If there was any exploitation to be done, Kearns did it at the expense of everybody else except himself and his fighter.

With some muscles now on his rangy frame, Dempsey fought 21 opponents in 1918, beating 17 on knockouts, 12 in the first round. He developed into a murderous puncher, one of the hardest two-fisted hitters in history, and although aggression was the basis of his style, he was far from being just a blind slugger. He had extremely fast reflexes and the bobbing and weaving of his head and torso made him a difficult target. But sheer ferocity was perhaps Dempsey's greatest ally in the ring. The hard times he had been through had taken mercy totally out of his soul and once the bell rang he believed in a philosophy of kill-or-be-killed. His highly strung temperament made him a bundle of nerves before a fight and when the action started he would all but hurl himself into the attack, almost like an uncaged panther going for his prey.

The unbridled fury with which he destroyed the much bigger and heavier Jess Willard on 4 July 1919, to win the heavyweight title captured the public imagination and it was Dempsey's good fortune that he became champion just as America entered a decade of unprecedented affluence and a preoccupation with entertainment which, in retrospect, bordered on the decadent.

Aided by the flair of George 'Tex' Rickard, an unusually

Luis Angel Firpo and Jack Dempsey shake hands before the start of their epic heavyweight fight at the Polo Grounds in New York in 1923.

perceptive promoter, Dempsey turned professional boxing into a multi-million-dollar business. Between 1921 and 1927, when he officially retired from the ring, Dempsey engaged in only eight bouts and no less than five of them drew live gates of more than a million dollars each. All at a time when income tax was a negligible factor and generations before television could give an event a worldwide audience.

Dempsey, at first, was not generally popular and many spectators paid to watch in awe as he assaulted his victims, hoping against hope that he would get beaten-up himself. There were allegations that he had avoided service in the American army during the First World War and he was plagued with ugly lawsuits by his first wife, a prostitute he had married while still an inexperienced youth. It was not until he had lost his title against Gene Tunney, and later after the controversial battle of the 'Long Count', against the same opponent, that Dempsey became a national hero. The uncomplaining way in which he accepted defeat against Tunney in the first bout and then later in the return fight in which his refusal to retire to a neutral corner after flooring his opponent (then a new rule) conceivably robbed him of a knockout victory, had much to do with the amazing affection the American public developed for him and which he retained until his death 56 years later.

Dempsey lived his long life to the full. He earned and spent millions of dollars, starred in the typical melodramas produced by Hollywood in the 1920s, and his second wife, Estelle Taylor, was herself one of the most celebrated screen actresses of her day. He later married Hannah Williams, a beautiful showgirl and model, who gave him two daughters, and he spent the final years of his life married to the much-younger Deanna Piattelli, a serenely attractive and sophisticated lady, who spent much of her time keeping a protective screen between him and his demanding public.

The savagery which made him such a great champion was never evident in his life outside the ring. Drunks often tried to pick fights with him during the many years he ran the restaurant at 1619 Broadway, New York, but he always managed to keep his sense of humour and his feared left hook remained retired.

There was the night, for instance, when he caught a burglar in his apartment and reporters wanted to know whether he had punched the miscreant.

'Of course not,' the man they called the 'Manassa Mauler' replied. 'I only had a couple of thousand dollars in the place and I've got to be paid more than that to hit someone!'

When I met him he was in his late seventies but still an impressive-looking man, tall with a shock of dark hair only streaked with grey. His ring-battered nose had been straightened by a plastic surgeon, and conservatively dressed and immaculately groomed, he looked and behaved like a successful businessman. Aware of his obligation to talk about the ring career which had made him one of the best-known people in the world, he recounted a few anecdotes and added some kindly comments about the modern champions.

I mentioned that I had once sent him a clipping of an article written by Mr C R Swart, then the South African State President, on the occasion he saw Dempsey knock out Georges Carpentier in boxing's first-ever million-dollar fight, and he assured me that he still had it somewhere around his place. By that time another queue of tourists had formed and we shook hands and moved on. There was a limit even on the time he could spend with the friend of a friend.

Our second meeting, the formal occasion at the Waldorf Astoria, was fleeting as there were too many other demands from far more important guests.

Fame can be a burden when you are nearly 80 years old and later that evening while Muhammad Ali and George Foreman were turning the dinner into a shambles by hurling insults at each other for the benefit of the cameramen, I caught my last glimpse of Jack Dempsey.

He was slumped in his seat, idly twirling an unlit cigar between the fingers of the one big hand. He did not seem to hear Ali or Foreman, who were fellow guests at the main table, nor did he seem to notice the flashing cameras. Perhaps he was remembering an era when fighters did their fighting in the ring.

Luis Firpo sends Jack Dempsey flying through the ropes in the first round of their world heavyweight title fight in 1923.

DIVISIONS

With 17 weight classifications, modern boxing has mushroomed far beyond its simple beginning in the eighteenth century. When James Figg was proclaimed champion of England in 1719 he was, in effect, champion of all boxing as there were no weight divisions. Standing six feet tall and weighing 185 pounds, Figg was clearly a heavyweight, even by today's standards (well, sort of).

But it was not until 1746 that anyone thought of classifying boxers according to their weight or size. This was the year that the lightweight class became more or less an official division in England. And yet the lightweight class of 1746 bore little resemblance to the lightweight division of today.

A small man was called a lightweight simply because of his size, not necessarily for his weight. The earliest lightweights were not taken seriously and usually fought in the preliminaries put on before the big fights.

Next to be given a descriptive tag were the medium-sized men. They were called 'middleweights'. Originally the English considered as middleweights all men too heavy to fight the lightweights but not big enough to take on the heavyweights.

Despite the division of boxers by weight and size, the only official championship fights were among the big fellows. In fact, there was no recognized champion in the lighter classes until the nineteenth century. Then, as boxing began to enjoy more popularity, recognition of the smaller men began, and public interest demanded that lightweight and middleweight championships be held.

In 1792, some English boxers began to call themselves 'welters'. 'Welter' was a horse-racing term and referred to an impost carried by a horse in a handicap race. A 'welter' weighed ten stone or 140 pounds.

It was not until the 1890s, after the widespread adoption of the Queensberry Rules, that a real effort was made to standardize weight divisions. Some sort of agreement was reached when British and American boxing authorities got together in 1910, but many of the limits set then have since changed.

In fact, for several years both before and after the date of the agreement, weight limits fluctuated a pound or two according to the weight of the contemporary champions. For example, Willie Ritchie raised the lightweight limit in 1912 from 133 to 135 pounds, while Bob Fitzsimmons increased the middleweight limit in 1894 from 154 to 158 pounds. In the same year, George Dixon raised the featherweight limit from 115 to 129 pounds.

Nowadays it is the sanctioning bodies, such as the World Boxing Association, the World Boxing Council, the International Boxing Federation and the World Boxing Organization, who stipulate the weight limits and determine if and when new divisions should be established.

The eight weight divisions established by mutual agreement in 1910 – heavyweight, light heavyweight, middleweight, welterweight, lightweight, featherweight, bantamweight and flyweight – have since grown to 17. Moreover, the so-called 'world titles' are now split between the various sanctioning bodies, which means that effectively there can now be 68 or more 'world' champions reigning at one and the same time.

The last weight classification to be officially recognized was the mini flyweight. At least, that is what the IBF calls it. The WBC has named it 'strawweight' and the WBA calls it the minimum weight division.

Once called the Cinderella class of boxing, the light heavyweight division has surprisingly become one of the most consistent. First established in 1903 by Lou Houseman, the then sports editor of the *Chicago Inter-Ocean*, the limit has never been increased above its original 175 pounds. And that is more than can be said of many of the other weight divisions.

The middleweight limit has been raised twice: first by Fitzsimmons from its original 156 to 158 pounds in 1894, and then to its present limit of 160 pounds in 1915. The welterweight limit was increased from its original 142 to 147 pounds in 1909, while the lightweight limit has moved up and down like a barometer. In the 1860s, the limit was 133 pounds but this went as high as 140 pounds before the turn of the century, only to drop back to 133 pounds soon

New York boxing commissioner Randy Gordon checks the weight of US superstar Oscar de la Hoya.

afterwards. In 1912, the limit was raised to 135 pounds.

The junior divisions, most of which were established by the WBA and its forerunner the National Boxing Association, have struggled for years to gain acceptance. The junior lightweight and junior welterweight classes were established by the NBA as long ago as 1922 but only gained real acceptance some 40 years later.

It took 150 years for boxers to be subdivided into three different weight categories, but it has taken fewer than 75 years for the number of weight divisions in boxing to be doubled. The following 17 weight divisions are generally recognized throughout the world today:

MINI FLYWEIGHT

Limit 105 lb, 47.62 kg, 7 st 7 lb

Also known as minimum weight and strawweight.
Established in June 1987.
First champion: Kyung-Yung Lee of Korea

LIGHT FLYWEIGHT

Limit 108 lb, 48.98 kg, 7 st 10 lb

Also known as junior flyweight.
Established in April 1975.
First champion: Franco Udello (Italy)

FLYWEIGHT

Limit 112 lb, 50.80 kg, 8 st

First established by the National Sporting Club of London in 1909, but only recognized in the United States in 1920.
First champion: Sid Smith (England)

SUPER FLYWEIGHT

Limit 115 lb, 52.16 kg, 8 st 3 lb

Also known as junior bantamweight.
Established in February 1980.
First champion: Rafael Orono (Venezuela)

BANTAMWEIGHT

Limit 118 lb, 53.43 kg, 8 st 6 lb

First recognized in Britain in 1886, in the United States in 1888.
First champion: Tommy Kelly (USA)

SUPER BANTAMWEIGHT

Limit 122 lb, 55.33 kg, 8 st 10 lb

Also known as junior featherweight.
Established in April 1976.
First champion: Rigoberto Riasco (Panama)

LIGHTWEIGHT

Limit 135 lb, 61.23 kg, 9 st 9 lb

Division dates back to the Prize Ring.
First champion: Jack McAuliffe (USA)

FEATHERWEIGHT

Limit 126 lb, 57.15 kg 9 st

Established in March 1890.
First champion Billy Murphy (Australia)

JUNIOR LIGHTWEIGHT

Limit 130 lb, 58.96 kg, 9 st 4 lb

Also known as super featherweight.
Established in November 1921.
First champion: Johnny Dundee (USA)

JUNIOR WELTERWEIGHT

Limit 140 lb, 63.50 kg, 10 st

Also known as super lightweight and light welter.
Established in November 1922 by *Boxing Blade*.
First champion: Pinky Mitchell (USA)

WELTERWEIGHT

Limit 147 lb, 66.67 kg, 10 st 7 lb

Established in October 1888.
First champion: Paddy Duffy (USA)

JUNIOR MIDDLEWEIGHT

Limit 154 lb, 69.85 kg, 11 st

Also known as super welterweight and light middleweight.
Established in October 1962.
First champion: Denny Moyer

MIDDLEWEIGHT

Limit 160 lb, 72.57 kg, 11 st, 6 lb

Established in July 1884.
First champion: Jack Dempsey

SUPER MIDDLEWEIGHT

Limit 168 lb, 76.20 kg, 12 st

Established in March 1984.
First champion: Murray Sutherland (Canada)

LIGHT HEAVYWEIGHT

Limit 175 lb, 79.38 kg, 12 st 7 lb

Established in April 1903
First champion: Jack Root (USA)

CRUISERWEIGHT

190 lb, 86.18 kg, 13 st 8 lb

Also known as junior heavyweight.
Established in December 1979.
First champion: Marvin Camel (USA)

HEAVYWEIGHT

Over 190 lb, 86.18 kg, 13 st 8 lb

First champion under Queensberry Rules: James J Corbett (USA).
Corbett beat the last bareknuckle champion John L Sullivan on 7 September 1892 to win the title.

DRAWS

Next to a 'no contest' or a 'no decision', a draw is the most negative result in boxing. Nobody wins; nobody loses. But while some fighters may consider it an honour to have held an opponent to a draw, winning is what professional boxing is all about.

Some of the early champions seemed to make a habit of boxing to drawn decisions. George Dixon, an early claimant to the world featherweight title, had an astonishing 45 drawn bouts in 130 recorded fights and the suspicion persists that many of these drawn decisions were either contrived or pre-arranged.

In the nineteenth century many fights were declared drawn when unforeseen circumstances forced stoppages. This was certainly the case in the two famous prize-fights between John C Heenan and Tom Sayers in 1860 and John L Sullivan and Charlie Mitchell in 1888.

The Heenan-Sayers fight, which was staged at Farnborough, on 17 April 1860, attracted a large crowd, including the Prince Regent, Lord Palmerston, the prime minster, and many other notables of Church and State.

'We have a fine morning for our business,' Heenan said to Sayers as the two men greeted each other warmly.

'We have indeed,' said Sayers. 'If a man can't fight on such a morning as this, he can't fight at all.'

Both men were capable fighters, but after two hours and 20 minutes the referee declared the match a draw when the crowd threatened to cut the ropes and invade the ring.

Bad weather caused the fight between Sullivan and Mitchell to be declared a draw after 39 rounds. It was fought under London Prize Ring Rules on the country estate of Baron Rothschild at Chantilly, France, on 10 March 1888, and the men were obliged to call it quits after three hours, ten minutes and 55 seconds of fighting. Heavy rain, which had started falling from the tenth round, finally forced the stoppage when the footing became almost impossible.

Only four contests for the world heavyweight title under Queensberry rules have ended in drawn decisions. Tommy Burns,

Featherweight George Dixon had an astonishing 45 drawn bouts in 130 recorded fights.

Above left: Tommy Burns was the first world heavyweight champion under Queensberry Rules to be held to a draw in a championship fight. Above right: Mike Weaver's fight with Michael Dokes in 1983 was the last heavyweight championship fight to end in a draw. Below: Marvin Hagler scores with a right jab in his world middleweight title fight with Vito Antuofermo in 1979, which ended in a draw after 15 rounds.

one of boxing's most forgettable champions, was held to a draw over 20 rounds by Philadelphia Jack O'Brien at the Naud Junction Pavilion, Los Angeles, on 28 November 1906.

Seven years later the heavyweight fight between champion Jack Johnson and challenger Jim Johnson at the Elysée-Montmartre, Paris, was declared a draw by referee Emil Maitrot when the defending champion broke his hand and was unable to continue after the tenth round.

The third heavyweight championship fight to end in a draw was the match between Mike Weaver and Michael Dokes for the WBA title at the Dunes Hotel in Las Vegas on 20 May 1983. Judges Harold Lederman and Larry Hazzard both scored the fight a draw but judge Jerry Roth had Dokes winning by four points.

'Mike Weaver and boxing history have always been an item,' Bert Sugar pointed out in his fight report for *The Ring*. 'Only a few heavyweight champions ever lost their first pro fight. Weaver is the only one to lose his first two. He won the heavyweight title with the shortest time remaining on the fight clock; he lost his title in the shortest time in boxing history. Now, he has fought a draw in his attempt to recapture the crown – only the third time in modern heavyweight history a heavyweight title fight has ended in a draw.'

Las Vegas also hosted two other highly controversial drawn fights. Marvin Hagler was convinced he had been 'robbed' when his middleweight championship fight with Vito Antuofermo in November 1979 was declared a draw after 15 rounds. And some called it the 'phoney war' when the WBC super middleweight title fight between Sugar Ray Leonard and Thomas Hearns was declared a draw in June 1989.

Scoring in the Hagler-Antuofermo fight was split right down the middle with judge Dalby Shirley favouring Antuofermo 144–142, judge Duane Ford scoring for Hagler 145–141 and judge Hal Miller calling it even 143–143. 'All this is going to do for me is make me meaner,' Hagler said afterwards. 'It only puts bitterness in me and keeps it there.'

There was no such bitterness after the Hearns-Leonard fight. 'I gave it my best shot,' Hearns said afterwards, perhaps feeling relieved he was still standing at the final bell. 'I am not upset about the decision. It was very close.'

Close it certainly was – so spare a thought for the judges in these superfights, who now carry an enormous responsibility with millions of dollars riding on the result. 'Shall we do it again?' Leonard asked Hearns after it was all over, and then added: 'No, let's go home and rest.'

Almost without exception, drawn decisions cause the antagonists to search for a scapegoat, and American promoter Dan Duva believed he had found one in British judge Mickey Vann when Julio Cesar Chavez held Pernell Whitaker to a draw in their WBC welterweight title fight in San Antonio, Texas, on 10 September 1993.

Vann was accused of deducting a point from Whitaker in the sixth round for 'an appalling low blow' without referee Joe Cortez issuing an official warning. The point deducted would have given Whitaker a majority decision win because judge Jack Woodruff had scored the fight 115–113 in favour of the defending champion, while judge Franz Marti had it even at 115–115.

Lady judge Eugenia Williams became the scapegoat in what was arguably one of the most controversial fights in heavyweight boxing history. No sooner had the unification title bout between Evander Holyfield and Lennox Lewis at Madison Square Garden in New York been declared a draw on 13 March 1999 than all hell broke loose.

The headline in *Flash*, the American trade paper, said it all: 'Lewis Mugged; Two Judges Turn Holy.' The mainstream media was even more vociferous. 'Robbery!' screamed the New York *Daily News*. 'It stinks!' declared the *New York Post*.

While Ms Williams had made Holyfield a two point winner, British judge Larry O'Connell had scored the fight a draw. Only South African judge Stan Christodoulou seemingly got it right when he made Lewis the winner by three points. Lewis was indignant: 'I was in total control. Total control. What did he do to me? Nothing. I was popping him with jabs all night. There was no doubt who won the fight.'

With three American groups declaring their intention to investigate the fight – Attorney General Eliot Spitzer claimed that either 'tampering or incompetence was involved' – the heads of the sanctioning bodies swiftly ordered a rematch.

DRUGS

It was common knowledge for years but it still came as something of a shock when Pinklon Thomas, the former world heavyweight champion, admitted that he had a drug problem.

'I just try to live one day at a time,' Thomas told me as we left the Roberto Clemente Coliseum in San Juan on a hot, humid day in September 1989. 'I'm doing the best I can, but I don't try to live beyond tomorrow. I don't even know if there will be a tomorrow.'

Five years later Mando Ramos, the former world lightweight champion, claimed that he fought on cocaine and heroin in a no-holds-barred article published in the September 1994 issue of *The Ring*. 'I never fought a fight without using alcohol or drugs,' Ramos told Pete Ehrmann. 'When I fought Ismael Laguna, I don't know how they even let me in the ring, I was doing so much cocaine.'

Ramos claimed he had been clean and sober for eleven years and that he had started an organization called Boxers Against Alcohol and Drugs in 1983 – the year he started to go straight.

Like so many boxers in the Americas, Ramos got hooked when he was young, and like Thomas and countless others, he found it awfully hard to break the habit. The tragedy is that more than half the boxers in the Americas now suffer from similar problems. Drugs have become the scourge of sport.

Some of the biggest names in boxing have admitted their addiction: heavyweights Michael Dokes, Tyrell Biggs, Tony Tucker, Gerry Cooney and Leon Spinks; junior welterweight Aaron Pryor; junior lightweights Sam Serrano, Antonio Cervantes and Rocky Lockridge. The list is endless.

Lockridge, a former two-time world champion, was forced to withdraw from a proposed fight with WBA junior lightweight champion Brian Mitchell in South Africa in 1989 because he was obliged to enter a drug rehabilitation centre. And yet it was only a year earlier that Lockridge was visiting schools in New Jersey to warn teenagers about the dangers of drug abuse.

Tony Tucker rips a right uppercut to the face of Eddie Lopez during their heavyweight fight in Las Vegas in 1984. Tucker later admitted that he had a drug problem.

And only a couple of weeks before Lockridge admitted his addiction, the then IBF world featherweight champion Jorge Paez was fined for failing to take a post-fight drug test following his title defence against José Mario Lopez in Mexico City.

Clearly the drug problem was getting out of control in boxing and this despite the fact that the World Boxing Council had launched a drug and alcohol awareness programme in 1988 by placing posters and pamphlets in gyms throughout the world and that later in the year the World Boxing Association passed anti-drug regulations making it mandatory for fighters in championship bouts to undergo an official urine test either before or after the fight.

This procedure is now accepted practice in all major championship fights. As early as February 1988, Vaughn Hooks, an unbeaten

Philadelphia light heavyweight, became the first boxer to be stripped of a title after testing positive for drugs. The urinalysis, after Hooks had won a disputed decision over Frankie Swindell for the USBA vacant title, showed that Hooks had traces of cocaine in his system. The decision was promptly changed to 'no contest' and the title declared vacant.

A year earlier, drug-testing conducted by the Michigan State Athletic Commission had showed that nearly one in five of the state's boxers used drugs. Alarmed, the Commission proposed stiffer penalties for violations, including a lifetime ban.

It was Bill Gallo, associate sports editor of the New York *Daily*

Gerrie Coetzee rocks Michael Dokes with a solid jab to the head during their WBA heavyweight title fight in Richfield, Ohio in 1983. Dokes later claimed he was on drugs at the time.

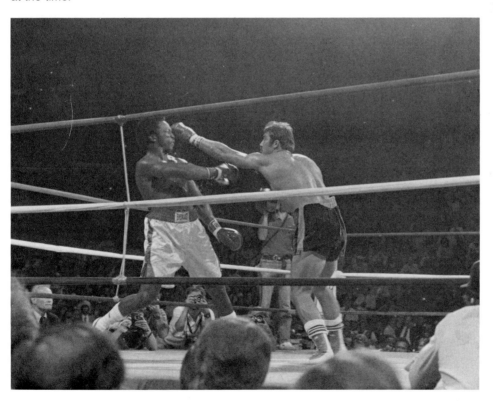

News, who first warned in print that boxing had a drug problem. 'Professional boxing is not becoming America's next big drug-problem sport, it already is, with estimates from knowledgeable ring figures that upwards of 20 per cent of all active fighters today have used drugs, some of them even going into the ring under the influence,' Gallo wrote early in 1984.

Michael Dokes later blamed his drug addiction for his defeat at the hands of Gerrie Coetzee in their WBA world heavyweight title fight in Richfield, Ohio, in September 1983.

'Definitely, it was the cocaine,' Dokes said. 'I had to have it because I was living in the fast lane, where drugs go along with fast cars and fast women. My daily routine was to go out and buy coke like someone else would buy vegetables.'

Dokes, who was knocked out in the tenth round, foamed at the mouth during his fight with Coetzee, and when I spoke to him at the post-fight press conference he was almost incoherent. The American heavyweight later claimed the cocaine did not show up in the post-fight drug tests because none were held that night in Richfield, Ohio.

Ten years ago it was merely a whisper but today drug usage has become common practice among many boxers. Kennedy McKinney, an Olympic champion who went on to win the IBF world junior featherweight title in 1992, suffers from calcium deficiency because he was once addicted to cocaine.

McKinney tested positive for drugs after his fight with Joe Martinez in July 1990. The Nevada State Athletic Commission suspended McKinney for six months and his backers persuaded him to enter a drug rehabilitation clinic.

This is not to suggest that every boxer is hooked on drugs. The then WBO junior welterweight champion, Hector Camacho, reacted angrily in 1989 when American reporters questioned him about his alleged drug problem. 'I don't look like a drug addict and I don't act like a hoodlum. I might talk like one, but there's a difference,' he said.

The first boxer to test positive for anabolic steroids was IBF heavyweight champion Frans Botha, who failed a urine test conducted by the Bund Deutscher Berufsboxer (German Professional Boxing Association) following his fight with Axel Schulz for the vacant title in Stuttgart on 9 December 1995.

Frans Botha, the South African heavyweight, was the first boxer to test positive for anabolic steroids following his fight with Axel Schulz.

Sterling McPherson, manager of Botha, later claimed the test in Stuttgart was shoddily done. 'We weren't sure if there was anybody in the room from the IBF or if there was even anybody there in an official capacity,' he said. 'No one had a badge. A woman there said she was the official doctor, but she didn't show anything to prove it, so already I was worried about getting a fair shake and we weren't even out of the building.'

Bobby Lee, president of the IBF, admitted before the second sample was tested in the United States that it was a complicated case. 'This is our first experience with anabolic steroids,' he said. Lee could have added that the test was done upon the insistence of the BDB. Only after the results of the tests were disclosed did American boxing commissions declare their intention to start testing boxers for steroids.

After much deliberation, the IBF decided not to strip Botha of his title but fined him $50,000 instead. Schulz and his promoters were

Pinklon Thomas, the former WBC heavy-weight champion, has been battling against a drug habit for years.

not impressed and took their case to a New Jersey court.

'The IBF cannot fail to disqualify a fighter who has taken drugs before a fight,' Dickinson Debevoise said in handing down his ruling. In the event, the IBF had no option but to strip Botha of the title. The result was also changed to 'no contest'.

ROBERTO DURAN

Roberto Duran is a man of many moods – and his mood for most of 1989 was mean. Although he had already been pencilled in for boxing's next big superfight, the legendary Latin had a chip on his shoulder the size of Mount Everest.

Duran was still simmering from the less-than-royal treatment he had received from the press and public in Panama after he had beaten Iran Barkley to win his fourth world title in February 1989.

It seems that Duran bad-mouthed just about everyone when he returned home after the fight. He also demanded that a large statue

Roberto Duran and Wilfred Benitez trade blows during their WBC super welterweight title fight in 1982.

of himself be erected in his honour in Panama City. 'I want the recognition now,' he said, 'not after I'm dead.'

It was not the first time Duran had been at odds with his fans or the media. After he quit in the eighth round of his return fight with Sugar Ray Leonard in November 1980, Panamanian fans threw stones at his house and called him a homosexual.

Duran, now fat and fortysomething but still fighting, has never forgotten those dark days nor the way the world's leading boxing promoters dropped him like a hot potato. 'They're all a bunch of pirates,' he said, not bothering to conceal his contempt. 'Whatever they offer you, they always expect five or six times as much in return. They live off us boxers – and they give nothing away.'

But Duran, who shocked the boxing world when he beat Barkley only four months short of his 38th birthday and 17 years after he had won his first world title, was also capable of showing compassion.

We got a rare glimpse of it early in 1989 when he visited Estaban DeJesus, the first man to beat him in the professional ring, at his home in San Juan, Puerto Rico. DeJesus was dying of AIDS at the age of 37 and in a touching gesture, Duran kissed him on the cheek – a last farewell from a great warrior to an honoured adversary.

Duran seldom if ever showed such compassion in the ring. A product of the ugly barrios of Panama City, his sadistic upbringing as a street urchin was later reflected in the way he thought and fought. Time and again his pre-fight predictions would consist of 'I will kill him'. And when he knocked out Ray Lampkin to retain the world lightweight title in March 1975, he glanced at the badly beaten boxer being carried off to hospital and then turned to tell television viewers: 'The next time I send him to the morgue.'

Duran not only had the look of an assassin when he entered the ring, he had the same burning desire to 'waste' his opponents and for 13 years he proved invincible. Only the third fighter to win four world titles, he won 21 of his first 24 contests on knockouts and quickly became known as 'Manos de Piedra' or 'Hands of Stone'.

A one-time shoeshine boy, Roberto became the original 'macho man' of boxing. He won the world lightweight title in 1972 when he knocked out Ken Buchanan in the 13th round of a controversial fight at Madison Square Garden in New York. Duran was careless with his punching and hit Buchanan low several times, prompting TV commentator Reg Gutteridge to remark afterwards: 'That proves that British boxers can't take it – in the balls!'

After 12 successful defences, Duran relinquished the title in 1979 and a year later defeated Sugar Ray Leonard to win the welterweight title in a thrilling fight in Montreal.

'It's the single most amazing thing I've seen in my lifetime in boxing,' said American TV commentator Alex Wallau. 'And Duran did it two weight classes above his prime weight, and at a time when Leonard was in his prime. I don't think anybody can truly appreciate how phenomenal that is.'

The rematch five months later left Duran in disgrace when he turned his back on Leonard and quit in the eighth round. And this from a macho man who really did knock down a horse with a right hand (he also kayoed the wife of an opponent when she charged him after he had knocked out her husband in a Panama City ring).

'To make any man quit is an achievement,' Leonard said later. 'To make Roberto Duran quit seemed impossible. It was better than knocking him out. I outclassed him, humiliated and frustrated him. He couldn't take it mentally. I didn't hurt him or make him bleed. I just made him look a fool before millions.'

'Now I've seen everything,' said Ray Arcel, Duran's famous American trainer. 'If any guy had told me Duran even knew how to quit I'd have spat in his eye.'

Arcel recalled the impression Duran first made on him. 'Right from the very start I saw that he was a natural fighter,' Arcel said. 'He could think in the ring, which is very important. It was a natural reaction, sharp and fast.'

A further setback for Duran came in 1982 when Wilfred Benitez outboxed him for the WBC junior middleweight title, and when he lost to Kirkland Laing later in the same year it looked as though Duran had reached the end of the road. But Roberto regained much lost prestige when he knocked out Davey Moore in eight rounds to win the WBA junior middleweight title in a savage fight in 1983.

A points loss to Marvin Hagler did his reputation little harm but a second round knockout at the hands of Thomas Hearns in 1984 virtually brought his career to an end. Duran remained inactive in 1985, returned to the ring in 1986 only to lose to Robbie Sims and then caused a major upset in 1989 by beating Barkley for the WBC middleweight title.

Meanwhile Duran had been sparring with the US Internal Revenue Service. The nightmare began in 1988 when the IRS sent Duran two cheques totalling $1.6 million in refunds for overpayments on his income taxes between 1977 and 1984. Duran, bless his soul, promptly cashed them both.

However, when a third cheque arrived for $3.4 million even the boxer realized something was wrong. He sent it back immediately for a reassessment and the US government then demanded that he

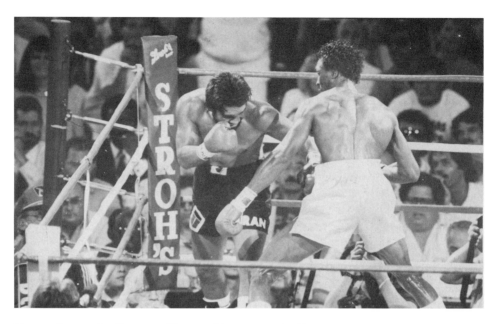

Above: disaster for Duran as Thomas Hearns knocks him out in the second round of their fight for the world junior middleweight title in 1984. Below: still winning fights at the age of 41, Duran has his arms held aloft after stopping Ken Hulsey in Cleveland, Ohio.

repay $1.54 million given to him by mistake.

Amid all the confusion, American promoter Bob Arum came to Duran's rescue by offering him a third fight with Leonard. In one of those amazing coincidences that happen every now and then in boxing, it meant that the first superfight of the 1980s would also be the last. How's that again? Well, the first superfight of the 1980s was between Duran and Leonard in Montreal on 20 June 1980 and the last featured the same fighters at The Mirage in Las Vegas on 7 December 1989.

Duran claimed at the time that nobody could have done what he had as a fighter, and when told that Leonard always wanted to meet him in a third match, simply smirked. 'He's full of shit,' he said. 'If he wanted me so badly how come it took him nine years?'

Leonard tried to play down the bad feeling between the two boxers, but when pushed by reporters he exploded in mock anger: 'Okay, I hate the son of a bitch. The guy always disturbs me. He's a bad man. Duran walks around thinking he owns the world and that when he puts his foot down, everything should come to a halt. The guy is just weird.'

Leonard proved his superiority by again beating Duran on points. And yet, was anybody really superior to the Latin legend?

Even at the age of 43, Duran still proved a handful for Vinny Pazienza when he challenged the American tough guy for the IBC super middleweight title in January 1995. 'I have to respect him,' Pazienza, 12 years younger, said afterwards. 'He fought a helluva fight.'

EXHIBITIONS

Once they were a good source of income for both champions and challengers, but when television turned the world into a global village, they quickly lost their appeal. Exhibition bouts clearly belong to the past – and yet there was a time when they caused almost as much excitement as the real thing.

Probably the most successful exhibition tour ever undertaken was that of Jack Dempsey, the former world heavyweight champion. From 19 August 1931 until 31 March 1932, Dempsey engaged in nearly 100 exhibition bouts across the United States that drew record attendances and gate receipts.

'The USA was in miserable shape,' recalls Bob Soderman, the American boxing historian. 'Banks were collapsing right and left and businesses were laying off workers on a daily basis. The politicians were dispensing nothing but platitudes and the public was sadly coming to the realization that things were only going to get worse.'

And yet, despite the great economic Depression, the magic of the Dempsey name still drew large crowds wherever he boxed. A total of 23,322 fight fans were in attendance at the Chicago Coliseum on a cold February night in 1932 to watch Dempsey box a four-round exhibition with King Levinsky. Paid admissions totalled $74,199 – still the largest amount ever grossed from an exhibition bout.

There was, of course, no official decision rendered but a poll of writers at the ringside showed that 18 favoured Levinsky while only two thought Dempsey was the better boxer.

The next largest crowd for an exhibition bout was recorded on 12 November 1946 in Honolulu, Hawaii, when 10,075 people turned up to watch Joe Louis, the then world heavyweight champion, box a total of six rounds with Cleo Everett and Wayne Powell.

Louis had boxed countless unrecorded exhibitions for the US Armed Forces during the Second World War and he continued to appear in exhibition bouts during 1946 and 1947. The upshot was that when Louis was matched with Jersey Joe Walcott in December 1947, the New York State Athletic Commission was at first prepared to sanction it as a mere ten-round exhibition bout.

Pressure from press and public forced the commission to reconsider their decision, which was just as well because in the event Louis only retained the title by the skin of his teeth, winning on a hotly disputed split decision over 15 rounds. Joe was so embarrassed by his poor performance he even tried to leave the ring before the decision was announced.

King Levinsky, the American heavyweight, whose exhibition bout with Jack Dempsey in 1932 set the record for both the largest attendance and the biggest gate.

Jersey Joe Walcott, whose first fight with Joe Louis in 1947 was originally planned as a 10-round exhibition.

Oddly enough, a previous Louis title defence (against Abe Simon in Detroit in March 1941) ran into similar trouble when the Michigan Boxing Board refused to recognize it as a championship contest. 'This is not sanctioned as a championship bout,' Commissioner Hettche told the media. 'We are listing it only as a 20-round exhibition.'

Fortunately, others refused to accept the commission's ruling because not only did Simon give Louis a hard fight, the giant boxer was still on his feet at the start of the 13th round.

'If a contest is worth while permitting at all under the rules of a state, it should merit the wholehearted support of the men behind it. Otherwise why charge fight patrons regular prices to see an exhibition?' Nat Fleischer, the highly respected American boxing writer, asked afterwards.

Jim Jeffries, an earlier heavyweight champion of the world, also had reason to regret an exhibition bout he engaged in over four rounds with Jack Munroe in Butte, Montana, on 19 December 1902. Jeffries had been taking life very easy following his second victory over Jim Corbett in San Francisco several months earlier and was not in the best of shape, either physically or mentally.

Munroe, on the other hand, was in good condition and had a local reputation as a fighter to uphold. This he did by roughing Jeffries up at close quarters and putting the champion on the floor in the fourth round. It was a push, rather than a punch, that put Jeffries down and the big fellow was up in a jiffy – but the news was flashed around the world by Associated Press.

In truth Munroe was little more than a run-of-the-mill fighter and when he was given a title shot on 26 August 1904 – largely on the strength of what had happened in their exhibition bout – Munroe appeared to suffer stage-fright and made little attempt to fight back. Jeffries knocked him out in the second round.

Last of the great heavyweight champions to appear in a series of exhibitions was Muhammad Ali who, after he had lost the world title to Joe Frazier in New York in March 1971, engaged in no fewer than 28 exhibition bouts around the world during 1971 and 1972.

Perhaps the most extraordinary exhibition bout was that between John L Sullivan and James J Corbett on the stage of the Grand Opera House in San Francisco on 26 June 1891. Not because Sullivan was then heavyweight champion of the world and Corbett was the man destined to beat him, but because John L insisted that they appear on stage in evening dress, not boxing trunks. The men sparred four rounds. At the end of the second Corbett returned to his corner and told his chief second Billy Delaney: 'Billy, I can lick this fellow.' A year later he did.

FAMILIES

For some, boxing is not merely a sport but a family tradition – and if it's proof you need check the history of the Sands of Australia, the Turpins of England, the Famechons of France, the Arrendondos of Mexico or the Toweels of South Africa.

These families were not only steeped in boxing tradition, but in the case of the Famechons both the fathers and/or uncles and their sons became champions. Nor does tradition demand that the sons follow exactly in the footsteps of the fathers. For example, Lou Duva's son Dan had become one of the top boxing promoters in the world before his untimely death in 1996, while his father has long been regarded as one of the best trainers.

Latest in a long line of families who regard boxing as a tradition are the McNeeleys of Massachusetts in the United States. Heavyweight Peter McNeeley was named as the first man to fight Mike Tyson following Tyson's imprisonment, while his father Tom McNeeley challenged Floyd Patterson for the world heavyweight title in December 1961. McNeeley's grandfather Tom was also a fighter, so the tradition goes back for at least three generations.

Patterson knocked out Tom McNeeley in the fourth round after he floored McNeeley eight or nine times. 'Until the day I die, I can say I fought for the heavyweight championship of the world,' McNeeley said afterwards. 'How many guys can say that?'

The Famechons of France were a household name in boxing in

Vic Toweel traps Manuel Ortiz against the ropes during their world bantamweight title fight in Johannesburg in May 1950. Vic was one of five brothers who followed in their father's footsteps and became boxers.

Europe in the 1940s and 1950s. Brothers Ray, André and Emile were all highly successful, with Ray (the youngest) winning the European featherweight title in 1948 and challenging Willie Pep for the world title in 1950. Ray's nephew, Johnny Famechon, was destined to win the world title his uncle couldn't when he beat José Legra in London in 1969.

At last report, only one of the six Sands brothers is still alive in Australia. Middleweight Dave was the first to go, killed in a road accident when he was 26 and at a time when he was on the verge of a world title shot. Ritchie, Russell, Alfie and George all died of natural causes. Only Clem, the eldest of the most famous fighting family in Australian boxing history, is still living.

The exploits of the Toweel family of South Africa are legendary. Papa Mike boxed briefly himself before becoming a trainer for his five sons (Maurice was crippled but still became a top-class manager and promoter).

Of the others, Vic Toweel became world bantamweight champion in 1950, Willie held Robert Cohen to a draw for the same title in 1955, Jimmy won the South African lightweight title in 1949, and Fraser lost four edge-of-the-seat thrillers to Willie Ludick for the national welterweight title. Alan had half a dozen or so professional fights but made his name as a manager and trainer.

The Turpin brothers brought much pride and glory to Britain when Randolph beat the great Sugar Ray Robinson for the world middleweight title in 1951 and elder brother Dick won both the British and Empire middleweight titles in 1948. Younger brother Jackie also boxed with modest success.

Sadly, Randolph held the world middleweight title for only 64 days.

FAT FIGHTERS

Call them blubberweights if you will but fat fighters cannot be taken lightly. Many have become world champions, some have proved a touch troublesome for fighters greater than themselves, while others have added welcome humour to what is essentially a serious business.

George Foreman made more money and friends as a 'fat fighter' than he did when he was lean and hungry. But money, they say, is the root of all evil and money has already caused the downfall of more than one champion.

Add the name of Buster Douglas to the list. The former world heavyweight champion was guaranteed $24 million for defending his title against Evander Holyfield in Las Vegas in October 1990 and literally took the money and ran. Well, sort of. Douglas was so poorly conditioned the chances are he wouldn't have been able to run to the nearest pizza parlour.

There is an old axiom in boxing that a fighter needs to be 'hungry' to make it to the top. Trouble is, once he's there he's now likely to eat himself out of condition (Riddick Bowe is a prime example).

The story goes that when Douglas approached John Johnson to manage him in 1984, the 46-year-old manager held up an empty plate. 'I told him it was empty,' Johnson later recalled, 'but if he paid the price, some day there'd be a million on it.' That day arrived six years later and by the time Douglas climbed into the ring with Holyfield, the plate was already full to overflowing. And there, I suspect, lies the rub.

Nobody – and particularly not a lazy-boned fighter like Douglas – is likely to go through the deprivation and rigours of training when he knows he has $24 million in the bank.

Douglas tipped the scale at a blubbery 246 pounds, causing Lou Duva, Holyfield's trainer, to quip: 'They'll have to roll him in and roll him out.' They very nearly did. Douglas moved so slowly as he 'marched' to the ring, it looked like a slow-motion replay – and he took even longer to get off his back after Holyfield had knocked him out in the third round.

The fight will probably go down in boxing history as another victory for obesity ... and goodness knows we've had enough fat cats pretending to be champions to last us a lifetime. There was Primo Carnera in the 1930s, Abe Simon in the 1940s, Don Cockell in the 1950s, Buster Mathis in the 1960s, Mike Schutte in the 1970s, Leroy Jones in the 1980s, and a toss-up between George Foreman and Riddick Bowe in the 1990s.

At least Carnera had the frame to carry his 260–270 pounds, as did Jess Willard (245 pounds) before him, but guys like Cockell, Mathis, Jones and Foreman were clearly fat when they challenged for the title.

The first fat fighter to make a name for himself was probably Willie Meehan, a squat, blubbery American heavyweight who had actually started his boxing career in 1909 as a flyweight. In 1917 Meehan caused a major upset when he beat Jack Dempsey, who was destined to become world champion two years later. Meehan won on points over four rounds in Oakland, California.

In three subsequent bouts Dempsey managed to reverse the loss before twice being held to a draw. In their last fight in September 1918, Meehan again beat Dempsey on points over four rounds in San Francisco. Clearly the Fat Man had the Manassa Mauler's number.

Another celebrated fat fighter was 'Two Ton' Tony Galento, an American heavyweight who was active in the 1930s and 1940s, and who shocked the boxing world when he floored the legendary Joe Louis in the third round of their world heavyweight title fight in New York in June 1939. Louis climbed off the floor to batter Galento into submission in the fourth.

Tony Galento and Lou Nova square up at the weigh-in for their fight in Philadelphia in 1939. Galento won on a knockout in the 14th round.

A balding, five-foot nine-inch powerhouse of a man, Galento was based in Orange, New Jersey, and fought all the top heavyweights of his time. Tony did almost everything wrong. He reportedly trained on beer, did his 'roadwork' in an old Chevvy, and had the audacity to dismiss even Louis as a 'bum'. However, Galento had a powerful left hook and the strength of half a dozen men and among his victims were top heavyweights like Lou Nova, Natie Brown, Harry Thomas and Al Ettore.

Buster Mathis was a much better boxer than his size would suggest. Many are convinced Mathis would have been the Olympic champion in 1964 if a thumb injury had not kept him out of the Tokyo Games. Mathis turned professional the following year and at one stage his weight dropped to a svelte 220 pounds. However, by the time he fought Joe Frazier for the New York version of the world heavyweight title in March 1968, Mathis was again tipping the scales at 240 plus.

Mathis was surprisingly nimble on his feet for a big man and was essentially a boxer. 'That guy was unreal,' Rodney Bobick later told a writer. 'He could do things other heavyweights only dream about and despite his size and weight "Big Daddy" [Buster's nickname] could really roll.'

In September 1972 when he was long past his best as a boxer, Mathis was matched with Claude McBride for the mythical 'super heavyweight championship of the world'. According to American promoter Pat O'Grady, whose brainchild it was, the minimum weight limit for the division was 240 pounds. McBride was knocked out in the third round.

Tony Tubbs, who briefly held the WBA heavyweight title for fewer than nine months after beating Greg Page in April 1985, was another big fellow with a weight problem. In fact, after flopping like a beached whale through several of his fights, Tubbs had a weight clause written into his contract for his world heavyweight title fight with Mike Tyson in Tokyo in March 1988 that restricted him to a limit of 235 pounds. In the event, Tubbs came in at 238. Not that it made much difference. Tyson knocked him out in the second round.

FATHERS AND SONS

There were tears in his eyes when Ray 'Boom Boom' Mancini spoke at the press conference shortly after he was knocked out by Alexis Arguello in the 14th round of their WBC lightweight title fight in Atlantic City in October 1981. 'I'm very disappointed I didn't win this fight for my father,' Mancini said. 'I guess the Good Lord didn't see it was the time for me to win yet. But I'll be back.'

And, sure enough, eight months later he was. A wide grin split Mancini's face as he savoured the cheers of the fans following his one-round knockout victory over Arturo Frias in Las Vegas. 'It feels good to hear people calling me champ,' the new WBA titleholder admitted.

But not nearly as good as he felt on an afternoon in Youngstown, Ohio, when he was presented with his world championship belt. Larry Ringler of the Warren, Ohio *Tribune Chronicle* described the scene.

'The moment was 40 years in the making,' Ringler wrote. 'When it came, even Mother Nature seemed impressed. Dark clouds broke and the wind calmed. In the hush that fell upon Federal Plaza Wednesday afternoon, Ray "Boom Boom" Mancini officially became a world champion.

'It didn't matter to Mancini or about 2,000 adoring fans that the championship belt came in a plain brown grocery bag. Or that the microphone temporarily went dead during the presentation by the World Boxing Association vice-president Bob Lee.

'What mattered was that the hefty gold-plated belt came home to Youngstown. And in a very special way to Mancini's father, Lenny, the original Boom Boom.'

The story of the Mancini family, father and son, is a moving tale of heartbreak, raw emotion and true grit. Later they even made a movie about it and like all true stories it was hard to beat. Consider some of the ingredients:

When he was ten, Ray gave his father what became one of Lenny's most precious possessions. It was a block of wood he had made at

Ray Mancini, the former WBA lightweight champion, playfully taps his father, Lenny, on the chin with his right hand. Lenny was a leading lightweight in the 1940s.

school, a piece of two-by-six cut at an odd angle. A photograph of a grinning Ray was pasted at one corner, and across the top was inscribed CHIP OFF THE OLD BLOCK.

Ray often did things like that. When he was 13, he wrote a poem for his father, entitled 'I Walk in Your Shadow'. The final stanza reads:

> I want to feel this man's pains
> I want to be locked in this man's chains
> I want to be his model and live with his great name;
> For I am this man's son, and I'll never bear shame.

When he was 15, Ray announced that he wanted to train for the Junior Olympics. 'He was wearing his father's old trunks and old shoes in training, literally trying to walk in his father's footsteps, and finally I asked him if he wanted me to go up and get the old mouthpiece, too,' his mother Ellen recalled.

In the years that followed, Mancini experienced a whole range of emotions – from the bitter disappointment of losing to Arguello when he so wanted to win a world title for his father, to the joy of the Frias victory when his ambition was achieved, to the dark despair of the Kim tragedy when the Korean died following their world title fight in Las Vegas.

The Mancinis became the best-known father and son relationship in boxing in the 1980s, but there are others and there have been many more down the years. It seems only natural that most boxers' sons would want to follow in their fathers' footsteps and make a name for themselves in the ring. But when the father also happens to be a millionaire, it takes a special kind of person to make the effort.

Marvis Frazier, son of former world heavyweight champion Joe Frazier, was such a person. 'To be a boxer,' Marvis said, 'my father just told me you got to be mean and lean, and you can't take no stuff.'

When Marvis was about 14, he stopped by his father's gym in North Philadelphia, put on the gloves and a headguard, and climbed into the ring with his dad. 'My father nailed me with a hook,' Marvis

Father and son Phil and Harold Johnson share a unique record. Both were knocked out by Jersey Joe Walcott, both in fights in Philadelphia and both in three rounds – but 14 years apart.

later recalled with a laugh. 'But he reached out and caught me before I fell.'

Marvis Frazier became a good amateur but only a moderate professional. He was never able to match the wonderful feats achieved by his father – but at least he tried.

Harold Johnson, on the other hand, achieved far more than his father – except against one man: Jersey Joe Walcott. Both Harold and his dad Phil were knocked out by Walcott, both in fights in Philadelphia and both in three rounds – but 14 years apart. Walcott knocked out the father on 22 June 1936 and the son on 8 February 1950.

It is a pity Archie Moore and Harold Johnson reached their peak at the same time. Johnson always had to play second fiddle to Moore but he did eventually receive international recognition as world light heavyweight champion when he outpointed Doug Jones in May 1962. A year later Johnson lost the title to Willie Pastrano in a closely contested fight.

'Harold's the greatest defensive boxer I've ever seen,' Pastrano said afterwards. 'He's a perfectionist.'

Of course, not all boxers' sons become boxers themselves. Joe Louis's son Joe Jr became a lawyer after graduating from Boston University, while Gene Tunney's boy John became a United States senator. Rocky Marciano Jr was a batboy with the Los Angeles Dodgers baseball team. Rocky Sr always wanted to be a professional ballplayer but finished up as a fighter.

No fighter who has won a world title has ever had a son who also achieved that distinction but not for the want of trying. Included in the list of famous fathers and sons in boxing are Marcel Cerdan and Marcel Jr, André Famechon and son Johnny, Bob Fitzsimmons and Young Bob, Jack London and sons Jack Jr and Brian, Pat O'Grady and son Sean, Jersey Joe Walcott and Jersey Joe Jr, Davey Hilton and sons Davey, Alex, Matthew and Stewart, and Ubaldo Sacco and his son Ubaldo Jr.

However, the only father and son team to referee a Golden Gloves tournament at the same time was Johnny LoBianco and his son Al. The men established the record in 1980 at the New York Golden Gloves tournament in Madison Square Garden.

FICTION

The difference between fact and fiction in the fight game has become almost indistinguishable. Not surprising when so much fiction has been based on fact and so many in boxing try to imitate fictional characters in order to attract the attention of the media.

'Boxing and literature might not seem to be likely bed-fellows yet the sport of pugilism has attracted many famous writers down the ages and fight literature has its own masters and bards,' says Peter McInnes, the British boxing historian.

Moreover, much of their work has been based on actual events with both the *Iliad* and *Odyssey* offering long, detailed descriptions of boxing contests. Plato in the *Dialogues* and Aristotle in his *Nicomachean Ethics* both discuss classic fistic confrontations, while in Virgil's *Aeneid* and the *Epigrams* of Martial, boxing is recommended as 'a manly attribute, practised by men of skill and courage'.

Strictly speaking, these great Greek and Roman writers were the first fight reporters. Others like Lord Byron, Victor Hugo, William Thackeray, Samuel Johnson, George Bernard Shaw and P G Wodehouse later also wrote about or referred to the fight game.

According to Shaw, Thackeray 'loved a prize fight as he loved a fool'. However, when it was reported that Thackeray was among the spectators at the Heenan–Sayers fight at Farnborough in April 1860, he denied his presence in an anonymous poem he wrote for *Punch*.

Lord Byron, on the other hand, was proud of his association with prize-fighting and personally investigated the home of boxing's first Golden Era by visiting Greece. Byron recorded the attitude of the fashionable young men of his day when he wrote in his *Hints from Horace*: 'And men unpractised in exchanging knocks must go to Jackson ere they dare to box.'

In his *Dictionary of the English Language*, Samuel Johnson claimed that 'box' came from the Welsh word *bock* and signified a blow to the head given with the hand. He added that 'to box' is 'to fight with the fist' and that 'a boxer' is 'a man who fought with his fists'.

George Bernard Shaw, who wrote *Cashel Byron's Profession* at the age of 26, later admitted that he researched the book by 'wading through *Boxiana* and the files of *Bell's Life* at the British Museum'. Shaw later befriended Gene Tunney when Tunney became the first heavyweight champion of the world to show an interest in literature.

Not all the great works on boxing received instant recognition. Ernest Hemingway's *Fifty Grand*, the story of a fixed fight, was first rejected by both *Cosmopolitan* and the *Saturday Evening Post* before being printed in the *Atlantic Monthly* in 1927.

Ring Lardner's *Champion*, which was published in 1929, was destined to become his best-known work despite his own view that he had written better stories. *Champion* received even more critical acclaim when it was made into a movie starring Kirk Douglas and Arthur Kennedy in 1949. 'Still one of the great movies about the fight game,' declared Steven H Scheuer in *Movies on TV*.

Supporting the theory that some of the best boxing fiction is based on fact was the runaway success of Budd Schulberg's 1947 novel *The Harder They Fall*. The story line closely resembled the unfortunate fate of Primo Carnera, the former world heavyweight champion who started his career as a circus strongman. Made into a movie in 1956 starring Humphrey Bogart, Jan Sterling and Rod Steiger, *The Harder They Fall* received surprisingly good reviews.

Of the more recent boxing novels to be published, M S Hunter's *The Final Bell* 'is different from anything ever written about the Sweet Science', says Steve Farhood, editor-in-chief of *The Ring*. Nor is it difficult to understand why. The book focuses on New York City welterweight Stormy Rhodes, who goes on national television after winning the world title to announce that he is gay.

Improbable as that may seem to some, the story line is not entirely fictional because Kid Chocolate, the handsome black Cuban who won the world featherweight title in 1930, was well known in boxing circles as a homosexual.

FILMS

Thomas Alva Edison was not merely an inventor. Edison also had a sharp eye for business and knew how to promote the goodies he invented. And so one of the first things he did after perfecting the Kinetoscope, an early motion picture camera, was to film an exhibition bout between Mike Leonard and Jack Cushing in 1894.

Satisfied that the contraption actually worked, Edison then decided he needed a 'name' fighter to appear in front of the camera.

The best-known prize-fighter of the day was John L Sullivan, the old bareknuckle heavyweight champion, whose most famous boast was that he could 'lick any son of a bitch in the house'. And it was to Sullivan that Edison turned for help. Unfortunately, Sullivan rejected Edison's offer because he felt the fee was not big enough.

Jim Corbett, the man who had beaten Sullivan for the title, was more reasonable. Corbett, who fancied himself as an actor and was terribly vain, readily accepted the opportunity to be recorded on film.

And so on 7 September 1894, as Edison's primitive movie camera rolled, Corbett squared up to Peter Courtney for six two-minute rounds in the Black Maria, the name given to Edison's weird-looking studio in Orange, New Jersey.

Working to a pre-arranged script, Corbett knocked out Courtney in the sixth round and was paid $4,700 for his work. But as he was about to catch the train back to New York, Corbett was accosted by the local sheriff, who had been tipped off about the illegal prize-fight and wanted to arrest someone involved.

'Don't you recognize me?' Corbett asked. 'I'm Maurice Barrymore.'

The sheriff stared in puzzlement. 'Maurice Barrymore, the actor,' Corbett added and the sheriff turned on his heel and left.

The film of the Corbett–Courtney bout was never shown publicly but Edison had proved that boxing was an ideal subject for the Kinetoscope and, since the whole episode was reported by the *New York World*, the idea of filming prize-fights soon became an obsession with many movie-makers.

Two years later the first attempt was made to film a major fight outdoors when Bob Fitzsimmons was matched with Peter Maher near Langtry, Texas, in a fight advertised as for the heavyweight championship of the world.

Dan Stuart, the promoter, had no intention of paying the boxers anything extra for the movie rights and when Fitzsimmons became aware of what was happening he grew angry.

'Where do we come in?' he asked Stuart.

'You don't,' the promoter replied.

Bob Fitzsimmons and Jim Corbett exchange left jabs during the first world heavyweight title fight to be successfully filmed in Carson City, Nevada in March 1897.

'Corbett got the best part of five grand for a mere exhibition,' said Martin Julian, the boxer's brother-in-law.

'Your contract makes no mention of photographing the contest,' Stuart pointed out. 'You boys are getting paid to fight not act.'

'If there isn't anything in it for me,' said Fitz, 'then there won't be no moving pictures.'

Fitzsimmons kept his promise by knocking out Maher in 95 seconds of the first round, the fight ending even before the camera operators could get the Kinetoscope started.

Fitzsimmons was later involved in the first world heavyweight title fight to be successfully filmed. This took place in Carson City, Nevada, on 17 March 1897 when Fitzsimmons challenged Jim Corbett for the title. Enoch J Rector photographed the fight on 38mm film for the Veriscope, a machine especially built for use outdoors.

They also built a special box at the ringside to house the cameras.

Many notorious characters of the Wild West attended the fight but Bat Masterson, the famous Western marshal, and his deputies relieved spectators of their guns and other weapons before they entered the wooden arena. Fitzsimmons knocked out Corbett with his famous solar-plexus punch in the 14th round.

The film was a huge success and made a great deal of money all over the world. Unauthorized copies appeared on the scene and even fakes were made, with actors playing the roles of Fitzsimmons and Corbett.

Sixty-one years later, Jim Jacobs, the well-known American film collector who was destined to become the first manager of Mike Tyson, discovered a print of the old film in a barn in New Jersey. Much of the nitrate-based film had disintegrated and Jacobs spent months piecing together the knockout in the 14th round.

'It was like a jigsaw puzzle,' Jacobs said when he gave me a strip of the original film in his New York editing room in August 1970. 'But thanks to modern technology we were able to restore it to a reasonable condition and we used the sequence in *Legendary Champions.*'

The film of the Corbett–Fitzsimmons fight proved so popular that an attempt was made to film the world title fight between Fitzsimmons and Jim Jeffries at Coney Island, New York, on 9 June 1899. The big difference was that the fight was held indoors and the primitive cameras used failed to capture the images of the fighters.

Undaunted, the film producers restaged the fight, using two actors to play the part of champion and challenger. The result was downright hilarious and nobody was really fooled.

Yet another attempt was made to film indoors on 3 November 1899 when Jeffries defended the title against Tom Sharkey. The heat of 400 arc lamps almost cooked the contestants. The lights were so low that Jeffries was able to reach up and touch the lamps with his glove.

And yet Jeffries and Sharkey fought 25 gruelling rounds under these trying conditions, with Jeffries taking the decision. Less than a week after the fight the hair of both men began to fall out. But despite the technical problems the big breakthrough had been made and filming fights quickly became a profitable business.

Soon the importance of the films began to influence the way men fought, and when Jack Johnson defended the world heavyweight title against Stanley Ketchel in 1909 it was clearly intended that the fight should go the limit for the benefit of the movie cameras.

Ketchel, however, had other ideas and shot across the ring in the 12th round to drop Johnson with an overhand right. Johnson was furious. Quickly regaining his feet, he rushed at Ketchel and smashed him in the face with a straight right. The blow was so powerful that four of Ketchel's teeth were sheared off, embedded in Johnson's glove as he withdrew his fist.

Pre-arranged fights became less fashionable after that but the films lost none of their popularity because of it. If anything, they became an even bigger attraction and when the film of the Johnson–Jeffries fight caused race riots in several American cities in 1910, the US Congress passed a law prohibiting the interstate transportation of fight films.

The law stood on the statute books for 28 years before President Roosevelt signed a bill on 1 July 1940 to remove it. 'When President Roosevelt signed the repeal measure he did away once and for all time with an obnoxious situation, one that bred contempt for law and order,' said Nat Fleischer, the famous editor and publisher of *The Ring* magazine.

Sadly the films did not always serve to resolve the great controversies that often arose in big fights. It was only years later that someone thought of timing the film of the famous 'long count' in the second fight between Jack Dempsey and Gene Tunney in 1927 to establish beyond doubt that Tunney had been on the canvas for 14 seconds.

And Jack Johnson's widely publicized claim that his fight with Jess Willard in 1915 was fixed is not supported by the evidence available in the film of the fight. The film was never shown in the United States at the time and Johnson took advantage to claim that he had thrown the fight.

The black boxer pointed to the photograph which shows him lying flat on his back and declared that he was shielding his eyes from the hot Cuban sun as he allowed the referee to count him out.

But the film of the fight shows that Willard dropped Johnson with a pretty good right hand to the jaw and that only seconds after the famous photograph was taken, Johnson rolled over on to his side.

The film, which was the first to include close-ups shot from the ringside, also clearly shows that Johnson was a weary champion as he answered the bell for the 26th round and that Willard was in full command of the fight.

Johnson sold a written confession to Nat Fleischer in 1916 for $250 but Fleischer, who witnessed the fight from the ringside, never believed it. Fleischer allowed 52 years to pass before he decided to publish the confession in *The Ring* in 1968.

Jack Johnson used this photograph to substantiate his claim that his fight with Jess Willard in Havana, Cuba, was 'fixed'. However, the film of the fight proved otherwise.

FIRSTS

There is something special about being first, and while not all nice guys finish last, it's the fellows upfront that history will remember. The following is a roll-call for boxing:

First boxing book published: *A treatise upon the useful science of defence* by Captain John Godfrey, 1747. First boxing annual: *Boxiana* by Pierce Egan, 1812–29. First boxing magazine: *Boxing Reviewed* by Thomas Fewtrell, 1790.

First Olympic gold medallist to win a professional world title: Frankie Genaro, who won the flyweight title at the 1920 Olympics in Antwerp, and the NBA world flyweight title in 1924. Real name: Frank Di Gennara.

First set of written rules for boxing: as agreed by favoured gentlemen at Broughton's Amphitheatre, Tottenham Court Road, London, on 16 August 1743. The seven rules became known as Broughton's Rules.

First woman to judge a world championship fight: Eva Shain, who was one of three judges for the heavyweight championship fight between Muhammad Ali and Earnie Shavers at Madison Square Garden, New York, on 29 September 1977.

First belt awarded in boxing: Tom Cribb was presented with a belt by George III after he had beaten Tom Molineaux at Copthall Common on 18 December 1810.

First world championship fight to be filmed: James J Corbett *vs* Bob Fitzsimmons at Carson City, Nevada, on 17 March 1897. Fitzsimmons knocked out Corbett in the 14th round.

First world championship fight to be broadcast on radio: Jack Dempsey *vs* Georges Carpentier at Boyle's Thirty Acres, Jersey City, on 2 July 1921. Dempsey knocked out Carpentier in the fourth round. Ringside commentators: Major Andrew White and J O Smith.

First black man to win a world championship: George Dixon, who was nicknamed 'Little Chocolate' because of his colour, won recognition as world featherweight champion when he knocked out Nunc Wallace in the 18th round at the Pelican Club, London, on 27 June 1890.

First black man to win the heavyweight championship of the world: Jack Johnson of Galveston, Texas, when he stopped Tommy Burns in the 14th round of their championship fight in Sydney, on 26 December 1908.

First black man to referee a world heavyweight title fight: Zack Clayton of Philadelphia, when he acted as the third man in the heavyweight championship fight between Jersey Joe Walcott and Ezzard Charles at Municipal Stadium, Philadelphia, on 5 June 1952. Walcott won a unanimous points decision over 15 rounds.

First international heavyweight championship fight: John C Heenan of the United States *vs* Tom Sayers of England at Farnborough, on 17 April 1860. The men fought 37 rounds with a referee and five without when the referee quit to avoid assault from the unruly crowd. Fight was declared a draw when the crowd tore down the ropes and entered the ring.

First black man to win a British boxing title: Andrew Jephta, the son of a Cape Town cabinet maker, who knocked out Curly Watson in the fourth round in London on 25 March 1907 to win the British welterweight title.

First black South African to promote a world championship fight: Stanley Vokwana, who promoted the WBA junior lightweight title fight between Samuel Serrano and Nkosana 'Happyboy' Mgxaji at the Goodwood Showgrounds, Cape Town, on 14 April 1979. Serrano won on a knockout in the eighth round.

First black South African to win a world championship: Peter 'Terror' Mathebula, who won the WBA flyweight title by outpointing Tae Shik Kim over 15 rounds in the Olympic Auditorium, Los Angeles, on 13 December 1980.

First man to win two undisputed world titles in two separate weight classes in one fight: Barney Ross, when he beat Tony Canzoneri on a split decision over ten rounds at Chicago Stadium in Chicago on 23 June 1933. Both the world lightweight and junior welterweight titles were at stake. It was also the last time the lightweight title was contested in a fight scheduled for ten rounds.

Tony Canzoneri (left) and Barney Ross pose for photographers before their fight in Chicago in June 1933. Both the world lightweight and junior welterweight titles were at stake.

First death recorded in a world championship fight: Walter Croot died of a brain injury following his world bantamweight title fight with Jimmy Barry at the National Sporting Club, London, on 6 December 1897. Barry knocked out Croot in the 20th round and the British boxer struck his head on the floor as he fell.

First heavyweight to regain the world title: Floyd Patterson, when he knocked out Ingemar Johansson in the fifth round at the Polo Grounds in New York on 20 June 1960. Patterson had lost the title to Johansson the year before when the Swede knocked him out in three rounds in New York.

First brothers to hold world titles in the same weight division at the same time: Gaby and Orlando Canizales of Houston, Texas. Gaby, the elder by five years, won the WBO bantamweight title by knocking out Miguel Lora in two rounds on 12 March 1991. Orlando had already won the IBF bantamweight title three years earlier when he stopped Kelvin Seabrooks in 15 rounds on 7 July 1988. Orlando was still IBF champion when his brother Gaby won the WBO version.

Orlando Canizales (right) and his brother Gaby were the first brothers to hold world titles in the same weight division at the same time.

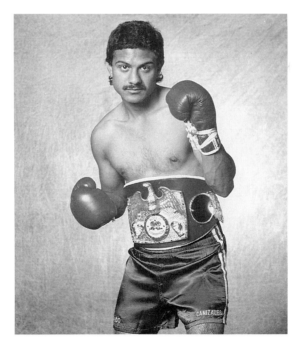

Stan Christodoulou was the first man to referee world title fights in every weight division.

First man to referee world title fights in every weight division: Stan Christodoulou of South Africa became the first referee to score a unique grand slam when he officiated in the WBA super middleweight title fight between Victor Cordoba and Vincenzo Nardiello in Paris, on 13 December 1991. With this contest, Christodoulou completed a lifelong ambition to referee world title fights in each of boxing's 17 weight divisions.

First heavyweight championship fight in which gloves were used: John L Sullivan *vs* James J Corbett at the Olympic Club, New Orleans, on 7 September 1892. Corbett won on a knockout in the 21st round.

First man to challenge for the world heavyweight champion-ship without professional experience: Pete Rademacher, the 1956 Olympic heavyweight champion, who challenged Floyd Patterson for the world heavyweight title in his first professional fight at Sick's Stadium, Seattle, on 22 August 1957. Patterson knocked him out in the sixth round.

First world heavyweight championship fight to be filmed in three dimensions (3D): The return bout between Rocky Marciano and Jersey Joe Walcott at Chicago Stadium, Chicago, on 15 May 1953. Marciano retained the title on a first-round knockout. The film was produced by Winik Films of New York.

First man to use oxygen in his corner during a heavyweight championship fight: James J Corbett, who had oxygen administered to him during his fight with James J Jeffries at Mechanics Pavilion, San Francisco, on 14 August 1903. Jeffries won on a knockout in the tenth round.

First fight to be televised: Len Harvey *vs* Jock McAvoy at Harringay Arena, London, on 4 April 1938. Harvey won on points over 15 rounds. The TV signal was not seen by the public.

First publication to rate boxers: *The Ring* magazine, the American monthly which was launched by its editor-publisher, Nat Fleischer, in 1922. First issue to carry ratings of boxers was the February 1925 edition of the magazine.

First world championship fight to end in a one-round knockout: Terry McGovern knocked out Pedlar Palmer in two minutes 32 seconds at the Tuckahoe Arena, New York, to win the world bantamweight title on 12 September 1899.

GEORGE FOREMAN

George Foreman was convinced he was dying. Oppressive heat had turned the Roberto Clemente Coliseum in San Juan into a cauldron. As the exhausted boxer lay in the dressing room, near-naked and fighting for breath, he began to hallucinate.

Only minutes earlier, the big fellow had stumbled from the ring following a 12-round points loss to Jimmy Young. Now, as he lay in a cold sweat, he underwent the religious experience he claims enabled him to be born again and allowed him to answer a higher calling.

'I met with Jesus Christ Himself,' Foreman said afterwards. 'It tore me apart not being a Christian. Scared me a little, too. I actually died, then life came back into me after a moment's time.'

To everyone's surprise, Foreman promptly retired as a boxer and founded a church in an impoverished section of Houston. The puncher had become a preacher, and for the next ten years never laced on a boxing glove. Instead, he gave sermons in his Church of The Lord Jesus Christ, while his personality changed perceptibly from surly introvert to friendly foe.

Foreman insists he took not the slightest interest in boxing during the ten years of his retirement. 'My church was running out of funds

George Foreman, who twice won the world heavyweight title, claims the only reason he returned to the ring was to raise funds for his church.

in 1987,' he says. 'That was the only thing that could've inspired me to get back in the ring.'

Most sportswriters at first had difficulty in taking him seriously as a born-again boxer. Foreman, they said, was fat and foolish. Some even made jokes. 'Foreman is so fat,' they wrote, 'that if he was lying on a beach, Greenpeace would drag him back into the ocean.'

'They were wondering if a 38-year-old could come back,' Foreman says. 'They forgot that after I retired and took a job as a minister, God Almighty kept looking after me.'

It was only when Foreman began beating guys like Bert Cooper, Everett Martin, Gerry Cooney and Adilson Rodrigues that he gained some respect. Even so, there were still plenty of sceptics around.

When one accused him of fighting tomato cans, he quipped: 'Not just tomato cans – there've been some bean bags, too!'

From the outset of his comeback, Foreman purposely played on two things: his age and his appetite. 'I was once on a diet for two weeks running,' he said, 'and all I lost was two weeks.' And after he predicted he would knock out Evander Holyfield in two rounds to win the world heavyweight title, he added: 'And in between we're going to have cheeseburgers!'

Foreman, who had promised to weigh less than 250 pounds for the Holyfield fight, eventually gave up the ghost. 'Why bother to weigh heavyweights?' he asked. 'What's the point except for people to applaud?' Not many applauded when Big George tipped the scale at 257 pounds.

Mind you, Foreman has always been a big man. He looked enormous the first time I saw him fight in Madison Square Garden in August 1970. George Chuvalo was his hapless victim that night and the memory of it all still lingers.

Foreman battered Chuvalo into defeat in three rounds. No knockdowns, you understand, because nobody back then ever knocked Chuvalo down. However, Foreman's firepower had the Canadian rocking defenceless on his heels.

Then, on 22 January 1973 Foreman stunned the boxing world by hammering Joe Frazier into defeat in Kingston, Jamaica. Frazier was sent crashing to the canvas for six counts before referee Arthur Mercante stopped the slaughter in the second round.

If Foreman gave the impression of being a sadist of sorts, he had only himself to blame. As he now readily admits, back in the 1970s he was surly, arrogant and angry. And what's more, it showed.

When Foreman arrived at the weigh-in for his title defence against Joe Roman in Tokyo in 1973, it annoyed him that Roman was smiling and joking with the media. 'What the hell you got to smile about?' he demanded.

'I'm Puerto Rican,' said Roman, 'and Puerto Ricans are happy people. We like to talk and smile.'

'Well, don't make any jokes when I'm around,' said Foreman.

'Oh yeah, and since when is a Puerto Rican scared of a Texas nigger?' Roman shot back.

Foreman never forgave Roman for the remark. He knocked the Puerto Rican out in less than a round and even struck Roman while the challenger was on the canvas. No wonder muscleman Ken Norton froze with fear when he faced Foreman for the title seven months later. Foreman handled the powerfully built Norton like a child, knocking him out in the second round.

'I've moulded a monster,' said Dick Sadler, Foreman's trainer, after the fight. 'I've taken the best of Joe Louis, Jack Johnson and Rocky Marciano and rolled it all into one.'

Muhammad Ali was to prove Sadler emphatically wrong when he took the title from Foreman in the famous 'Rumble in the Jungle' in October 1974. It's a fight Foreman prefers not to talk about, except to say that he felt like a prisoner in Zaire.

Sixteen years later Foreman was back, trying at the age of 43 to regain the title some claim he lost under 'mysterious' circumstances. 'I've become better in my 40s than I was at 24,' he said. 'And besides, I'm just a growing boy. I won't reach middle age until I'm 75.'

But the thought of Foreman, a 42-year-old fat man, winning the heavyweight championship of the world by beating Holyfield literally frightened the hell out of boxing men everywhere. 'It gives me the fits,' said George Zeleny, the then editor of *Boxing Monthly*. 'It would be a monumental disaster for boxing if Foreman were to regain the world title.'

The Ring magazine was so sceptical the editors only gave Foreman a top-10 rating when the Foreman–Holyfield fight was signed and sealed. Reluctantly *The Ring* slotted Foreman in at number ten.

'In a sport where 30 is old and 40 is ancient, George Foreman has beaten the odds,' declared the *New York Times*. Well, not quite. Holyfield convincingly beat him on points over 12 rounds, and if that wasn't bad enough Tommy Morrison also turned the trick in a WBO heavyweight title fight two years later.

Michael Moorer was convinced he could not lose when he chose to defend his WBA and IBF heavyweight titles against Foreman 17 months later. But 5 November 1994 is a date that will for ever be etched in the history of sport (and not because of some fellow called Guy Fawkes).

It was the day that the 45-year-old Foreman made every middle-aged man walk tall. The day the big fellow regained the championship he had lost 20 years before by knocking out Moorer in the tenth round. *Boxing News* caught the mood when it described Foreman as 'the world's most valuable antique'.

Oh well, as Jersey Joe Walcott used to say when asked how a man of 37 could be heavyweight champion of the world: 'I ain't old, just ugly.'

George Foreman addresses a press conference before his controversial heavyweight championship fight with Axel Schulz in Las Vegas.

GAMES

Little did the Roman Emperors of old realize what they were starting when they used to declare: 'Let the games begin!' The games – whether Olympic, Pan-American, Commonwealth, Asian, African or Goodwill – have become a showcase for sport.

According to the Greek historian Herodotus, the Egyptians participated in 'games comprising every form of contest' long before the Greeks and the Romans. Many historians believe the ancient Olympics probably only began about 1000 BC and at a time when there were already other games like the Pythian, Nemean and Isthmian.

The early games were exclusively for Greeks – the ancient Olympics were actually a religious festival, created to celebrate the great festival of Zeus – but by the year 146 BC the Romans had begun to participate.

There was a time when the games were considered so important that all wars among Greek city states were suspended to enable them to take place. However, because they were considered a pagan festival during a time when Christianity was gaining acceptance, Emperor Theodosius decided to suspend them in AD 394.

Some 1,500 years later a French nobleman named Baron de Coubertin revived the concept with the first modern games in Athens. An idealist, De Coubertin believed that 'the most important thing is not to win but to take part'.

Fat chance! In the very first Olympiad in 1896, King Constantine of Greece celebrated Greece's only gold medal by running around the track himself! And it is common knowledge that international politics has marred the Olympics ever since.

Nationalism first reared its ugly head at the London Oympics in 1908 when British and American officials were guilty of constant bickering, and when the games were awarded to Nazi Germany in 1936 there was widespread opposition.

Typical was the open letter to the American Olympic Committee written by Nat Fleischer, editor and publisher of *The Ring*, which was published in the October 1935 issue of the magazine.

How can you gentlemen, with any regard for the principles of democracy, equality and social, racial and religious freedom which we foster in this country, call upon Americans to condone the actions of Germany, and approve the unsportsmanlike action of the Hitler government?

Yes, it is quite true that *The Ring* has been banned from general circulation in Germany. But *The Ring* is proud of this distinction. Catholics and Jews have had a rather difficult time of it in Germany. It is not merely a matter of being permitted to earn a living over there. It is a matter of being permitted to live.

Sending an American team to a meet in that country would be tantamount to approval of the policies of the Hitler government. It would be an open insult to every Catholic and Jew in the United States, a blow to every sponsor of fair play, regardless of race and creed.

Despite Fleischer's emotional appeal, the Americans still sent a team to represent them. Things got even worse in the post-war years and by far the blackest mark of all was the massacre of Israeli athletes at the 1972 Olympic Games in Munich.

Although boxing was one of the original Olympic sports, since the revival of the modern Olympics in 1896 it has been tolerated merely on sufferance ... or so it would seem.

IOC president Juan Antonio Samaranch delivered the 'death sentence' at the close of the 1992 Olympic Games in Barcelona when he said: 'Boxing will eventually lose its position as an Olympic sport.'

Samaranch could have added that it already had on at least two other occasions. When the ancient games were revived in 776 BC boxing was not a regular feature. It was not until the 23rd Olympiad in 688 BC when Onamastus won the championship that boxing regained its place among the other contests.

And when the modern Olympics were revived in 1896 boxing was not on the menu. The first time the sport was featured was in the 1904 Olympic Games in St Louis and then almost as an afterthought (all 28 entrants were from the United States). Worse still, when the Olympics were held in Stockholm in 1912, there was no boxing because the sport was banned by Swedish law at that time.

Not until the post-war years did Olympic boxing champions make names for themselves as professionals in any great number. Only four men who were successful in the seven Olympiads held between 1904 and 1936 were later recognized as world professional champions: Frankie Genaro (USA), Fidel LaBarba (USA), Willie Smith (South Africa) and Jackie Fields (USA).

This is not surprising considering the way some of the early boxing squads were selected. A case in point was Fred Gilmore of Chicago, who entered the 1904 Olympic Games even though he had never before boxed in competition. Moreover, there were so few entrants in the 1908 Olympics that the boxing competition was completed in one day.

By far the two best Olympic boxing champions were Laszlo Papp of Hungary and Teofilo Stevenson of Cuba.

Papp was the first man to win three gold medals in Olympic boxing. He won the middleweight title in 1948 and the light middleweight title in 1952 and 1956. Papp was permitted to turn professional at the age of 31 and was undefeated in 29 bouts. He was European middleweight champion from 1962 to 1965 when he was ordered to retire by the Hungarian government.

Stevenson also represented a communist country at the games and became the only other three-time Olympic gold medallist by winning the heavyweight title in Munich in 1972, in Montreal in 1976 and in Moscow in 1980.

At one time Stevenson was offered a million dollars to turn professional, but the Cuban heavyweight remained loyal to his country. 'Why do I need a million dollars when I am already a hero to eight million of my people in Cuba?' he asked.

Other games have also adopted the Olympic concept. One of the earliest was the Empire Games (now known as the Commonwealth Games) which were first held in Canada in 1930. Only those countries once belonging to the British Empire or the present Commonwealth of Nations may participate. Like the Olympics, the Commonwealth Games are held every four years.

The American equivalent is the Pan-American Games, which were conceived during a meeting of the American Congress in Buenos Aires, Argentina, in 1940. The first Pan-American Games were scheduled to be held in Buenos Aires in 1942 but because of the Second World War they did not take place until 1951.

The games are conducted by the Pan-American Sports Organization under the rules of the IOC. As many as 28–30 nations are involved.

GAMESMANSHIP

Gamesmanship in boxing is alive and well. Who says so? Chris Eubank, the former WBO middleweight and super middleweight champion. Eubank was the victim of a psychological ploy in his title defence against Steve Collins in March 1995, and was so upset at losing the mind game (not to mention his title) that he later accused Collins of 'cheating'.

When Eubank learned that Collins had been working with Irish hypnotist Tony Quinn, he seriously considered calling off the fight – especially after Collins had acted irrationally at the weigh-in. 'I understand he's under hypnosis,' Eubank told reporters, 'which is very unfair as far as boxing is concerned.'

'I was never under hypnosis, but Chris believed I was,' Collins said after beating Eubank on points. 'Talk about taking the bait – he swallowed the fishing rod as well.'

Eubank can comfort himself in that he is not the first boxer to fall victim to a psychological ploy – or gamesmanship as they prefer to call it in the trade. Muhammad Ali was a master at playing mind games and others before him also attempted to exploit boxing's dirty tricks department.

One of the earliest recorded acts of gamesmanship in the ring happened in the heavyweight fight between Tom Cribb of England

and Tom Molineaux of the United States at Copthall Common, on 18 December 1810.

Under the rules of the fight, a round ended when a man went down. The fallen fighter was then allowed 30 seconds in which to regain his feet and come up to the 'scratch'. But when Molineaux sent Cribb crashing to the ground to end the 28th round, the British champion failed to respond to the umpire's call of 'time'.

Instead Jem Ward, one of Cribb's seconds, rushed across the ring and accused Bill Richmond, the American's cornerman, of concealing two bullets in Molineaux's fists in an attempt to increase his punching power.

A full four minutes passed before the accusation was proved to be false and by then Molineaux's great chance of winning had been lost. Moreover, while Cribb had fully recovered thanks to the extended time between rounds, the American was shivering from the cold, wet weather.

Fifty-five minutes later, in the 33rd round, Molineaux sank slowly to the ground and whispered to Richmond through swollen, blood-splattered lips: 'I can fight no more.'

More than a hundred years later Jimmy Johnston, the British-born, American-based boxing manager, pulled off an even neater trick. Johnston was managing South African heavyweight George 'Boer' Rodel and shrewdly manipulated Rodel into a fight with Jess Willard, only three months after Willard had killed Bull Young in a fight in Vernon, California.

As Johnston walked over to inspect Willard's gloves before the start of the fight, he began a conversation with the big fellow. 'Reckon you'd best take it easy tonight, Jess,' he said.

'Why?' the fighter asked.

''Cos my fighter's got a bum ticker,' Johnston replied.

'What's he doin' in here then?' Willard asked.

'You know, the usual story, lack of coin,' Johnston told the man destined to become the next heavyweight champion of the world.

Willard believed the yarn and for the next ten rounds hardly laid a glove on the South African. The bout was held under the prevailing no-decision rules but newspapermen at the ringside were unanimous that Rodel had done enough to win.

George 'Boer' Rodel, the South African heavyweight, whose manager tricked Jess Willard into believing he had a weak heart.

Later, when Willard learned how he had been conned, he demanded a rematch. And so, 42 days after their first bout, the men squared up to each other again in Milwaukee. With handcuffs off, Willard knocked out Rodel in nine rounds.

Still not convinced that Willard was the better man, Rodel met the American in a third fight in Atlanta in April 1914. It proved to be Willard's last fight before he beat Jack Johnson for the world title exactly a year later, and Rodel's decline – or was it Willard's improvement? – was best illustrated by the result. The ex-cowboy kayoed Rodel in six rounds.

Gene Tunney attempted a psychological ploy that nearly backfired when he challenged Jack Dempsey for the heavyweight championship of the world in Philadelphia on 23 September 1926.

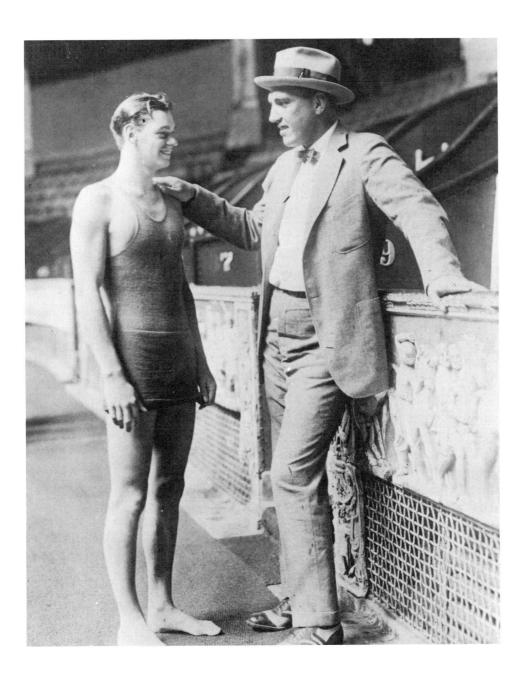

Jess Willard and ace American swimming star Johnny Weissmuller. Willard was a former world heavyweight champion.

Tunney claimed that he took a plane from his training camp in Stroudsburg to the fight because it had been raining and he didn't want to make the long automobile trip on slippery roads. But considering that flying was still innovative in 1926 and the weather had turned unpleasant, many suspect he went through with the flight in an attempt to unsettle Dempsey.

'I got airsick,' Tunney admitted afterwards. 'That great old pilot, Casey Jones, who flew me, lost his way in the clouds. It was one of the worst airplane rides anyone ever had and I was shaking and pale and green when I got to Philadelphia.'

The word got around that Tunney was scared to death but Gene had fully recovered by fight time and proceeded to outbox Dempsey easily over ten rounds. It was one of the biggest upsets in the history of boxing.

As already mentioned, Muhammad Ali (aka Cassius Clay) was a master of mind games. However, Ali needed the help of his famous trainer Angelo Dundee when Henry Cooper dropped him with a left hook only seconds before the end of the fourth round of their heavyweight fight at Wembley Stadium, London, on 18 June 1963. The American was still in a daze as he stumbled to his corner.

'You can see on the film as plainly as anything that in Clay's corner his helpers broke a phial right under his nose and you see him recover,' Cooper claimed in his autobiography.

More important, perhaps, was that Dundee suddenly 'discovered' that Ali had a split glove. By the time referee Tommy Little had been called to the corner and reported to a steward who went to the back of the hall to find a spare set of gloves (only to discover there weren't any), at least a minute and three-quarters had elapsed.

Fully recovered, Ali answered the bell for the fifth round and proceeded to stop Cooper on cuts.

Years later, I asked Angelo Dundee on camera whether he had cut Ali's glove in the corner. 'The stitching near the thumb started to come apart in the first round,' he said, 'but I told Muhammad to keep his fist closed so no one would notice. And then after Cooper dropped him just before the bell in the fourth round and he came back to the corner in a bad way, I opened the stitches in the glove a little more. I even took some of the horsehair out of the glove before calling over the referee. No, I didn't cut the glove ... but I used it to our advantage.'

GIANT BOXERS

In boxing, yesterday's giants are tomorrow's pygmies (well, sort of). Men who were considered giant boxers at the turn of the century would hardly merit a second look today, and for the simple reason that most modern heavyweights seldom stand less than six feet tall. Many stand considerably taller including George Foreman (6ft 3in), Frank Bruno (6ft 3in), Tony Tucker (6ft 4in), Lennox Lewis (6ft 5in), Riddick Bowe (6ft 5in) and Jorge Luis Gonzalez (6ft 7in).

None of these men are now described as giants. In fact, they are fairly average by today's standards. In the past – and as recently as the 1940s – any heavyweight standing much taller than six feet was considered a giant and so men like Fred Fulton (6ft 5½in), Primo Carnera (6ft 6½in), Jess Willard (6ft 6in), Buddy Baer (6ft 6½in) and Vittorio Campolo (6ft 6½in) were looked upon in awe.

A big powerful man and a beautiful boxer, Fulton was among the first of the big men with all the equipment needed to become a champion. Arguably his best performance was recorded on 19 June 1917 when he battered the great Sam Langford into defeat in seven rounds in Boston. Actually, it was about the only bright spot in Fulton's career.

A year later Jack Dempsey knocked Fulton out in 19 seconds, which caused Arthur 'Bugs' Baer to quip in the New York *Evening World*: 'Fulton would do better selling advertising space on the soles of his shoes.'

Several of these so-called giants came from strange backgrounds. Willard was in his mid-20s when he drove a team of six horses into a small town in Oklahoma, only to learn about the defeat of Jim Jeffries at the hands of Jack Johnson.

The local barman asked Willard why he didn't try his hand at boxing. The cowboy gave it a moment's thought and said: 'Why not?' Five years later Willard was the heavyweight champion of the world.

Few of the bigger men enjoyed much success. All had the same thing in common: they were poor athletes. Among them were Gil Anderson (7ft 250lb), Jim Cully (7ft 4in, 275lb), Henry Johnson (7ft 2in, 265lb), Milo Maligoli (7ft, 270lb), Ben Moroz (7ft 1in, 302lb), Ewart Potgieter (7ft 2in, 326lb) and John Rankin (7ft 4in, 269lb).

South African heavyweight Ewart Potgieter moved remarkably well for a big man and quickly grasped the basics of boxing, but Irishman Jim Cully was a good example of how inept most of these big fellows really were in the ring.

Cully was discovered while working as a doorman at a circus in Ireland and for his own sake should have stayed there. Instead, after only two fights in Ireland, Cully was shipped to the United States in 1948 in the belief that fight fans would pay handsomely to see the Irishman in action.

Cully's backers evidently envisaged another Primo Carnera buildup. But the plan backfired when, after winning his first fight in the States, a young heavyweight named Red Pierce, who was just out of the amateur ranks, battered Cully all over the ring, broke his nose and stopped him in three rounds.

Cully's performance was so inept that the New York State Athletic Commission decided that the Irishman knew so little about boxing that it would be dangerous for him to continue with a boxing career. Cully never fought again.

GLOVES

Two things – a set of written rules and a pair of boxing gloves – gave prize-fighting its first look of respectability and both were the brainchild of one man. John Broughton, later to become known as

Above: Primo Carnera, the former world heavyweight champion, squares up to Walter Neusel of Germany in 1935. Below: Ewart Potgieter, the giant South African heavyweight, dwarfs his diminutive trainer, Johnny Holt, during a public workout.

the 'Father of Boxing', published his Rules and invented the first pair of boxing gloves in 1743.

Broughton's Rules (all seven of them) governed boxing from 1743 until 1838, when a new code – the London Prize Ring Rules – was adopted. But Broughton's gloves (or mufflers, as they were then called) were used only for sparring and it was not until 1818 that gloves were first used in a fight between two Englishmen at Aix-la-Chapelle in France.

A French publication, dated 9 October 1818, reported that the men put up a great fight. 'The two champions were built like Hercules and were naked to the waist,' the report read. 'They entered the ring with their hands guarded with huge padded gloves.'

Although the two 'champions' were not named and no mention was made of Broughton, it is likely the gloves used were mufflers. Broughton had started to instruct men in self-defence at an amphitheatre he had erected in Hanway Yard, Tottenham Court Road, London, in 1742. And it was a year later that he invented mufflers to minimize the risks of facial damage to his students, many of whom came from aristocratic families.

As he put it in an advertisement for his academy, instruction 'will be given with the utmost tenderness ... for which reason mufflers are provided that will effectively secure pupils from the inconvenience of black eyes, broken noses, and bloody jaws'.

It is thought that Broughton invented the boxing glove after studying the Olympic type of *cestus* (or hand-wrapping) on a Greek statue. Broughton's concept was certainly not new. What was new was the padding he used: the mufflers were stuffed with lamb's wool or horsehair and weighed about ten ounces. This was a far cry from the various hand-wrappings used in the Ancient Olympics or the deadly *cestus* used by Roman gladiators.

The bloodthirsty Romans would have been bored to death with a modern prize-fight even of the fiercest kind. They did not want winners and losers, only survivors. And so instead of youngsters competing for laurels and the olive branch, as in the Ancient Greek Olympics, Roman gladiators fought to the death for gold prizes.

The 'glove' of the era was the *cestus*, essentially similar to the Himas Oxys (which was first used from 300 BC) but with sharpened metal studs extending even to the wrist-straps.

Small wonder that fist-fighting itself ultimately died the death it deserved after Rome's decline and fall. Several hundred years passed before it was resurrected and when it was brought back to life in England in the eighteenth century it was strictly a bareknuckle sport. Gloves only became mandatory when the Marquess of Queensberry Rules were drafted in 1865 and officially adopted in 1892.

Even so, skin-tight gloves were often used during the latter half of the nineteenth century. Made of the best French kid without seams in the back and laced without the aid of eyelets, the gloves were made to order to fit snugly the hands of the men who were to use them.

The weight of the gloves varied but stake matches were usually fought with two-ounce gloves. Skin-tight gloves remained popular until the turn of the century and the last two-ounce-glove fight took place between Jimmy Briggs and Tony Daly at the Windsor Theatre, Boston, on 22 May 1903. Among those who helped popularize the use of gloves was John L Sullivan, the first American heavyweight to capture public imagination. Sullivan is unique in that he fought the last heavyweight championship fight with bareknuckles (against Jake Kilrain in 1889) and the first with gloves (against James J Corbett in 1892). Sullivan and Corbett both wore five-ounce gloves.

A D Phillips, the doyen of early American boxing writers, saw most of Sullivan's fights and claimed in an article he wrote for *The Ring* magazine in 1939 that Sullivan preferred to use gloves:

'Of the 50 or more bouts that Sullivan fought during his career, only three were fought with bare knuckles, one was with skintight gloves, and one with one-ounce gloves. All the rest were with gloves weighing two to five ounces,' Phillips declared.

Nowadays the weight of the gloves varies between eight and ten ounces for fights above the middleweight limit and between six and eight ounces for fights below. In June 1991, IBF junior bantamweight champion Robert Quiroga told reporters he would never defend his title with six-ounce gloves again following the near-tragedy in his bout with Kid Akeem Anifowoshe. 'This is my fourth fight with six-ounce gloves and I'm going to ask the IBF to stop using them,' he said.

A contemporary drawing of Jim Corbett knocking out John L Sullivan in the first world heavyweight championship fight in which gloves were used.

But in trying to design a safer glove, more attention was focused on the thumb rather than the weight. The New York State Athletic Commission became the first boxing commission to make the thumbless glove mandatory. The rule went into effect on 15 January 1982 but was subsequently suspended after Madison Square Garden was forced to cancel a tournament at the Felt Forum because many of the boxers had refused to wear the new gloves.

Dan Golomb, the then chairman of the Everlast equipment company, claimed the thumbless glove was nothing new. 'A manufacturer had a patent on one in 1890, twenty years before my father started Everlast,' he said, 'but the gloves never took hold.'

Arguments for and against the use of the thumbless glove raged around the world. 'The thumbless glove is strictly a puncher's glove,' said Willie Pep, the former world featherweight champion. 'It's not for a defensive fighter. He can't do all the things that he could do if he had a regular glove.'

Floyd Patterson, the former heavyweight champion of the world and at the time a member of the New York State Athletic Commission, disagreed. 'The principal place for boxing injuries is not the brain, as so many people think, but the eyes,' he said. 'I was thumbed in the eye accidentally when I was fighting, and I know how bad it can be.'

By 1986 the thumb-attached glove, and not the thumbless glove, had won wider acceptance. 'We are satisfied that the use of gloves with a restricted thumb serves a dual purpose,' said IBF president Bobby Lee, 'in that it does not hamper the fighters' ability to perform, yet it protects them from career-threatening injury.'

In 1987 Dr David J Smith, of the Wills Eye Hospital in Philadelphia, disclosed that of 166 boxers he had examined, 34 had significant eye problems. Dr Smith described the findings as particularly disturbing because the average age of those he had examined was 24. By then most American boxing commissions had already made use of the thumb-attached glove mandatory.

GOLDEN GLOVES

The birth of what is probably the most famous amateur boxing tournament in the world was a direct result of anti-boxing protesters overstepping the mark in the state of Illinois in 1923.

It happened when the anti-boxing lobby forced the closure of a programme which the Illinois naval force had attempted to hold on the ship *Commodore*. Boxing had been banned in that American state for nearly 20 years but because of the reformers' unpopular action the influential *Chicago Tribune* published an editorial taking them to task. The newspaper added that it would sponsor an amateur boxing tournament in order to test the existing legislation.

The entry list was so large that the tournament ran for nearly a week in March 1923. A total of 424 boxers was recruited from universities, gymnasiums, parks, playgrounds and YMCAs.

The test tournament was vigorously attacked by such anti-boxing men as the Rev W S Fleming of the National Reform Association and Arthur Burrage Farwell of the Law and Order League. And when threats were made to stop it, an injunction was obtained from Judge Ira Ryner.

Despite the success of the tournament, the *Chicago Tribune* decided not to renew it until boxing in the state was legalized. This was done in April 1926 and, on 8 May 1927, the *Tribune* carried a story by Walter Eckersall.

'A mammoth amateur boxing tournament, open to all fighters registered with the Amateur Athletic Union, will be conducted by the *Tribune* next winter. Proceeds of the meet will go to some charity to be named later,' Eckersall wrote, and added: 'It is planned to give the champions gold boxing gloves with a diamond inserted.'

That first official Golden Gloves tournament in Chicago was a huge success.

Writing in the *Chicago Tribune* on 10 March 1928 Eckersall reported that 'five thousand folks, the largest crowd ever to watch amateur boxing in Chicago since the sport was legalized, occupied every foot of vantage in the Ashland Boulevard auditorium' and added that 'it was an orderly crowd which enjoyed the fights immensely. It cheered the honest efforts of the contestants, it cheered the victors, and it cheered the losers.'

The name Golden Gloves had been suggested by Captain Joseph M Patterson when the New York *Daily News*, a sister publication of the *Chicago Tribune*, held a similar tournament in 1927. And since March 1928 the Golden Gloves tournament has been held without interruption every year.

In the beginning the tournament was restricted to boxers from Chicago and New York but later other newspapers also became involved. In fact, since the formation of the Golden Gloves Association of America Inc in 1964, the national tournament has been held in a different city each year.

Writing in *Sport* magazine in March 1947, the famous *Chicago Tribune* sports editor Arch Ward described the Golden Gloves as 'a

Many great American boxers first made a name for themselves in the Golden Gloves. Cassius Clay (aka Muhammad Ali) was voted the outstanding boxer of the East-West tournament in 1960. Cassius is on the far right.

highroad to glory, a rough and rocky road to be sure, but a path that can lead to fame and fortune – a gateway to a championship'.

Ward was responsible for giving the Golden Gloves international status when he invited the French Boxing Federation to send a team of eight boxers to Chicago in 1931. That visit led to similar series with Germany, Ireland, Poland, Italy and finally a team from Europe that was sent over by the International Amateur Boxing Federation.

Ward claimed that the Golden Gloves was amateur to the teeth. 'The kids who show up for the elimination tournament bouts frequently wear trunks tailored by their mothers, and have their fathers act as seconds,' Ward said. 'Nobody – but nobody – is paid. The proceeds go to charity.'

Over the years, the Golden Gloves tournaments have raised vast sums of money for charities and other worthy causes. In 1936 the Golden Gloves paid all expenses of the United States Olympic team for the Games in Berlin.

'Every youngster, who wants a chance and can prove his right to recognition, is cared for,' Nat Fleischer, the editor and publisher of *The Ring* pointed out in May 1941. 'Free training, free medical care, close observation by a competent staff of trainers, plenty of wholesome food while in training – these necessities are given each lad while he remains in the competition.'

The Golden Gloves has also introduced numerous safety measures and innovations. The sub-novice class idea was a stroke of genius and the introduction of mandatory drug testing in 1987 was a bold move to protect the status of the tournament.

And yet, even though the introduction of drug testing happened to coincide with the arrival of crack cocaine on the streets of New York, the results of those first tests were astounding by any standards. Of the 744 boxers in the New York tournament that year, only half a dozen failed the test.

Tall, lean 20-year-old Mark Breland probably became the greatest Golden Glover of all time when he won a record fifth straight New York Golden Gloves title in 1984, stopping Victor Laguer in 42 seconds of the first round at Madison Square Garden.

In winning the welterweight title for the fourth consecutive year (Breland won the 139-pound novice title in 1980), the New Yorker equalled records that were previously established by such Golden Glove greats as Vince Shomo, Howard Davis, Mitch Green, Alex Ramos and Davey Moore. As luck would have it, Shomo refereed the Breland–Laguer fight.

For 15 minutes Breland remained in the ring as photographers took his picture and officials presented him with a special award – a large championship belt.

Breland later went on to make a name for himself as a professional, but the first Golden Glove champion to win a world title was Barney Ross when he beat Tony Canzoneri for the lightweight title in 1933. Other Golden Glovers who were destined to become well-known professionals were heavyweight Joe Louis, light heavyweight Gus Lesnevich, middleweight Tony Zale, welterweight Sugar Ray Robinson and featherweight Petey Scalzo.

Lou Winston, a great friend and supporter of the Golden Gloves movement, was once asked to describe a Golden Glover:

A Golden Glover may be a little fellow or a giant. He may be a tender 18-year-old or a matured young man of 26. He may be gaunt or lean, but is mostly muscular. He may be a sixth-grade drop-out or a student attending college.

He may be a boy who travels more than 100 miles five nights a week, merely to train ... he may be rich or of wealthy parents, or have a mediocre income. He may be a boy taking his initial airplane flight, or be quartered in a hotel for the first time. He is the type of fellow who expends every ounce of energy in the ring for a medal or trophy, instead of fighting for cash.

ROCKY GRAZIANO

The record books show he was born Thomas Rocco Barbella on New York's East Side on 1 January 1922; that he turned professional in 1942, won the world middleweight title five years later, and fought 83 bouts before he retired from the ring in 1952.

But the books do not tell you that he was once a real-life hoodlum who on his own admission was heading for a cell on Death Row before he turned to boxing; nor that he had deserted the US Army and was AWOL when he began to make headway as a boxer under the borrowed name of Rocky Graziano.

And yet by the time he died at the age of 68 in 1990, Graziano had captured the heart of the sports world, warts and all. Moreover, he had seen his autobiography, *Somebody Up There Likes Me*, made into a movie starring Paul Newman, and he was financially independent.

The stigma of having his boxing licence revoked by the New York State Athletic Commission in 1947 for not reporting an alleged bribe was all but forgotten when he was elected to the Boxing Hall of

Fame in 1971, and his willingness to admit his past mistakes had endeared him to millions the world over.

'I had three careers,' Graziano once told a writer. 'A robbing career, a fighting career, and an acting career.'

There were few niceties about his style. In fact, Sol Gold, a member of the Tony Zale camp, was so concerned before the first Zale–Graziano fight in 1946 about Rocky's dirty tactics he suggested that 'the referee sit outside the ring, just like it used to be in England. Then, if Rocky wants to play rough, Zale can show him just what rough and dirty fighting is all about.'

Gold listed three fights in which Graziano allegedly broke the rules. He accused Rocky of grabbing world welterweight champion Freddie Cochrane by the throat, choking him with his left hand while hitting him with his right; of knocking down Bummy Davis with a punch well after the bell and then striking him while he was helpless on the canvas; and of failing to go to a neutral corner after he had floored Marty Servo, whom Graziano struck the moment his hands left the canvas.

'There hasn't been a fight in which Graziano has not broken one or more rules,' said Gold.

Gold need not have worried. After surviving a second round knockdown, Zale came back in the sixth to score a sensational knockout. A right to the pit of Rocky's stomach turned the trick. The punch virtually paralysed Graziano and a follow-up left hook sent him crashing to the canvas.

It was the first of three ring classics. Zale was knocked out himself in the return fight but gained revenge in the rubber match by stopping Graziano in three rounds. Somebody once suggested that the films of the fights should be put in a time capsule.

It was after Graziano won the world middleweight title in Chicago in July 1947 that Rocky grabbed the microphone and spoke those unforgettable words: 'Hey, Ma – your bad boy done it. I told you somebody up there likes me.'

'Everybody liked Rocky,' Sugar Ray Robinson recalled years later. 'He was out of the Lower East Side of New York, a real Dead End kid who walked and talked like one.'

'Yeah.' Graziano once said. 'Everybody likes me. Even the black

Rocky Graziano took a bad beating when he lost the world middleweight title to Tony Zale in 1948.

people, all over the country, for some stupid reason, like me.'

Robinson fought Graziano in the twilight of Rocky's career in 1952 and claimed in his autobiography that the Big Man who ruled the mafia in Chicago at the time had offered him a million dollars to take a dive.

'I'm sorry,' Robinson said he replied. 'I guess I'm too stupid to be anything but a winner. But it was nice of you to ask me. Not many people get a chance to turn down a million dollars.'

Robinson came off the canvas in the third round to knock out Graziano with a left-right combination to the jaw. 'Sugar Ray *must* be good,' Rocky said afterwards, 'because he knocked *me* out in three.'

Graziano was always brutally frank. 'To be a fighter you can't be a smart guy,' he once said. 'To get in the ring with anybody you got to be a little wacky.'

And when New York boxing commissioner Eddie Eagan took his boxing licence away in 1947 for failing to report an alleged bribe, Rocky exploded like the hoodlum he once was. 'I'll kill the bastard,' he threatened. 'I'll get a gun. I'll kill the sonofabitch. The sonofabitch should be dead.'

In later life Graziano not only made money doing TV commercials, he was also well paid to chat to the high-rollers at the Playboy Hotel and Casino in Atlantic City two nights a week.

It was Graziano's appearance on the Martha Raye television show that was largely responsible for changing his lifestyle. Rocky was an instant success. Even so, he once asked Miss Raye whether he should take some acting lessons.

'You do that, Goombah, and you'll be out of a good job,' she said. 'If those marbles ever fall out of your mouth you're in trouble,' she advised, referring to the 'dese and doze' idiom in which Graziano spoke and the fact that Rocky was always playing himself on screen.

Graziano once told a writer what it was like appearing on the show. 'Like there's this line where somebody says I must toss the salad. How am I supposed to know that toss means mix the salad? So I throws it way across the stage against the wall, and it takes ten minutes to stop everybody laughing!

'I was so nervous I could have died but then it's over and they're slapping my back and Martha hugs me and says, "You done great, Goombah" and that became my name in the script.'

GYMNASIUMS

Somebody once called them workhouses of sweat – and he certainly got that right. Their origin is almost as old as the sport itself but they only became fashionable when boxing was revived in England in the eighteenth century and men like James Figg, John Broughton,

They call them workhouses of sweat and their origin is almost as old as the sport of boxing itself.

George Taylor, Daniel Mendoza and John Jackson established their own boxing academies.

Figg used his famous calling card, engraved by his friend, the celebrated William Hogarth, in 1716, to announce that he 'teached fencing, singlestick and boxing', while Broughton made use of the pages of the February 1747 issue of *The Daily Advertiser* to make it known that 'Mr Broughton proposes, with proper assistance, to open an academy at his house in the Haymarket, for the instruction of those who are willing to be initiated in the mystery of boxing ...'

Clearly fascinated, the British aristocracy were quick to support such establishments. For example, among the many notable patrons of John Jackson were the Dukes of York and Clarence, the Duke of Queensberry and Lord Byron. All attended Jackson's academy at No 13 Old Bond Street in London.

And what the Fives Court was to England, what Tom O'Rourke's old Broadway Athletic Club was to New York, the White Horse Inn in Sydney was to Australia: a mecca for men who wanted to box. It was after Jem Mace went to Australia in 1877 that Larry Foley's hotel achieved fame as a gymnasium. The two great bareknuckle champions joined forces and started a boxing school, but oddly they taught the Marquess of Queensberry Rules and nothing else.

Boxing gymnasiums have become an essential part of the sport since then. Most were found in the poorer areas and the most famous, Stillman's of New York, was downright grotty. The gym at 919 Eighth Avenue was a monument to squalor. Spitting on the floor was prohibited but virtually everything else was allowed and the boxers smoked heavily.

The grimy windows were never opened and when on a memorable occasion in the late 1920s the then world heavyweight champion Gene Tunney demanded fresh air, Lou Stillman flatly refused, claiming 'that stuff kills people'.

They demolished Stillman's Gym in the 1960s and today Gleason's Gym, which is situated in Brooklyn, close to the waterfront, is unquestionably the best in New York. The neighbourhood is undeniably tough, the entrance to the gym dark and dingy, but working out in Gleason's can open a great many doors for a young boxer. Four full-sized boxing rings are often in use simultaneously and there is every chance of rubbing shoulders with a world champion.

Many of the more famous gymnasiums in the world have either closed their doors or been demolished. Miami's Fifth Street Gym is a case in point. Muhammad Ali was one of six world champions who used to train there. Hot, dirty and decaying, it was demolished several years ago.

The gym was on the second floor of a ramshackle building and by early afternoon the place was like a hothouse as the sun baked the flat tin roof. The floor was a weathered grey, bleached by 30 years of sweat, while the locker room had a gaping hole in the ceiling.

Angelo Dundee was the last of the great trainers to make use of the Fifth Street Gym; nowadays he and his fighters work out at a youth centre in North Miami – smaller, cleaner and a lot more hospitable.

The old-timers remembered it as Johnny Papke's Gym, where

Lennox Lewis does most of his training for his big fights in the United States.

Cleveland's finest fighters did their time-honoured workouts on the second floor. Situated on the corner of Lexington Avenue and East 55th Street, the battered brick building had housed a boxing gym for as long as anyone could recall.

Nobody goes to watch the fighters train there any more. Some boxers still show up at the newly named Loft Boxing Club but the old gym clearly belongs to another era and is dying by the day.

Luna Park Gym in Buenos Aires already has. Tito Lectoure, who first made a name for himself as a matchmaker in the mid-1950s, closed the doors of the gym for the last time in November 1987. One of the problems was the location of the gym in downtown Buenos Aires.

Most boxers come from the poorer neighbourhoods and the lack of support was blamed on the tendency of Argentine boxers to return to their local gyms to train. Something similar has happened to the Thomas à Becket in London's Old Kent Road. Once a thriving gymnasium, it is now more of a museum – and this despite concerted efforts to keep it alive.

The truth is that gyms come and go just like everything else in life. The Kronk Gym in Detroit, once one of the most successful and famous in the world, has clearly seen better days. And yet there was a time in the 1970s and 1980s when Emanuel Steward virtually turned it into a fight factory and produced one world champion after another.

A big, simple structure held in place by an iron frame, the Maranon Gym in Panama City has also seen better days. Once a seedbed of champions – Roberto Duran often trained there in his younger days – the atmosphere today is subdued compared to the furious activity of the past.

When Brian Mitchell, the former WBA and IBF junior lightweight champion, opened a spanking new gym in Booysens, Johannesburg, in 1995, he insisted on state-of-the-art facilities. 'It's a fallacy that boxing gyms should be rundown places in some dark back street,' Mitchell said. 'Boxers should have modern equipment and feel comfortable as it is hard enough coming to the gym every day to go through the rigours of training.'

The spanking new World Gym in Las Vegas is popular for the same reasons. 'Strength and tone used to be taboo for boxers,' said manager Kevin Cyrus. 'Now fighters and trainers realize it makes sense. There are still some hardcore, old-fashioned trainers that don't want their fighters doing it, but most of them now can see the benefits.'

Even so, Johnny Tocco's more modest Ringside Gym on Charleston and Main was still doing good business until his death in 1997. The gym wasn't large but it was big enough . . . and besides, Tocco was always on hand to offer advice if needed.

MARVIN HAGLER

Asked why he was growing a beard before his fight with Mustafa Hamsho, British middleweight Alan Minter replied, 'It makes me feel evil.'

Marvin Hagler, who took the world title from Minter in a brief and bloody battle at Wembley Stadium in London in September 1980, never needed to grow a beard to feel evil.

Marvin had his own formula for getting into a mean mood. He isolated himself on a bleak, windswept island at the very tip of Cape Cod. Hagler had been going there to train since 1977 and the desolate, eerily silent island helped turn him into a monster.

'I've got meaner since I've become champion,' Hagler said in 1983. 'They're all trying to take something from me that I've worked long and hard for, and I like the feeling of being champ. There's a monster that comes out of me in the ring. I think it goes back to the days when I had nothing. It's hunger. I think that's what the monster is, and it's still there.'

Those who know him claim that Hagler had a split personality. His half-brother Robbie Sims once told a writer how Marvin had made a shrine out of his championship belt. The belt was stored away in a

Marvin Hagler lashes out with a left during his world middleweight title fight with Alan Minter in London in September 1980.

case and once a year the boxer would put it under the Christmas tree.

'He would put it there and then get down on his knees and open up the case for a few minutes, take a look at the belt, probably say a prayer, and then put it back. You wouldn't see it again until the next Christmas,' Sims told Bill Lyon of the *Philadelphia Inquirer*.

Hagler was always a very private person. That's something I discovered personally while in Monte Carlo for the Corro–Antuofermo world middleweight title fight in June 1979. Hagler was scheduled to fight Norberto Cabrera on the same bill.

I spotted Hagler in the foyer of his hotel before the fight and offered my hand in friendship. Hagler gave me a cold stare that went right through me. He neither took my hand nor responded to my greeting. Later I discovered that this was typical of the man. 'The

Hagler was one of the greatest southpaws in the history of boxing.

week of a fight, even we dread to go near him,' said Hagler's co-manager Pat Petronelli.

Marvin admits that his childhood may have had something to do with his personality. 'Animals were the only friends I could relate to,' he once said. 'Maybe the only friends I really liked. I was always by myself.'

Not only did Hagler like to be alone as a fighter, he was also fiercely proud of what he had and what he was. So proud that when an American television network refused to call him 'Marvelous', he went right out and legally changed his name to Marvelous Marvin Hagler.

The champion had come a long way from his modest start as a

professional in Brockton, Massachusetts, in May 1973. In those days Hagler fought whomever and wherever he could. His only two losses before Sugar Ray Leonard beat him in his last fight came in Philadelphia in 1976. The first, against Bobby 'Boogaloo' Watts, was so scandalous Hagler actually benefited from the publicity.

Hagler later dispatched Watts and Willie Monroe, the other man judged to have beaten him, in two rounds apiece.

Hagler got his first title shot in November 1979 but his fight with Vito Antuofermo was declared a draw. 'I won the fight,' Hagler insisted. 'It hurt, but I just went back to school. Back to work. I felt as though, if I missed that shot, I'd never get another opportunity.'

Marvin got his second title shot a year later and had to travel to London for the opportunity. Unfortunately, the crowd turned ugly when Hagler stopped Minter in the third round, and unruly fans pelted the ring with beer bottles and other debris. 'Here I was at the moment of my glory, the things I'd been waiting for all my life and I was deprived of it by those small people,' the bitter boxer said afterwards.

Seven successful defences later Hagler fought Roberto Duran in Las Vegas in November 1983 in what was to be the first of three superfights (the others were against Thomas Hearns and Sugar Ray Leonard). However, instead of adding to his glory, Hagler was made to look downright ordinary, even though he won the decision.

Marvin was mugged right there in the middle of the Caesar's Palace ring, under the full glare of the television lights and as countless millions looked on, by a scruffy-looking, bearded Duran. Hagler had entered the ring as one of the most menacing men in boxing: a champion whose mere stare was often enough to intimidate his opponents.

He left it just over an hour later with a swelling beneath his left eye, a cut on his brow and the myth of his invincibility exposed for all to see. If he felt naked, it was easy to understand why. The carefully cultivated image of 'destruct and destroy' lay in tatters.

Hagler regained some of that respect when he knocked out Juan Domingo Roldan, Mustafa Hamsho, Thomas Hearns and John Mugabi. But then came the showdown with Sugar Ray Leonard in April 1987 and despite being wobbled in the ninth round, Leonard won the split decision. Bitterly disappointed, Hagler viewed the videotape of the fight only once.

'I almost threw a chair at the TV,' he admitted. 'I know in my heart I won that fight. I still have a bad taste in my mouth about how that ended up, and how the organizations handled my situation.'

Brooding and bitter, the boxer they called Marvelous put himself in a prison of his own making. 'He's a very proud guy,' said Pat Petronelli. 'To him, this is the end of the world.'

Marvelous Marvin Hagler never fought again.

HALLS OF FAME

The concept is almost as old as the sport of boxing and yet there are more Halls of Fame in the United States of America than the rest of the world combined.

The International Boxing Hall of Fame in Canastota, New York, is by far the most successful even though some of the others have been in existence much longer. For example, the World Boxing Hall of Fame in Los Angeles was first established by Everett Sanders in 1979 yet still does not have its own boxing museum. The International Boxing Hall of Fame in Houston, Texas, has been planning a 90,000-square-foot museum with a five-storey rotunda since 1988.

Meanwhile the World Boxing Hall of Champions opened in the Metz Plaza in Las Vegas in June 1993. A host of internationally famous boxing champions and personalities attended the opening ceremonies. With more than 1,500 items on display, the museum is open daily. Housed in eight rooms are gloves, trunks, robes, posters, photographs, programmes and paintings from the past 100 years of boxing.

Not to be outdone, Madison Square Garden in New York launched

Muhammad Ali speaking to guests at the Rochester Boxing Hall of Fame in 1994.

its Walk of Fame in September 1992. The Walk honours the greatest athletes to have performed in the world's most famous sports arena, and boxing is well represented.

Formed in 1982, the International Boxing Hall of Fame erected the Basilio-Backus Boxing Showcase in August 1984. The showcase included two lifesize bronze statues of Carmen Basilio and Billy Backus and also housed mementoes, posters and a seven-minute colour video. It was an instant success.

In June 1989 the Hall of Fame was opened with more than a dozen former champions on hand for the ribbon-cutting ceremony. Both the crowds and the facilities have grown in size each year.

According to the organizers, 'the excitement of the weekend reaches its peak with induction ceremonies on Sunday. It is truly boxing's greatest annual festival.'

The Induction Weekend in June has become a tribute to the sport of boxing and its great champions. Fans from all parts of the United States and abroad gather and celebrate in an array of exhilarating activities. The organizers call it 'a one-of-a-kind happening'.

At last count, the Boxing Hall of Fame collection included 500 newspapers from the American west and east coasts covering many title fights from before the turn of the century to the present; hundreds of championship boxing programmes, press releases, photo files and boxing books. One of these, a rare copy of *Physical Culture and Self Defense*, was written, published and signed by heavyweight champion Bob Fitzsimmons in 1901.

In many respects the town of Canastota is an unlikely setting for the Hall of Fame. A typical American country town, it is situated 20 miles from Syracuse in New York State.

'The enthusiasm of Canastota inhabitants was unbelievable,' Simmy Lewis of *Boxing World* magazine reported after attending the 1994 Induction Weekend. 'On Sunday a procession of bands, fire engines and drum majorettes paraded just before the induction ceremony.

'Canastota is truly a hub of boxing. They claim their mission is to honour and preserve boxing's heritage, chronicle the achievements of those who excelled, provide an education experience for visitors and operate their facility in a manner that enhances the image of the sport.'

Long may they succeed.

IMPOSTORS

Impostors are not new to the prize ring but modern technology and instant communications have made it more difficult for them to get away with their deception. Even so, some still manage to slip through the net, which is why the World Boxing Council has recommended that a boxing passport be carried by active

Felix Trinidad, the hard-hitting IBF welterweight champion, with promoter Don King.

professionals throughout the world.

As recently as May 1993 – and only one fight before he became the IBF welterweight champion – Felix Trinidad knocked out a man he thought was Terry Acker but who is now listed in his record as 'opponent unknown'.

It was only when the real Terry Acker showed up in Puerto Rico to fight Simon Brown three months later that the fraud was uncovered. The unknown opponent whom Trinidad knocked out in one round was a fat blond with a gold tooth and a big scar across his back.

A similar scam was attempted in an IBF championship fight in Korea in 1984. A boxer claiming to be IBF flyweight champion

Alberto Castro turned out to be a man named Joaquin Caraballo. Castro, who was training in Panama for a title defence at the time, blew the whistle on the scam when he learned that he had supposedly lost his title to Kwan Sun-Chon.

To their credit, the Koreans reacted quickly once they learned the truth. The Seoul Municipal Police Force's bunko squad promptly arrested the promoter, the boxer and his manager.

World welterweight champion Kid McCoy attempted a similar scam back in 1896 when he arrived in Cape Town on board a steamer from England under the name of Harry Egan. The Kid's real name was Norman Selby, but the shrewd American was planning to pose as a mediocre boxer until he could lure the local champion into the ring. And then, with the odds nice and juicy, he would finally show the suckers what the real McCoy could do.

'Only 23 years old in 1896, McCoy had been forged in a hard school and he was a ruthless, self-centred man who had no scruples in or out of the ring,' Chris Greyvenstein wrote in *The Fighters*, his history of South African boxing.

'There was a strong streak of cruelty in his make-up and it was said that he often toyed with opponents in order to prolong their agony and humiliation. As a boxer McCoy was superb and to this day he is rated among the greatest fighters in the annals of the ring.'

But McCoy had hardly stepped on South African soil when he discovered that his deception could never work. The *Police Gazette* and other overseas publications that covered the fight game were freely available in all the major cities and McCoy was immediately recognized as the first world champion ever to visit South Africa.

McCoy had only one fight in South Africa. He knocked out Bill Doherty in nine rounds in Johannesburg on 26 December 1896.

'We were quite unprepared for the magnificent physique he displayed,' the Johannesburg *Star* commented after the fight. 'Never perhaps could the old adage "appearances are deceptive" be better applied than in his case. To the ordinary observer he appeared of the overgrown and delicate order. However, all these adverse opinions were at once flouted when he stripped his sweater and presented to the spectators a perfect model of humanity.'

INJURIES

One of the best investments the World Boxing Council has ever made was probably the donation of $700,000 to the UCLA-based SPAR (Safety and Performance Advancement through Research) in 1983. The object, to establish a sports medicine foundation for the prevention and treatment of injuries in boxing, has already paid handsome dividends.

SPAR has launched many studies, ranging from drug-testing to efforts to minimize long-term brain damage, to developing mouth-guards that will absorb more shock from a blow. The research facility is currently studying the level of electrolytes and neuro-excitory amino acids in the brain during different stages of concussive damage.

'It's conceivable that understanding these events can allow us to protect the brain,' Dr Gerald Finerman, an orthopaedic surgeon and director of sports medicine at UCLA, told Robert Cassidy of *The Ring* magazine.

Preliminary findings from a similar study which was started in 1986 at Johns Hopkins University indicate that amateur boxers, who are obliged to wear headguards in the ring, are not suffering any detectable chronic injuries to the brain. None of the 500 males in the sample has encountered any unusual medical problems.

'Maybe professional boxing has to look at headgear, but I don't see any interest in that yet,' said Dr Robert Voy, a Las Vegas physician who has played a leading role in organizing the study and securing its financing.

The Johns Hopkins study drew its sample from six American cities and the participants are examined every two years by representatives of the Baltimore-based university. The idea for the study originated in 1983 when Dr Voy was with the United States Olympic Committee.

'The American Medical Association had just voted to ban amateur boxing and I put in for a research grant at Colorado Springs to study the long-term effects of the sport on its participants. That led to the US Amateur Boxing Federation getting $1.2 million through the US

Olympic Foundation to start the Johns Hopkins study,' Dr Voy said.

Both these research programmes are indicative of how safety-conscious boxing people have become in the last two decades. Besides reducing the number of rounds in world championship fights from 15 to 12, suspending fighters who have suffered knockouts or technical knockouts, and making the thumb-attached glove mandatory in all title fights, the commissions, boxing boards and other interested parties have looked beyond the obvious in an attempt to make the sport safer.

The New Jersey State Athletic Commission was the first to require cornermen to wear surgical gloves and in 1987 also insisted that the boxer's mouthguard be replaced during the round in the event it comes out. In addition to pre-fight medicals, many commissions also require a fighter to pass an annual physical examination, which often includes a CATscan or MRI and sometimes a neurological assessment.

Progress has been slow but sure. In 1981 the Canadian Minister of Sport, Gerald Regan, ordered a government study that recommended ringside doctors be given the right to stop a fight at any time to examine a boxer. In 1985 the National Boxing Safety Center was officially opened by New Jersey governor Thomas Kean at the United Hospitals Orthopedic Center. 'New Jersey is blazing a path for other states and boxing commissions to follow,' Kean said.

In 1986 Dr Anthony Storace, of the Department of Orthopedic Surgery of the New York Medical College, was awarded a grant of $15,000 by the New York State Athletic Commission to research boxing headgear. 'We have been surprised by some of the test results obtained,' Dr Storace said. 'For example, we are reasonably certain that current headgear works against the boxers' interest for certain types of punches.'

In 1987, Dr David J Smith of the Wills Eye Hospital in Philadelphia recommended that boxers undergo mandatory annual eye examinations. Of 166 professional boxers examined before fighting in Atlantic City, Dr Smith said 34 had significant eye problems.

But detached retinas, once a common injury in boxing, have been drastically reduced since the introduction of the thumb-attached glove. And according to Dr Vincent Giovinazzo, an ophthalmologist and consultant to the New York State Athletic Commission, technological improvements have resulted in retinal problems being successfully treated with laser surgery.

Brain damage (or subdural haematoma) remains the most frightening injury of all as it is often fatal. But rest assured that the boffins of boxing are working on the problem. In fact, two significant advances were made in 1990. It was decided that every boxer in California would be required to take the state's neurological examination, which is designed to detect brain damage at an early stage, and the World Boxing Council ordered weigh-ins to take place on the eve of title bouts to allow for the boxer's rehydration, rest and recuperation before entering the ring.

The trend of holding weigh-ins 24 hours before a fight has now spread worldwide.

JUNIOR DIVISIONS

In the beginning the purists dismissed them as synthetic and when the New York State Athletic Commission abolished them in 1930 many stood up to cheer – including Nat Fleischer, the then editor and publisher of *The Ring* magazine, and one of the most influential boxing men of his time.

According to Fleischer, the junior divisions were the brainchild of Englishman William A Gavin, who had gone to America to establish an International Sporting Club and who insisted that boxing would greatly benefit by the additional titles. It was Gavin who persuaded the New York State Legislature to insert the junior weight classes in the bill that legalized boxing in the state of New York in 1920.

'The original New York Boxing Commission therefore had no option but to accept these junior titles and all other portions of the law introduced in the Legislature by Senator Walker. As the writer was a member of the committee that drew up the boxing rules, now part of the law, permit me to say that the original draft of the regulations did not contain any reference to junior titles,' Fleischer declared in an editorial in the July 1946 issue of *The Ring*.

When the Walker Law was enacted in 1920 the regulations provided for five junior divisions – junior flyweight, junior bantamweight, junior featherweight, junior lightweight and junior welterweight – but only the junior lightweight and junior welterweight classes gained any kind of acceptance.

Johnny Dundee was matched against George 'KO' Chaney on 18 November 1922 for the first junior world championship to be contested in New York. Dundee was declared the winner on a foul in five rounds and in the words of ring announcer Joe Humphries, he became 'the new junior lightweight champion of the world'.

The National Boxing Association (forerunner of the World Boxing Association) had already decided before the closure of its convention in New Orleans on 19 January 1922 that it would not

It was Tippy Larkin's fight against Willie Joyce in Boston on 29 April 1946 for the junior welterweight championship of the world that gave junior titles a second chance.

recognize the junior flyweight, junior bantamweight and junior featherweight divisions.

However, with Dundee having already been proclaimed junior lightweight champion by the New York State Athletic Commission, the NBA accepted an offer from Mike Collins, publisher of *Boxing Blade*, to invite his readers to pick 'the best man in the world at 140 pounds' and to provide a $2,000 championship belt for a junior welterweight champion.

After the votes were counted, Pinky Mitchell of Milwaukee was proclaimed the new champion. 'No one really took the title seriously, and the 5ft 11in Mitchell almost never defended it. He fought above 140 pounds on all but a few occasions over the next four years, and made sure the bout would be "no decision" before he allowed himself to reach or dip below the figure,' Herb Goldman pointed out in the June 1980 issue of *The Ring*.

When Mitchell finally agreed to defend his 'title' against Mushy Callahan in Vernon, California, on 21 September 1926 he promptly lost it. Callahan outpointed him over ten rounds.

With champions like Dundee and Mitchell, there is little wonder that the junior divisions did not gain much acceptance and when Tod Morgan, who won the junior lightweight title in 1925, was knocked out in the second round of a championship fight with Benny Bass in New York on 20 December 1929 it was literally the last straw.

'Among the rumors in circulation before the match started was one that it would end in the second round with Bass the winner on a knockout,' James Dawson wrote in the *New York Times*. 'Similar rumors have been circulated in advance of other matches in which attempts were made to designate the round in which a match would end, but few were so accurately fulfilled as was last night's.'

After calling for an investigation into the fight, the New York State Athletic Commission abolished the junior weight divisions on 31 December 1929. Four days later, Edward B Foster, chairman of the NBA's championship committee, recommended the abolition of the junior weight classes by the NBA.

The NBA itself took no action and member states held junior title fights for the next five years. Even so, it was not until the

Massachusetts State Athletic Commission sanctioned a fight between Tippy Larkin and Willie Joyce in Boston on 29 April 1946 for the junior welterweight championship of the world that junior titles got a second chance. Both the NBA and the New York State Athletic Commission had agreed to recognize the winner as champion.

Larkin's success (he beat Joyce on points over 12 rounds) was eventually followed by a revival of the junior lightweight title in 1959 and when the World Boxing Council was established in February 1963 and then began its war to the death with the WBA in 1968, junior divisions were created at the drop of a hat.

In a stroke of genius, the WBC decided to name most of their new divisions 'super' instead of 'junior', which may have made them easier to market but greatly added to the fans' confusion.

KNOCKOUTS

If we accept that boxing as a sport has been practised in one form or another for 8,000 years and more, knockouts are a relatively recent innovation. There was no such term in prize-ring days and there are still countless cases of the term being misused today.

American boxing historian Nat Fleischer always insisted that when a fighter had been stopped – 'whether by tossing in the sponge, through the action of a referee, because of injuries or any cause other than fouling' – he had been knocked out.

British boxing historian Gilbert Odd held a different view. 'In Great Britain and the rest of Europe a truer definition exists, the record being marked RET when a boxer has retired or RSF when the bout is stopped by the referee,' he said.

Just how important the definition is can be gauged by the fact that the two fastest knockouts on record could not possibly have involved a count. Paul Rees stopped Charlie Hansen in Brisbane,

Australia, on 19 June 1991 in five seconds. The men had exchanged only one set of blows when Hansen complained of double vision to referee Alan Simpson, who immediately stopped the fight. A ringside doctor diagnosed Hansen as having suffered a scratched eyeball.

Three years later Ever Beleno of Colombia set a national record when he knocked out Guillermo Salcedo in five seconds in Sincelejo, Colombia, on 16 September 1994. Clearly no count was involved.

Until these two fights took place the fastest knockout on record was always accepted as the ten-and-a-half-second stoppage of Ralp Walton by Al Couture in Lewiston, Maine, on 23 September 1946. (Couture was halfway across the ring as the bell sounded and struck Walton as Ralp was still adjusting his mouthpiece.)

Double knockouts have become even rarer and largely because referees are inclined to declare them no contests, technical draws or technical knockouts. None has occurred in a world title fight. The closest was when world lightweight champion Ad Wolgast and his challenger Joe Rivers landed blows simultaneously in the 13th round of their championship fight in Vernon, California, on 14 July 1912.

Both boxers fell to the canvas but what happened next depends on whose version you accept. Some historians claim that neither boxer would have been able to rise before the count of ten, while others insist that Wolgast was struggling to his feet when referee Jack Welch gave him a helping hand with his left and continued to count Rivers out with his right.

Photographs of the historic fight appear to confirm the latter version and also reports that Rivers was claiming a foul (the pictures show him holding his groin while sitting on the canvas).

There is no controversy surrounding the claim of the oldest man to score a knockout. Walter Edgerton, who was also known as 'Kentucky Rosebud', was 63 years old when he knocked out John Henry Johnson in four rounds at the Broadway Athletic Club in Philadelphia in February 1916. Johnson was 45 years old.

Boxers who scored 100 or more knockouts during their careers include Archie Moore (145), Young Stribling (126), Billy Bird (125), George Odwell (114), Sugar Ray Robinson (109), Banty Lewis (108) and Sandy Saddler (103). Moore, Robinson and Saddler all held world titles during their careers.

The record for the fastest knockout in a world heavyweight title fight is a toss-up between the 55-second stoppage of Jack Finnegan by James J Jeffries at the Light Guard Armory in Detroit on 6 April 1900 or the 60-second knockout of Sonny Liston by Muhammad Ali at the St Dominic's Youth Center in Lewiston, Maine, on 25 May 1965.

Both bouts are the subject of controversy. Few accept that the Jeffries–Finnegan fight was a genuine championship match; it is usually dismissed as an exhibition bout. And the time of one minute for the Liston knockout is disputed. A check of the videotape clearly shows Liston being put down at one minute and 42 seconds, and referee Jersey Joe Walcott only declaring the fight over at two minutes 12 seconds.

Walcott was all for allowing the men to fight on until Nat Fleischer, who was assisting the knockdown timekeeper at the ringside, drew his attention to the fact that Liston had already been on the canvas for longer than ten seconds.

Michael Dokes, the former WBA heavyweight champion, holds the record for the fastest knockout in a world heavyweight title fight.

Assuming the official time of one minute flat is incorrect – the evidence is irrefutable – then the fastest knockout in a world heavyweight title fight belongs to Michael Dokes, who stopped Mike Weaver in one minute and three seconds at Caesar's Palace in Las Vegas on 12 October 1982.

The Dokes–Weaver fight was also steeped in controversy and referee Joey Curtis was strongly criticized for his handling of the contest. In a rematch five months later the men fought a 15-round draw.

LEGISLATION

In an ideal world, each country would have its own Boxing Control Act, legalizing the sport and making the licensees answerable to state-appointed officials. But since we do not live in an ideal world, the next best thing is the hotchpotch of boxing boards, commissions and federations that attempt to control the sport.

Sadly, the world's two greatest democracies have done little to set an example. Boxing has never been legalized in Britain and the sport has been banned and unbanned on a number of occasions in the United States.

While 'fighting' is evidently illegal in Britain, a 'contest' is not. At least that was the interpretation of Sir James Vaughan when he sat in judgement of a manslaughter charge brought against Jimmy Barry following the American's ill-fated fight with Walter Croot in London in 1897. (Croot died after striking his head on the floor in the 20th round.)

Sir James explained that there was a 'thin partition' between what is termed a 'fight' and a 'contest' and decided that the two men had been engaged in a 'contest'. A further test case in 1901 confirmed this somewhat convoluted interpretation of the law.

However, the fact that the sport still skirted the lines of legality in England was emphasized on the December night in 1919 when Georges Carpentier knocked out Joe Beckett in one round at Holborn Stadium. As Carpentier was having his hands taped, a plain clothes detective came into his dressing room to issue the customary warning that preceded all British boxing shows at the time; a warning that all the principals could be put on trial for manslaughter if there was a death in the ring.

Carpentier knew no English, so Victor Beyers, a French sports-writer and friend of the boxer's manager, François Descamps, translated the police warning like this: 'I am here as head of the British police to wish you well and express the hope that you will beat Beckett.'

Georges Carpentier (left), the French heavyweight who challenged Jack Dempsey for the world title in 1921, with American baseball star Babe Ruth.

There were smiles and much bowing all round. Later, much later, Beyers confessed that if he had relayed the detective's message accurately, the tensed-up Carpentier would probably have knocked his block off. A neat bit of diplomacy, yet the fact remained that English law still operated – even though covertly – against boxing.

Meanwhile a long line of American senators has kept the myth of federal control of professional boxing alive in the United States. As recently as 1994 three bills were under consideration by the US government. Among them were the Professional Boxing Corporation Act of 1993, the National Boxing Corporation Act of 1994 and the Professional Boxing Safety Act of 1994.

The Professional Boxing Safety Act was approved by both the U.S. Senate and the House of Representatives in October 1996, but the other two bills have so far been passed at state level only. This in turn has led to a number of anomalies.

'You can be suspended in New Jersey and you can go to a state that doesn't have a boxing commission and you can fight,' said Larry Hazzard, chairman of the New Jersey State Athletic Commission. 'If you're really talking about protecting the fighter, why allow fights in states that do not have a commission?' asked Richard DeCuir, executive officer for the California State Athletic Commission.

The answer would appear to be federal control of boxing but not everyone in the United States thinks it would be a good idea. 'Boxing may be a sewer, but until the politicians cleanse themselves, the Roto-Rooter man is not coming from the Senate,' said Michael Katz, boxing writer for the New York *Daily News,* in 1992.

A list of the laws that governed boxing in the state of New York between 1859 and 1920 might explain why. In 1859, the first anti-boxing law was passed in the state. In 1881, the penal code was amended to make boxing 'a crime against the peace' and punishable by a heavy fine and imprisonment for up to three years. In 1894, the courts ruled that boxing was legal in bona fide athletic clubs. In 1895, promoters in New York seized upon the idea to stage regular shows on a club membership basis.

In 1896, the Horton Law was passed, amending the code to prohibit 'sparring exhibitions' under the club membership plan and substituted 'sparring exhibitions with gloves of not less than five ounces in weight, by a domestic incorporated athletic association, in a building leased by it for athletic purposes only'.

In 1897, fly-by-night promoters took advantage of the law and tickets were sold indiscriminately with the word 'membership' printed on the face. In 1898, Governor Roosevelt declared that 'the commercialism of boxing had brought disgrace upon the state' and asked for the repeal of the Horton Law. Roosevelt added that fake fights were frequent and that 'the sport, as now conducted, is degrading'.

In 1899, several deaths in Buffalo, gangster attacks in rings in New York City and upstate, and big betting coups following fake fights, brought about a strong editorial stand against the sport by many leading newspapers. In August 1900, the Horton Law was repealed the day following a fight between James J Corbett and Kid McCoy in Madison Square Garden, in which 'collusion' was charged.

Between 1900 and 1910, boxing in the state was conducted on a club-membership basis. Promoters and spectators both suffered at the hands of the police with frequent arrests and bodily injury. In September 1911, the Frawley Law was passed. The law established an athletic commission, composed of three members, who were granted full power to control boxing.

In March 1915, the Frawley Law was amended with the passage of the Malone Law, which abolished the unpaid commission and created a new commission, with each of its three members receiving a salary of $3,000. In 1916, the Frawley Law and Malone Law were viciously attacked by both public and press. Charges were brought against the chairman, who was absolved after a trial by a special investigator.

In 1916, a bill to repeal the laws failed. In 1917, no fewer than seven bills were introduced in an attempt to repeal the Frawley Law. In May 1917, Governor Whitman ordered the commission not to issue any more licences to clubs or boxers. In November 1917, the Frawley Law was repealed.

Between 1918 and 1920, boxing again went underground in the state of New York and raids and arrests were frequent. In 1918, an attempt was made to legalize boxing but the bill failed to pass. In April 1920, the Walker Law passed by 91 votes to 46 and boxing was back with a bang.

Offbeat incidents have often influenced decisions either to legalize or outlaw boxing. A case in point was the passage of the Boxing Control Act in South Africa in 1923. Political party affiliations were suspended for the debate and heated discussion for and against the proposal had the backers of the bill in a state of despair one moment and delight the next.

At the end of the first day it looked as if the cause was lost but that night a young girl was raped and her escort beaten up, and many suspect that it was the stark report of the outrage in the next morning's *Cape Times* that changed the whole attitude in the House of Assembly.

The highly respected John X Merriman entered the debate in favour of boxing and it was soon agreed that had the young man had a knowledge of self-defence he might have been able to protect his unfortunate girlfriend. Legalizing professional boxing, it was argued, would result in more young South African men taking an interest in 'the noble art of self defence'.

'Opposition to the proposal crumbled and Parliament legalized professional boxing through the promulgation of an Act which, with amendments from time to time, has stood since,' Chris Greyvenstein wrote in his book *The Fighters*.

On the other hand, a bizarre drinking incident resulted in all boxing being banned in Iceland in 1956. 'A group of our best professional boxers were spending the evening in a restaurant,' Sigurdur Magnusson, general secretary of the Icelandic Sports Federation, told Kate Battersby of the *Sunday Telegraph* in 1994.

'After they became drunk, fighting broke out between them and fellow diners. The police were called and an incident followed in which at least two policemen were very seriously injured, one of them incapacitated for life.'

So great was the public and parliamentary outcry that all boxing was banned in Iceland soon after.

SUGAR RAY LEONARD

Perhaps the hardest thing Sugar Ray Leonard had to do after he battered Thomas Hearns into defeat in 14 rounds on an autumn night in Las Vegas in September 1981 was to face his son, seven-year-old Ray junior.

Little Ray was clearly alarmed as he cast his eyes over the features of the man he adored. Leonard may have won, but not without paying a price. His left eye was swollen shut, his lips cut and bruised, and he was desperately tired as he faced his son in the dressing room.

'Daddy, why do you keep on fighting?' the little boy asked. 'Why don't you take up another sport?'

Leonard forced a smile on his battered and bruised face. 'Like what?' he asked.

'Like basketball.'

Nearly ten years later Sugar Ray was still fighting – or making the third comeback of his career, to be more precise – and with more than a hundred million dollars in the bank, the wonder was why.

'A fighter never knows when it's the last bell,' Leonard once told a writer. 'He doesn't want to face that. We have distorted views, pictures of how our lives should be.' And in that picture Sugar Ray Leonard was not merely a multi-millionaire or a corporate entity; he was the greatest fighter of all time, a superstar in the most macho of all sports.

To understand why men want to fight you need to know where they've come from and why they would rather be somewhere else. Sugar Ray often went hungry as a little boy because his family did not have much. He remembers eating mayonnaise sandwiches at home.

'They weren't good but they filled the stomach,' he said. 'I remember not going to school on some days because I didn't have clothes to wear, and what I had was so ragged it was embarrassing.'

No wonder Leonard learned more about life while boxing than he

Sugar Ray Leonard was a money-spinner from the moment he turned professional in 1977.

ever did in the classroom. Not only did it enable him to travel the world as a teenager, it taught him things some people never learn in a lifetime.

Leonard was only 16, and in Italy with a US amateur boxing team, when a bunch of local kids touched his skin and hair in sheer disbelief. 'I think the children either felt that I was a god or were telling one another that I was the reason their moms always said to use soap,' Ray said. 'I really wish I could relive that, because it was a beautiful experience.'

It seems Leonard always had charisma, even though some boxing writers accused him of being a creation of the media. I recall how he got the biggest cheer of the evening when he made his entrance to the Richfield Coliseum on the night Gerrie Coetzee knocked out Michael Dokes to win the heavyweight championship of the world in September 1983.

Leonard looked immaculate as he made his way to the ringside in a dress suit and bow-tie. And when someone told him it was time to get ready for the big fight (he was doing the commentary for an American TV network), he checked his gold watch and flashed his million-dollar smile. 'Gotta go get my make-up on,' he said.

Of course, not everyone in the media fell for Leonard's charm. Irving Rudd, the legendary American press agent, called Ray a 'prick' in his book *The Sporting Life*. 'Do you think I was too hard on him?' Rudd asked when we later spoke about it in New York.

Rudd admitted upfront that he did not like Leonard, whom he thought lost his youthful sweetness when American boxing promoter Don King took him into the men's room at Yankee Stadium in 1976 and 'showed him one hundred grand in cash'.

Leonard was a money-spinner from the moment he turned professional in 1977. A year earlier he had won the Olympic light welterweight title in Montreal. And by 1979 he had won his first world title – the WBC welterweight championship. Leonard suffered his first defeat at the hands of Roberto Duran a year later, only to humiliate the 'Hands of Stone' in a rematch in November 1980.

Victories over Larry Bonds, Ayub Kalule, Thomas Hearns and Bruce Finch followed and then Leonard was forced into retirement because of an injury to his retina. Sugar Ray remained in retirement

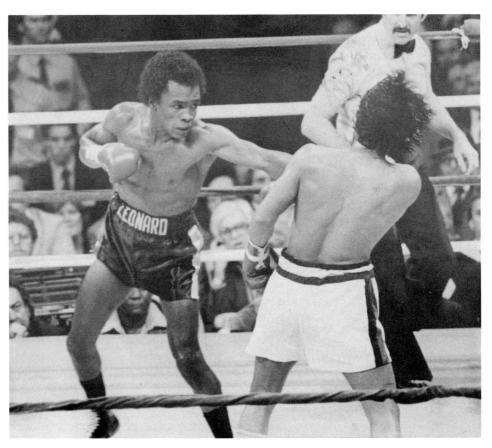

Sugar Ray drives Roberto Duran to the ropes during their 'no mas' fight in New Orleans in November 1980.

for two years before returning to the ring against Kevin Howard in May 1984. Leonard stopped Howard in the ninth round but it was an unsatisfactory performance and he again hung up his gloves.

Nearly three years passed before Leonard decided to challenge Marvin Hagler for the world middleweight title. To nobody's great surprise, many experts began to question his sanity. After all, Hagler was supposedly invincible, but Marvin's 'Destruct and Destroy' image had not fooled Sugar Ray.

Angelo Dundee, who was then Leonard's guru, claimed that one of the reasons Ray would beat Hagler was because Marvin was in the habit of crossing his legs in the ring. 'Ray's gonna nail him,'

Dundee predicted. 'Hagler won't be able to get out of the way.'

As usual, Dundee was right and Leonard won a points decision over 12 rounds. And just when the boxing world thought they had seen the last of Leonard, he popped up again to challenge Donny Lalonde for the WBC light heavyweight title and the then newly created super middleweight title. Leonard, who weighed in at his career highest with the admitted aid of two pockets full of silver dollars, survived a fourth-round knockdown to score a ninth-round TKO.

Finally came rematches with Hearns and Duran, and then a last hurrah against Terry Norris in Madison Square Garden. Leonard's decision to challenge Norris for the WBC junior middleweight title was based more on sentiment than economic sense. 'I want to be able to tell my kids that I fought in Madison Square Garden,' Leonard said when asked for an explanation.

It proved to be Leonard's last fight. Norris beat him on points over 12 rounds.

JOE LOUIS

Joe Louis became heavyweight champion of the world at a time when there was a gentlemen's agreement among boxing men that a black man would never again be permitted to win the title. And the fact he was able to break through that barrier says more for Joe Louis the man than any of the many records he subsequently established as champion.

Louis, who died in Las Vegas in April 1981 at the age of 66, did more to advance the cause of the black man in sport than anyone except Jesse Owens.

When Louis retired as undefeated champion in 1949, an editorial in *Life* magazine credited him with having opened the doors not only for other black sportsmen but also for entertainers and for the appointment of Dr Ralph Bunche as the United Nations mediator in what was then called Palestine.

Louis achieved that success by hiding his emotions, speaking as little as possible in public and boxing with such perfection that many were in awe of his ability. Sadly, some were misled by Joe's quiet demeanour. Paul Gallico, the author and one-time sports editor of the New York *Daily News*, was among them.

Gallico described Louis as cold and expressionless. 'The crowd will never warm to him as they do to fighters who have the knack of letting the spectators fight along with them,' Gallico wrote early in Joe's career. 'He has been carefully trained in the sly servility that the white man accepts as his due.'

Gallico was wrong, of course. Louis knew better than most that he would have to walk a tightrope if he ever hoped to fight for the world heavyweight title one day. The 'stigma' of another black heavyweight champion was more than most boxing men were prepared to tolerate in the 1930s.

And all because of the way Jack Johnson had abused his position as champion some 20 years before. History has treated Johnson harshly. He was, according to American boxing historian Nat Fleischer, one of the finest defensive boxers ever to lace on a glove and a brilliant exponent of the so-called manly art.

But his affairs with white women and the provocative manner in which he thumbed his nose at the Establishment have assured him of a place in boxing history as the most hated champion of all time.

Joe and his handlers were wary of making the same mistakes – nor could they afford to. Louis once recalled his first meeting with promoter Mike Jacobs in 1934. 'He told me then there was a colour line – at that time a gentlemen's agreement – and that there wouldn't be another coloured champion,' Louis said.

It explained why Harry Wills, a talented black heavyweight, never got the chance to challenge Jack Dempsey for the title in the 1920s, even though promoter Tex Rickard went as far as to have tickets printed for the fight. And it explained why even those who did acknowledge Louis's greatness in the early days invariably apologized for Joe's race with the familiar words ... 'even though coloured'.

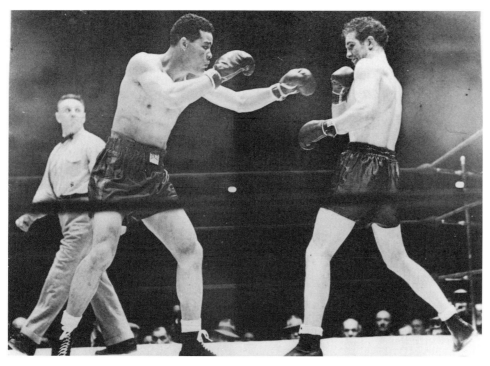

Joe Louis (left) was behind on points when he turned back the challenge of Billy Conn in June 1941 by knocking Conn out in the 13th round.

It took Benito Mussolini and Adolf Hitler finally to swing the balance of public opinion in Louis's favour in the 1930s.

When Joe fought Primo Carnera in 1935, at a time when Mussolini's troops were raping Ethiopia, many Americans viewed the bout as a battle against fascism. And when the 'Brown Bomber' met Max Schmeling in their famous return fight three years later, it was as though Democracy had suddenly pulled on a pair of boxing gloves and Nazi Germany was in the opposite corner.

'The atmosphere between Germany and America was very bad in 1938,' Schmeling recalled years later. 'There were pickets in front of my hotel every day and when I walked from the dressing room to the ring at Yankee Stadium, the crowd threw things at me and called me dirty names.'

Louis's colour became less of an issue to many Americans after Joe destroyed Schmeling in less than a round. Louis was largely accepted for what he was: a great heavyweight champion. For more than eleven years he ruled the boxing world with a firm-fisted dignity that wiped out the popular stereotype of the American black as a buffoon prone to stupidity and immorality if given money and fame.

As his confidence grew, Louis even occasionally showed his emotions, speaking more freely to the press and even appearing on political platforms as he actively campaigned in 1940 for Wendell Wilkie, the Republican presidential candidate.

Louis won over thousands more in 1942 when he donated his entire purse money for his fights against Buddy Baer and Abe Simon to the US Navy and Army Relief Funds. And all the while he kept putting together one of the finest records of any champion.

Then, after 25 successful title defences, he retired undefeated in March 1949, prompting American columnist Jimmy Cannon to write: 'Joe Louis is a credit to his race – the human race.'

MAGAZINES

Two hundred years after the first known boxing magazine – *Boxing Reviewed* by Thomas Fewtrell – was published in 1790, boxing's trade press is still flourishing. There are weeklies, monthlies, bimonthlies, quarterlies and annuals, all competing for a share of the market and published in half a dozen or more different languages.

But since it was in England that the first boxing magazine was published, it seems only fitting that the granddaddy of today's boxing publications should be British. *Boxing News*, the British weekly which was first published under the name of *Boxing* in 1909, is still going strong.

Under the editorship of Harry Mullan, *Boxing News* became more international in its coverage of the sport. However, the paper has never forgotten that its roots are British and it still serves British boxing better than any other publication on the market.

Even so, its position as the most popular boxing paper in Britain has been challenged on a number of occasions. In fact, shortly after it was launched on 11 September 1909, a weekly rival called *Boxing World* also entered the market. But when *Boxing World* failed to turn a profit, Frank Bradley incorporated it with his *Mirror of Life*, which he had successfully published since January 1900.

More recently, a colour tabloid called *Boxing Weekly* came on the market but died after a relatively brief life. *Boxing Monthly*, its sister publication, has proved to be a better stayer and under editor Glyn Leach continues to be one of the few successful all-glossy, full-colour boxing magazines in the world.

The first issue of *Boxing* sold out within two hours! Founded by a sports-minded aristocrat, Lord Camrose, it was edited by the celebrated Scot John Murray. '*Boxing* is not offered to its public with an apology,' Murray wrote in his first editorial. 'We claim it is wanted, and wanted badly. It will stand for good, clean sport. Its success or failure is in the hands of those who believe in sport of that character.'

The paper has had remarkably few editors. Claude Abrams is only the tenth in nearly a century. 'In the early days the staff of the paper were regarded as participants in, rather than commentators on, the boxing world. It was not unusual for the editor or his journalists to be invited by a promoter to act as referee,' Bob Mee wrote on the paper's 75th anniversary.

British boxing historian Gilbert Odd, who joined the staff in 1922 and had two spells as editor, told Mee how a London promoter once paid him a £5 bonus (more than a week's wages) for having the good sense to declare a local derby a draw.

'If you'd given it either way there would've been a riot,' the promoter told Odd. 'They'd have torn the hall apart and put me out of business.'

Odd thanked the promoter for his generosity but decided against explaining that the only reason he had declared the fight a draw was because he had been so terrified by the thought of finding a winner that he had forgotten to keep a scorecard and did not have a clue who was ahead on points!

The paper changed its name to *Boxing News* in 1946 and, like any worthwhile publication, prides itself on its independence and impartiality. Rows with promoters, managers, referees, boxers and the Board of Control are frequent and in 1994 the paper had to pay a huge out-of-court settlement for an alleged libel.

The Ring, the American monthly which was first published in February 1922, found itself in a similar unhappy situation on at least a couple of occasions while under the outspoken editorship of Nat Fleischer. 'Once, *The Ring* inferred that a British wrestler was incompetent. That cost *The Ring* $5,000. Once, *The Ring* warned certain promoters to stop using poor boxers under assumed names. That cost *The Ring* $10,000,' Fleischer admitted on the occasion of the magazine's 50th anniversary.

Fleischer was sports editor of the New York *Evening Telegram* when he started *The Ring*. 'There were important things I wanted to say which I could not say in the newspaper. I wanted a medium in which I could say it the way it was. So I decided to start a magazine of my own.'

American promoter Tex Rickard funded the project while Rickard's publicist Ike Dorgan assisted Fleischer with the production. When the magazine was launched on 15 February 1922 it was little more than a newsletter covering boxing in New York. But Fleischer solicited articles from top American sportswriters like Damon Runyon and Hype Igoe and, by 1927, *The Ring* had become so popular Fleischer was able to resign his position at the *Telegram*.

Fleischer's editorial column in *The Ring* soon became one of the most widely read and highly respected in boxing. The dandy little American capitalized on his success by calling his publication 'The Bible of Boxing'. Soon, others elsewhere in the world attempted to exploit the magazine's reputation.

Fleischer complained bitterly about imitators in an angry editorial he wrote in January 1935. After exposing a former Mexican correspondent who claimed that he was the owner of the authorized Mexican edition of *The Ring*, called *El Ring*, Fleischer added that there was a magazine in Australia that had also stolen *The Ring* name and trademark.

'There is another in Portugal, one in Spain and still another in

Italy,' Fleischer wrote. 'Not content with stealing the style and name and copyrighted lettering of *The Ring*, which has made its mark in international publications, these brazen imitators even go so far as to steal our stories and articles.'

Fleischer served as the magazine's sole editor and publisher for 40 years. And among its many achievements was that of being the first boxing magazine to publish world ratings in 1925. But sadly the magazine declined rapidly after Fleischer's death in 1972 and was involved in a nasty ratings scandal in 1977.

Bert Randolph Sugar gave the magazine back its self-respect when he took over as editor in 1979. 'In acquiring the rights to publish *The Ring* magazine, we are not just acquiring a magazine, we are acquiring the rights to a tradition; the tradition of Nat Fleischer and Nat Loubet,' Sugar wrote in his first editorial. 'These are the men

Bert Randolph Sugar, the colourful American boxing writer, publisher and editor, was nicknamed 'The Hat'.

who since 1922 have made *The Ring* not only "The Bible of Boxing", but, to a great many readers, boxing itself.'

Sugar made no bones about the fact that he was a nostalgia buff and one of the first acts was to bring back the old stylized *Ring* logo, complete with boxing gloves. He also introduced new graphics, new layouts and new writers.

Soon the bylines of many of boxing's greatest writers began to appear in the pages of the magazine – Paul Gallico, Dave Anderson, Red Smith, Barney Nagler, Budd Schulberg, W C Heinz, Bob Waters, Tex Maule – but Sugar's style was simply too rich for a magazine that was still financially unstable. Sugar was replaced as editor late in 1983 by Randy Gordon and when Gordon left to join the New York State Athletic Commission in 1985, Nigel Collins took over the editorship.

With debts estimated at one million dollars, circulation down to about 25,000 and its reputation at an all-time low, *The Ring* looked ready to take the ten count in 1989. Publishers Dave DeBusschere and Nicholas Kladis were reeling from court judgements that made them personally liable for the huge debts.

'Clearly, *Ring*'s legs are gone,' declared the *Village Voice*, the New York weekly.

It was then that Stanley Weston, a former *Ring* staff member and successful publisher, came to the rescue. 'I couldn't let the old girl die,' Weston said. After helping the magazine to regain some of its old glory, Weston sold his interests to Pennsylvania millionaire publisher Nick Karobots three years later. Included in the deal were Weston's other boxing magazines – *KO, World Boxing, Boxing '93*

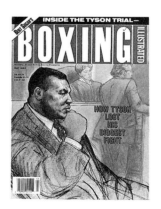

and *Knockout*.

Sugar, meanwhile, had joined *Boxing Illustrated*, the American monthly that was first published in 1958, and quickly turned it into his own fiefdom. Besides featuring himself on the cover and adding his name to the masthead, Sugar continued to conduct what José Sulaiman alleged was an on-going vendetta against the World Boxing Council and American promoter Don King.

A larger-than-life character straight out of a Damon Runyon novel, Sugar had a marvellous sense of humour and a racy style of writing. To prove it he published a picture of himself in the October 1988 issue of the magazine. The picture showed him being interviewed after the Tyson–Spinks fight in Atlantic City. A large card was draped around his neck with the words: 'I was wrong!' And the caption to the picture read: 'All writers picking Spinks deserved to be shot. That is, if, like this writer, they weren't half shot already.'

And later when Sugar offered to send 100,000 copies of *Boxing Illustrated* to American soldiers in the Gulf War, he admitted that he didn't know whether to laugh or cry when he learned from the US Defense Force that the Saudis might consider his magazine pornographic because it showed pictures of men wearing only boxing trunks.

'All my life I've waited for someone to call me pornographic,' Sugar said in mock seriousness, 'but when I told my wife she just passed it off as one of those things that happen in this crazy world of boxing.'

Mind you, Sugar has some way to go to match the achievement of Mike Collins, publisher of a now defunct Minneapolis weekly called *Boxing Blade*. Collins, who also happened to manage an overblown lightweight named Pinky Mitchell, offered to conduct a poll among his readers to pick 'the best man in the world at 140 pounds' and to provide a $2,000 championship belt when the National Boxing Association decided to recognize the junior welterweight division in 1922.

To nobody's great surprise, Mitchell topped the voting and was officially proclaimed world champion on 15 November 1922 – the first and only time that a world champion had been crowned by a boxing publication with official support.

MANAGERS

Managers are the middle men of boxing ... or used to be. Once, they not only controlled the lives of their boxers but called the shots when it came to negotiating a fight on their behalf. However, the role of a manager has been widely challenged in the 1990s and some boxers – the most notable example was Sugar Ray Leonard – have insisted on managing themselves while others have relied on promoters like Don King, Dan Duva, Bob Arum, Mickey Duff, Barry Hearn, Frank Warren and Barney Eastwood to conduct their affairs.

'There is no room for sentimentality in the boxing jungle. The young fighter needs someone to look after his interests, both in and out of the ring, and the appointment of his mentor can make or break him. The choice of the right man must be made with the utmost care,' Gilbert Odd warned in his book *Boxing – The Inside Story*, published in 1978.

Chris Eubank, the then WBO super middleweight champion, expressed a more militant view and urged his fellow professionals to 'take charge of their own careers before it's too late' when he spoke at a dinner in London hosted by the Professional Boxers Association in 1994.

'Boxers must remember that they are the employers, and behave accordingly,' Eubank said. 'We engage managers to negotiate on our behalf and to get us the best available deal, but the contracts belong to us.

'We are the employers. We pay them 25 per cent to handle negotiations, so that we are freed from that worry and responsibility, but too often we are made to feel like the employee. If boxers don't ensure that every detail of every deal is reported back to them, they risk ending up bitter, twisted and resentful.'

Boxers, by and large, are a restless lot, and few stay with their original trainer or manager throughout their career. Former world heavyweight champion Mike Tyson fired everybody from his manager to his bucket carrier when he decided to join Don King in 1988.

And yet some boxer–manager relationships are legendary. Could

It was Jack 'Doc' Kearns who was largely responsible for making Jack Dempsey a 'million dollar fighter'. The men later became bitter enemies.

anyone imagine Jack Dempsey without Jack Kearns? Well, actress Estelle Taylor did, and persuaded her husband to sack his long-time business associate in 1926. On the other hand, François Descamps and Georges Carpentier were inseparable, as were Joe Jacobs and Max Schmeling, Pop Foster and Jimmy McLarnin, and Cus D'Amato and Floyd Patterson.

When boxing as a sport was reborn in England in the seventeenth century it was fashionable to have a patron rather than a manager. Boxers only began to acquire managers towards the end of the nineteenth century and the then British heavyweight champion Jem Smith was one of the first to appoint a manager (John Fleming) to handle his affairs in 1887.

The golden age for managers came shortly after the turn of the century and many turned out to be larger-than-life characters. Among them were men like Tom O'Rourke, Jimmy Johnston, Jack Kearns, Lou Houseman, Pete Reilly, Al Weill, Cus D'Amato and Jack Hurley.

Houseman, a Chicago sports editor, both managed boxers and promoted fights and is best remembered for creating the light heavyweight division. Houseman matched his fighter Jack Root against Kid McCoy for the vacant title at the Light Guard Amory in Detroit in 1903 and Root became the division's first champion when he won on points over ten rounds.

Kearns made Dempsey boxing's first million-dollar fighter in the 1920s and then hounded the Manassa Mauler night and day when Dempsey refused to renew his contract in 1926. A smooth-talking, debonair fellow, Kearns reeked of class but boobed badly when he arranged for Dempsey to be photographed riveting a battleship while wearing patent leather shoes in the dying days of the First World War.

Joe Jacobs, the American Jew who gave a Nazi salute while standing in a German boxing ring with a cigar in his mouth in the 1930s, was an authentic Broadway character. Jacobs knew everyone from showgirls to millionaires, gangsters to cops, politicians to promoters.

'So far as his fighters were concerned, Joe was the perfect manager,' Walter Stewart wrote in the Memphis *Commercial Appeal* when Jacobs died in 1935. 'He demanded the promoter's pound of flesh – and sliced it off or no fight.'

It was Jacobs who cried 'we wuz robbed' when Max Schmeling lost on points to Jack Sharkey for the heavyweight championship of the world in 1932, and it was Joe who hopped into the ring screaming 'foul' when Sharkey struck Schmeling low in the fourth round of their first fight in 1930.

'If anyone made a case for a fight manager as an indispensable part of the business, it was old Pop Foster,' Ted Carroll wrote in the August 1940 issue of *The Ring* magazine.

Foster, who began training Jimmy McLarnin while he was still a young boy and became the lad's legal guardian when the future world lightweight and welterweight champion turned professional in 1923, always had a stock answer to promoters who attempted to downsize his purse demands. 'James is the card,' he would say. 'He's got to be paid.'

When Foster died in 1994 he left his entire estate to McLarnin.

Jimmy McLarnin, the former world welterweight champion, had such a close relationship with his manager Pop Foster that Foster became his legal guardian.

ROCKY MARCIANO

Barney Nagler, an American journalist who did much of his best work as a columnist for the *Morning Telegraph,* always insisted that Rocky Marciano was a man nobody knew. Peter Marciano, brother of the only heavyweight champion to retire without a single defeat, surprisingly agreed.

'All of the stories ever told about my brother Rocky were always very careful to protect an image that made him an all-American boy, who never swore, never got angry and never did anything except be nice to everyone,' Peter said in 1977. 'If Rocky was like they said he was he could never have been heavyweight champ. He never would have hit anyone.'

Well, not only did Marciano hit a lot of guys, he damn near killed Carmine Vingo when he knocked him out in six rounds in Madison Square Garden in December 1949. And he almost decapitated Jersey Joe Walcott with the murderous right that sent the defending champion sagging into the ropes in the 13th round of their heavyweight title fight in September 1952.

Rocky was also rumoured to have had strange sexual hangups, to be money mad – he evidently mistrusted banks – was paranoid about his balding pate and had a reputation as one of boxing's biggest freeloaders. And yet when he died tragically in a private plane crash on 1 September 1969 the men of the media wrote the kind of obituaries about him they usually reserved for saints.

Typical was the piece Arthur Daley, the distinguished American sports columnist, wrote for the *New York Times:* 'The Rock was a man of gentleness, kindness, compassion and affability. He brought dignity to the championship he held with such modest graciousness.'

We got a better insight of the man from Chris Greyvenstein, the South African boxing historian, who accompanied Marciano on a promotional tour in the Cape in 1967. 'He did not shave regularly and he was a careless dresser,' Greyvenstein recalled in *Boxing World* magazine in July 1980. 'The suite of rooms he shared with Frank de Lucca were also unbelievably untidy and with blissful

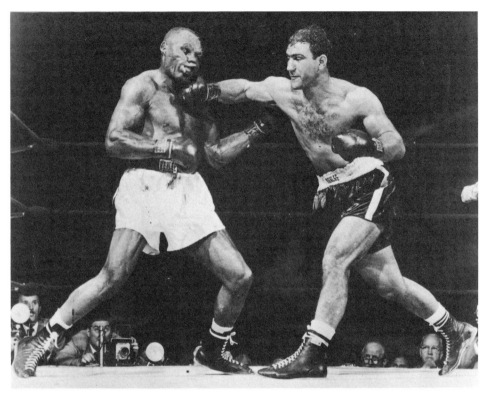

No need to measure the power of this punch as Rocky Marciano distorts the face of Jersey Joe Walcott during their world heavyweight title fight in 1952.

unconcern he received the most distinguished visitors while wearing nothing more than a pair of checkered underpants.'

But whatever his shortcomings as a man, few could fault him as a fighter. Physically, Marciano was at a disadvantage every time he stepped into a ring. Standing only five feet ten inches tall, he had the shortest reach of any heavyweight champion (only 68 inches) and next to Tommy Burns, he was also the shortest champion.

It meant that Marciano simply had to fight on the inside and to counter his lack of height, his trainer Charley Goldman persuaded him to bob and weave. 'He does so many things wrong, but I'm scared to change him much because I might take away what he's got,' Goldman once told a reporter.

Fortunately Marciano was a workaholic when it came to training.

He often spent three months at a time training for his big fights at Grossinger's while living in an old farmhouse on the edge of the airstrip. He hardly ever saw his family. 'That's the price I have to pay,' he would say.

Rocky always believed that his fight against Rex Layne in July 1951 was the turning point of his career. 'He was the strongest man I ever fought,' he said. 'There were times early on when he pushed me around as if I was a kid, but he tired quickly, and I got to know him with a good right hand. After I stopped Layne, people began to take me seriously.'

Knockout victories over Joe Louis, Lee Savold and Harry Matthews followed before Marciano challenged Walcott for the heavyweight championship of the world in Philadelphia on 23 September 1952.

Rocky Marciano (below right) and Roland LaStarza square up at the weigh-in for their world heavyweight title fight in 1953.

Behind on points going into the 13th round, Marciano unloaded what he later claimed was the best right-hand punch he ever landed in the ring.

'When I hit Walcott he just seemed to disappear in front of me and I really didn't quite know what had happened. Then, when I got to a neutral corner and turned around to see him dangling over the bottom rope, I just prayed he'd stay down for the count.'

Rocky defended the title six times. All except the first fight with Ezzard Charles – 'the man was as quick as a snake' – ended in knockout victories for 'The Rock'. And then, seven months after he had kayoed Archie Moore on 21 September 1955 he announced his retirement from the ring.

'I got worried about all those cuts around my eyes,' he explained. 'I dreaded going blind and I was also having a lot of pains in my back. And let's face it, I had seen too many good fighters making the mistake of hanging in there too long, having that one fight too many.'

Several attempts were made to get Marciano to change his mind.

Rocky once turned down an offer of $2 million to make a comeback. Instead, he remains the only heavyweight champion of the world to retire undefeated with 49 wins and no losses.

MEASUREMENTS

A boxer's vital statistics can look mighty impressive with all those detailed measurements of biceps, ankles, thighs, forearms and the rest. In fact, the first time I saw a tale of the tape, I was completely awed.

It listed the physical measurements of all the world heavyweight champions, and after checking the table I was convinced that Jess Willard and Primo Carnera must have been unbeatable. Their measurements suggested that they were little short of giants. Willard stood a lofty six feet six and one half inches while Carnera had an incredible reach of 85½ inches and a chest of 48 inches.

Mind you, I was only 12 years old at the time, so how was I to know that it's a boxer's ability, not his physique, that really counts in a fight.

Jim Jacobs, the American boxing manager who used to mastermind the career of Mike Tyson, once told me how uptight he had become after reading and hearing about Thomas Hearns's 'reach advantage' and 'height advantage' before his fight with Marvin Hagler.

'I'm always amazed at television announcers who tell their audience that so-and-so has a height advantage or a reach advantage,' Jacobs said. 'It has to be one of the most inane observations. It presumes that boxing history supports the concept that long-arm fighters win. Or, even more asinine, that the taller fighter usually wins.

'In my opinion, after watching a few thousand fights, the reason a fighter wins is because he has an *ability* advantage.'

Jacobs could have added that great fighters are not handicapped by their physical measurements; they invariably tailor their style to make the most of what they've got. Rocky Marciano's reach of 68 inches looks silly when compared to Willard's 83 or Carnera's 85½, but no one in his right mind would suggest that Willard or Carnera were better fighters than Marciano.

In his prime, Joe Louis seldom weighed more than 200 pounds but is there really anyone out there who believes that Louis would have been at a grave disadvantage against blubberweights like Greg Page, Tony Tubbs, Tim Witherspoon or Trevor Berbick?

If boxers were entering a Mr Universe competition instead of a ring, perhaps the tale of the tape would have some relevance. But despite the fascination many fans seem to have with the measurements of fighters, the figures are mostly meaningless.

I once asked Angelo Dundee, the American trainer, what advice he would give to a dwarf if he wanted to become a boxer. 'I'd tell him to get down lower,' Dundee said. 'That way he would be even harder to hit.'

I can think of several fighters who defied the laws of nature by making the most of their physical 'handicaps'. The immortal Jimmy Wilde, an early flyweight champion of the world, was one. Wilde looked like a walking skeleton when he stripped for action – his nickname was 'The Ghost with a Hammer in his Hand' – but once the bell rang he became a juggernaut in the ring. Where his punching power came from, goodness only knows, but he could take a man out with one blow — and often did.

So what if Tommy Burns stood only five feet seven inches; he was a world champion, wasn't he? And who cares that Carnera's waist measurement was 38 inches and the biggest ever for a heavyweight? The bum couldn't fight. The next time someone starts talking about a fighter's reach advantage or height advantage, tell him to check on the man's ability. He might find it doesn't measure up after all.

MEDIA

For more than 300 years boxing and the press have enjoyed a love–hate relationship. In fact, it would be fair to say that without the printed word, boxing as a sport would have remained in limbo when it died in AD 500.

On the other hand, editors discovered a long time ago that nothing increases circulation like a big fight. Pierce Egan, an early English sportswriter and boxing's first historian, drew attention to the fact in the eighteenth century.

Writing in his publication *Boxiana*, Egan observed that 'the most fashionable daily newspaper of the day has enjoyed a happy increase in sales' because of its coverage of the fights between Richard Humphreys and Daniel Mendoza. Mind you, big fights had been reported in print long before Humphreys and Mendoza began their series of bareknuckle bouts in 1787.

Prize-fighting, as boxing was then called, first caught the attention of the print media when James Figg reached the height of his fame.

A number of publications, including the *Daily Courant*, the *Tatler*, the *Spectator* and the *Guardian* began to carry items on boxing in their pages.

The *New York Clipper*, an early American tabloid, covered prize-fighting on a regular basis. The *Clipper* even published a column called 'The Ring' in which boxing news and even boxing items for sale were listed. A number of other publications also played an important role in the development of boxing in the United States.

Richard K Fox used his *Police Gazette* to make the sport one of the most popular in the United States before the turn of the century. Fox, who started the custom of presenting championship belts, is also remembered for his well-publicized feud with John L Sullivan, the last bareknuckle heavyweight champion.

But the media could work both for or against the sport, as was proved when Chicago newspapers led an attack on boxing following the alleged fake fight between Joe Gans and Terry McGovern in December 1900. Within two years the sport had been banned in the state of Illinois but, ironically, it was the *Chicago Tribune* that came to the rescue of boxing some 20 years later, when it sponsored the first ever Golden Gloves amateur tournament.

Sportswriters Walter Eckersall and Arch Ward were both instrumental in getting boxing unbanned in the state, and as sports editor of the *Tribune*, Ward went on to give the Golden Gloves international status.

More than anyone else, Jack London, the famous author and newspaperman, was responsible for triggering the 'White Hope Era' of boxing in calling for Jim Jeffries to come out of retirement to beat black heavyweight champion Jack Johnson in December 1908. London covered the heavyweight title fight between Johnson and Tommy Burns in Sydney, Australia, for the *New York Herald* and his lurid report was enough to stir any racist.

The *Herald* led London's ringside report with one of the longest headlines in the history of the newspaper business: 'Jack London Says Johnson Made a Noise Like a Lullaby with His Fists as He Tucked Burns in His Little Crib in Sleepy Hollow, with a Laugh.'

'The fight! There was no fight! No Armenian massacre could compare with the hopeless slaughter that took place in the Sydney stadium today,' London wrote. 'It was not a case of "Too Much Johnson", but of all Johnson. A golden smile tells the story, and a golden smile was Johnson's.'

After describing how Johnson humiliated the white champion and taunted Burns with 'an exaggerated English accent', London ended his report with an appeal. 'But one thing remains, Jeffries must emerge from his alfalfa farm and remove that golden smile from Johnson's face,' London wrote, then added: 'Jeff, it's up to you.'

'Nix, nothing doing,' was Jeffries's reply in a report from Los Angeles printed at the foot of the page. Another report from St Paul, Minnesota, headed 'John L Is Not Surprised' quoted Sullivan as saying 'the fight came out very much as I expected'. The old bareknuckle champion claimed that 'the negro can't assume the title, for the present day bouts cannot truly be styled prize-fights'. He was wrong, of course.

But if London was guilty of stirring race riots across the United States with his emotional appeal, New York boxing writers – Bat Masterson of the *Morning Telegraph*, Bill McGeehan of the *Tribune* and Charles F Mathison of the *Telegram* – were largely responsible for conducting a campaign that led to the sport being legalized in the state under the Walker Law of 1920.

'To Charlie Mathison, the Walker Law represented the salvation of boxing. He wrote the first draft of the law. He was one of its most enthusiastic advocates, and was the chief of staff of those who aided in drawing up the code of rules embodied in the measure,' Nat Fleischer said in 1941.

It was also a group of New York boxing writers who helped promoter Mike Jacobs and his Twentieth Century Sporting Club gain control of boxing in the state in the 1930s. They were Edward Frayne, sports editor of the *New York American*, Bill Farnsworth, sports editor of the *New York Journal* and Damon Runyon, a Hearst newspaper columnist for 30 years.

An article in the *New York World Telegram* of 13 August 1938 announced in a banner headline: 'Mike Jacobs admits Hearst writers share in boxing swag.'

The article claimed that in closing a new five-year contract with Madison Square Garden Corporation, Jacobs had paid one of the writers $25,000 for his 25 per cent share in the Twentieth Century Sporting Club. According to the report, the other writers had drawn their share after the Louis–Schmeling fight, leaving Jacobs as the sole king of American boxing.

Nearly 60 years later, the print media continues to snipe at promoters like Don King and Bob Arum and the so-called sanctioning bodies who control the sport, but with little apparent success – and probably because the major television networks around the world are happy with the present arrangement and the countless titles the sanctioning bodies have created.

American superstar Oscar de la Hoya is adept at handling the media.

MONEY

Hardly a year goes by in which boxers are not among the top money-makers in sport. In fact, in 1989 no fewer than six of the top ten money-makers in sport were boxers, proving yet again – as if proof were necessary – that boxing is the sport of big bucks.

But never forget that it was Muhammad Ali who triggered the megabuck era in boxing. It was Ali who broke the news that the government of Zaire would pay George Foreman and himself a total of $10 million to contest the heavyweight championship of the world in 1974.

Ali was in Venezuela to commentate for TV on the fight between Foreman and Ken Norton when he let the news slip. There was a touch of excitement in his husky voice as he delivered the following

Cassius Clay (aka Muhammad Ali), the man who made multi-million dollar purses commonplace in boxing. This picture was taken in 1964, before he won the world heavyweight title.

message with bated breath to the millions watching around the world: 'George Foreman and I have just been offered $5 million apiece – which is unbelievable – by the government of Zaire, formerly the Belgian Congo.

'And if Foreman can win this fight tonight – which I don't think he will – he will have to defend his title against me in the CON-GO!'

If the initial reaction of most television viewers was one of scepticism, they could be forgiven. After all, it was only three years previously that Ali and Joe Frazier were each paid a record purse of $2.5 million for their 'Fight of the Champions' in Madison Square Garden.

And considering that it took promoters 44 years to double the $1 million Gene Tunney received for beating Jack Dempsey in 1927, could the astronomical amounts paid to Ali and Frazier be doubled after a mere three years? The answer, of course, was yes.

Moreover, only eight years later the purses paid to Ali and Foreman for their 'Rumble in the Jungle' were to be doubled yet again. It happened in Las Vegas in 1982 when Larry Holmes and Gerry Cooney were each guaranteed a minimum of $10 million for their World Boxing Council heavyweight title fight.

Sportswriters in the 1920s were fond of describing Jack Dempsey as 'that million-dollar fighter', but Dempsey's entire ring earnings amounted to no more than $3.5 million. Jack's biggest purse was the $717,000 he received for his first fight with Gene Tunney in Philadelphia in 1926.

Mind you, the value of the dollar in the 1920s was much higher than it is in the 1990s. Inflation has dealt currencies a blow from which they will never recover. But even after making adjustments for inflation, many of the biggest purses paid in the past simply do not compare with the present.

Compared with the $13 million Sugar Ray Leonard got for each of his first two fights with Roberto Duran and Thomas Hearns, old-timers like Tunney and Joe Louis were probably short-changed. It was Ali who first made million-dollar purses seem commonplace in big-time boxing. Between 1971 and 1978, Ali took part in fifteen fights, each of which paid a million dollars or more in purse money.

Sports Illustrated gave its American readers a glimpse of things to come in 1964 when it published a picture of Ali in a bank vault with a million dollars at his feet. Taken before Ali became champion of the world, the picture was amazingly prophetic.

Fifty-eight years earlier, Tex Rickard had used a similar gimmick to clinch the first fight he ever promoted between Battling Nelson and Joe Gans in Goldfield, Nevada. Rickard had agreed to pay Nelson $20,000 – a fabulous purse in those days – and had wired confirmation that the money would be transferred to a bank in Salt Lake City or San Francisco.

Nelson could hardly believe his luck. 'Hold money,' he wired back. 'Am taking next train to Goldfield.'

When Nelson arrived in the tin-shanty mining town, Rickard had a surprise for him. Tex had taken $30,000 in gold pieces (the total amount of the two purses) and piled it up in the window of the local bank. When Nelson saw all that gold he could hardly take his eyes off it. He looked at it from every angle and was immediately sold on Rickard's proposition to fight Gans in Goldfield.

Inflation aside, the real reason why boxing has entered the age of megabucks is because marketing techniques have changed. Closed-circuit television, satellite transmission and pay-per-view TV in the United States and elsewhere have all increased the size of the viewing audience enormously.

Casino boxing has also contributed to the great rise in earnings. Millions, billions, trillions of dollars – that's what boxing has brought to Las Vegas, probably the gambling capital of the western world. 'Boxing transcends the sport and becomes a social event,' Alan Feldman, Mirage Resorts Inc vice-president of public relations, told the Las Vegas *Review-Journal* in 1994.

'Of all the events we do during the course of the year – with the exception of Barbra Streisand's concerts – none compares to boxing in terms of bringing in top-end gaming customers,' said Dennis Finfrock, MGM Grand Arena and Special Event vice-president.

'Let's get this straight,' said George Foreman before his heavyweight title fight with Axel Schulz in Las Vegas in 1995. 'The reason I'm in boxing is not because of the money part of it ... the money part of it ... the money part of it ... Somebody slap me on the back, I seem to be stuck.'

The money part of it is huge, and no one knew that better than Foreman. And besides, it was the money part of it that gave Foreman a reason to make a comeback in the first place. Clearly, the price of glory has become a price well worth paying.

MONUMENTS

Monuments are the most lasting tribute a sport can have and in this respect the sport of boxing has been well served. Many of boxing's monuments are housed in famous museums but many others can be found in the most unlikely places – ranging from a cemetery in Brisbane, Australia to an Olde World Pub in Kilcullen, County Kildare; from the cloisters of Westminster Abbey in London to a modern downtown shopping mall in Louisville, Kentucky.

Some of the earliest artefacts can be seen in national museums, such as the British Museum in London or the Terme Museum in Rome. A case in point is a vase depicting ancient Greek boxers (c. 600 BC) which is housed in the British Museum, while a lifesize bronze statue of Cleitomachus, a Roman heavyweight, who won the boxing at the 141st Olympic Games in 216 BC, is on display in the Terme Museum.

A figure of a Graeco-Roman boxer in fighting pose can be seen in the Atkins Museum in Kansas City, and a commemorative stone for John Broughton, the so-called 'Father of Boxing', who drafted what became known as Broughton's Rules in 1743, still exists in the floor of Westminster Abbey.

Impressive gravestones, modest plaques, historical markers and eye-catching statues are scattered throughout the world in homage to great fighters of long ago.

A sculpture of the legendary lightweight Joe Gans by Mahonri V Young used to stand in the entrance to Madison Square Garden in New York, and an historical marker on Half-mile pier in Mississippi

City commemorates the famous bareknuckle fight between John L Sullivan and Paddy Ryan in 1882. 'It ushered in the era of big-time prize-fighting. It caught the imagination,' said James Stevens, president of the Mississippi Historical Society in 1982.

Graveyards are also littered with monuments, from the impressive edifice erected in honour of old-time Australian heavyweight Peter Jackson, which still stands in Toowong Cemetery in Brisbane, Australia, to the haughty lion which stands atop Tom Cribb's monument, overlooking the Woolwich Ferry in London.

Perhaps the most poignant is the monument erected to 'Nonpareil' Jack Dempsey, whose burial site in Mount Calvary Cemetery in Portland, Oregon, was neglected until 1904 (eight years after his death).

It took a poem called 'The Nonpareil's Grave', written by M J McMahon, to trigger a public subscription drive that resulted in an imposing monument being erected. The last stanza of the poem, possibly the most famous in boxing, reads as follows:

> Oh, Fame, why sleeps thy favored son
> In wilds, in woods, in weeds,
> And shall he ever thus sleep on,
> Interred his valiant deeds?
> 'Tis strange New York should thus forget
> Its 'bravest of the brave'
> And in the fields of Oregon,
> Unmarked, leave Dempsey's grave.

More bizarre is the shrivelled and blackened right arm of Dan Donnelly, Ireland's greatest bareknuckle fighter, which rests in a glass case in The Hideout, an old pub in Kilcullen, County Kildare. Donnelly was reputed to have had the longest arms in the history of pugilism.

'It's said he could button his knee britches without stooping! You don't believe it? Well pay a visit to The Hideout in Kilcullen and see for yourself,' is the invitation extended to potential visitors by the Byrne family, present owners of the restaurant-museum.

Further south in Helston, Cornwall, stands the little stone cottage

Peter Jackson, the legendary Australian heavyweight, whose monument still stands in a graveyard in Brisbane.

in which Bob Fitzsimmons, the former world heavyweight champion, was born. The cottage, though thatched, is part of a row of terraced houses and plans are afoot to turn it into a museum. Fitzsimmons was born there on 26 May 1863 and there is a plaque above the front door which reads: ROBERT FITZSIMONS [name misspelt] CHAMPION OF THE WORLD 1897. BORN HERE IN 1863. PRESENTED IN 1937 BY A.W. WESTON ESQ.

Museums, whether devoted to an individual or to the sport in general, are now the in-thing. Among the best are the World Boxing Council Museum of Boxing in Mexico City; the International Boxing Hall of Fame in Canastota, New York; and the Jack Dempsey Museum in Manassa, Colorado. A Muhammad Ali Museum was launched in a downtown Louisville shopping mall in 1995.

The WBC Museum was opened in 1986 and is part of a complex with exhibits of other professional sports. The WBC claim the museum is unique and that there is no other like it in the world. In 1988 the WBC, in conjunction with the Mexico City Council, unveiled a beautiful sculpture in tribute to boxers. The statue of the boxer, his right arm raised towards the sky, is situated on Reforma Avenue, one of the most attractive and longest streets in Mexico City.

The Jack Dempsey Museum consists of a small frame and stucco house, originally built in 1880, and declared a monument in 1966. Adjacent to the museum is Jack Dempsey Park with a huge billboard depicting Dempsey in a fighting pose and the words: 'Home of Manassa Mauler – Jack Dempsey'. The one-room museum is filled with photographs, newspaper cuttings, the gloves Dempsey wore when he knocked out Luis Firpo and the shoes he used in the Gene Tunney fight. Admission is free but the museum is closed during the winter months.

Although no specific museum has been established for Joe Louis, the legendary 'Brown Bomber' and former world heavyweight champion, several busts and statues have been unveiled in his honour in the United States.

There is a statue of Louis in the entrance to Caesar's Palace in Las Vegas, a bust in Madison Square Garden in New York and two very impressive monuments in Joe's home town of Detroit.

Standing 12 feet tall and set on a marble base, a statue of Louis has been erected in front of Cobo Hall. A bronzed boxing glove Louis wore in the 1938 fight with Max Schmeling is displayed in a glass case next to the statue. At the push of a button, visitors can hear the radio commentary of the fight and the post-fight interview with Louis.

A giant 24-foot black fist and forearm of bronze was unveiled in the heart of Detroit in honour of Louis in 1986. The clenched fist swings from a pyramid frame in the centre of Jefferson Avenue and points across Hart Plaza towards the Detroit River.

MOUTHGUARDS

California can take credit for a number of innovative changes in boxing including the introduction sof the automatic timekeeper, a wider interpretation of the technical decision rule, and the compulsory use of mouthguards.

As American heavyweight Bert Cooper learned to his cost in his fight with Jeremy Williams at the Grand Olympic Auditorium in Los Angeles, in June 1994, if a boxer cannot keep his mouthpiece where it belongs, he runs the risk of disqualification under California rules.

Williams, who was leading on points on all the judges' scorecards, was 48 seconds into the seventh round when Cooper lost his mouthguard for the sixth time in the fight and was disqualified by referee Robert Byrd.

And yet, 80 years before, when British boxer Ted 'Kid' Lewis became the first fighter to wear a mouthpiece in an American ring, the practice was frowned upon. Lewis, who had begun using the mouthguard on a regular basis about a year earlier, found himself in frequent arguments with his opponents, referees and boxing officials.

As a boxer, Lewis invariably suffered torn lips because of his irregular teeth, which is why he decided to start using a mouthpiece in 1913. Until Lewis asked a dentist to make him one, boxers usually placed orange or lemon peel between their lips and teeth for protection.

The modern mouthguard was invented by Jack Marks, a London dentist, in 1902. However, mouthguards are known to have been used by the ancient Hellenic boxers about 1200 BC.

Research has shown that mouthguards do far more than simply protect the teeth. Manufactured from elastic, shock-absorbent material, mouthguards reduce injuries to the lips, tongue and cheek and also reduce much of the force that may be felt from a blow to the face or head.

In 1989, both the New York and New Jersey State Athletic Commissions adopted a mouthpiece rule similar to that in existence in California. It was decided that if a fighter's gumshield came out of his mouth during a round, the referee should stop the action, rinse the shield and replace it.

In 1993, the World Boxing Council made this rule mandatory in all WBC title fights and, as a result of research, developed a mouthpiece that offered even more protection and lessened the impact to the brain of blows to the head.

MOVIES

Whether art imitates life or life imitates art is debatable but few will deny that as an art form the movies have influenced a great many people since the turn of the century.

American junior welterweight Vinny Pazienza admitted as much when he claimed that he began boxing after watching the first *Rocky* movie. 'Now when I look at that damn movie, I don't know what made me do it,' Pazienza said in 1991. 'The guy takes a beating every fight and he can't put two syllables together.'

Few would rate the *Rocky* films as among the greatest of all time, but Pazienza's confession underlines the influence the cinema has had on the sport.

'Millions and millions of movie fans in the world during the entire history of the silver screen have cried, suffered and enjoyed boxing through the performances of some of the most beloved and greatest movie stars in history; filling our hearts with nostalgia and a deep respect and love for this noble sport,' the World Boxing Council acknowledged in 1994.

Sure enough, ever since Jimmy Clabby became the first boxer to appear in a movie in 1914 – *The Kidnapped Pugilist* produced by Carl Laemmle – there has been a certain buzz about boxing and the film industry. In fact, more movies have been made about boxers and boxing than any other sport.

In the early days of the cinema, the British produced some outstanding films based on Pierce Egan's stories of life in old London. Arguably the greatest was *The Call of the Road*, which dramatized the lives of some of the bareknuckle champions and was shot in Epping Forest on the very sites of the original fights.

Charlie Chaplin and Buster Keaton, immortal comedians of the silent films, used their genius for mime and control of movement to make wonderfully funny films with a boxing theme. Chaplin's *The Knockout* (1914) and *The Champion* (1915), and Keaton's *Battling Butler* (1924), set the tone for the many boxing comedies that were to follow with talented performers like Harold Lloyd (*The Milky*

Rocky (Sylvester Stallone) throws a punishing left at Clubber Lang (Mr T) in their title fight in *Rocky III*, an MGM/United Artists release.

Way), Danny Kaye (*A Kid from Brooklyn*), Ryan O'Neal (*The Main Event*) and Elliot Gould (*Matilda*).

But boxing is a serious business and the sport has best been served in dramatic movies – even those that have concentrated on the seedier side of the fight game – and this despite a tendency in the early days of cinema to cast well-known boxers in the leading roles.

Clabby's success in *The Kidnapped Pugilist* led to Kid McCoy playing the part of an 'opponent' in the D W Griffith classic *Broken Blossoms* (1919). Mind you, McCoy was a born actor and had earlier won high praise for his role as a detective in *The House of Glass*, which was released in 1917.

Among the many boxers to star in films were Jess Willard (*The Heart Punch* and *The Challenge of Chance*), James J Corbett (*The Midnight Man*), Jack Johnson (*False Nobility*), Victor MacLaglen (*The Informer*), Gene Tunney (*The Fighting Marine*), Jack Dempsey (*The Idol of Millions*), Billy Conn (*The Pittsburgh Kid*), Archie Moore (*Huckleberry Finn*), Muhammad Ali (*The Greatest*) and Max Baer and Primo Carnera in the 1933 MGM release *The Prizefighter and the Lady*.

Jack Dempsey also appeared in *The Prizefighter and the Lady* as a referee. Carnera was then the heavyweight champion of the world and his handlers insisted that he had to 'win' his fight with Baer in the movie. After much argument a compromise was reached whereby the 'fight' would end in a draw.

A year later Baer challenged Carnera for the title in Madison Square Garden Bowl in Long Island and won on a technical knockout in the 11th round after flooring the Italian 11 times.

Over the years many critics have been invited to rate the ten best boxing movies of all time, and although the order of merit is inclined to change from one critic to another, the same ten titles are invariably listed.

The Set-Up, starring Robert Ryan, Audrey Trotter and George Tobias and released by RKO in 1949, usually features somewhere near the top of the list, if not always in the number one slot. The movie tells of 72 minutes in the life of Stoker Thompson, a 35-year-old has-been heavyweight matched with the local hero in a small, dingy town. The running time of the film is also *exactly* 72 minutes, in other words, it is done in what is termed 'real time' and the viewer is reminded of this by the opening and closing shots of a clock.

Ryan, who was the heavyweight champion of Dartmouth University before he became an actor, is very comfortable in the fight scenes and gives a marvellous performance as the washed-up boxer.

Also near the top in most of the ten best lists is *Champion*, released by United Artists in 1949, and starring Kirk Douglas and Arthur Kennedy. In many respects *Champion* is similar to *Body and Soul*, which was released by United Artists two years earlier and which starred John Garfield and Lilli Palmer. Both are excellent boxing movies even though the fight sequences are, as usual, over-exaggerated.

Requiem for a Heavyweight and *Fat City* both tell the story of has-been boxers. *Requiem*, released by Columbia in 1962, starred Anthony Quinn, Jackie Gleason and Mickey Rooney, while *Fat City* (released by Columbia in 1972) features Stacy Keach and Jeff Bridges. The well-known American film critic Rex Reed praised the film for its 'splendid atmosphere and stunning performances'.

Most film critics agree that the first *Rocky* film, which won the Oscar for best picture in 1976, deserved all the praise it got. Starring Sylvester Stallone, Talia Shire, Burt Young and Carl Weathers, the message of the film was that the underdog can win. According to Desmond Ryan, the movie critic of the *Philadelphia Inquirer*, it was 'an entertaining, self-contained story of broad appeal'.

The four sequels that followed lacked the original impact, largely because they were no more than variations on the original theme.

A number of movies have been based on the lives of famous fighters and most have been huge successes at the box office. The first featured Errol Flynn in the title role of *Gentleman Jim*, a highly glamorized film biography of James J Corbett. Released by Warner Brothers in 1942, it was an extremely successful film with the flamboyant Flynn giving a breezy, confident portrayal of the first heavyweight champion of the glove era.

The success of *Gentleman Jim* led to the production of a film on the life of John L Sullivan, the last bareknuckle heavyweight champion. *The Great John L* was released by United Artists in 1945 and starred Greg McClure, Linda Darnell and Barbara Britton. Unfortunately Bing Crosby, who financed the film, made the mistake of selecting a colourless muscleman called McClure for the main role and neither he nor the scriptwriters were up to the task.

A low budget production called *The Joe Louis Story*, which was released by United Artists in 1953 and featured boxer Coley Wallace in the role of Louis, was equally bad. *The Harder They Fall* (released by Columbia in 1956) and loosely based on the life-story of Primo Carnera was not much better. It turned out to be Humphrey Bogart's last film and also starred Rod Steiger, Jan Sterling and Max Baer.

A far better movie was *The Great White Hope*, released by Twentieth Century-Fox in 1970, with James Earl Jones playing the role of Jack Johnson, the first black man to win the heavyweight championship of the world. 'James Earl Jones and Jane Alexander were terrific,' says Rex Reed, 'but the movie was a flop at the box office.'

Muhammad Ali's attempt to play himself in *The Greatest*, released by Columbia in 1977, was the only notable thing about the movie. Reviewing the film for the New York *Daily News*, Phil Pepe added a personal postscript: 'There's only one thing, and you're not going to

Muhammad Ali and Mira Waters in a scene from *The Greatest* in which Ali played himself and Ms Waters portrayed Ruby Sanderson.

like this, Muhammad. I know you're not going to believe it. But if I were you, I wouldn't count on adding an Oscar to your collection of trophies.'

Next to *Gentleman Jim*, the best boxing biography on film was arguably *Somebody Up There Likes Me*, the story of former world middleweight champion Rocky Graziano. Starring Paul Newman and Pier Angeli, the movie was released by MGM in 1957. Director Robert Wise was also responsible for *The Set-Up*. Newman was superb as Rocky.

Monkey on My Back, which was released by United Artists in the same year, was based on the life-story of Barney Ross. However, it was poorly marketed and virtually sank without trace.

Shot in stark black and white at a time when colour was fashionable, *Raging Bull* was considered the number one movie of the 1980s by many American film critics. The biography of former world middleweight champion Jake LaMotta, the film starred Robert De Niro and was directed by Martin Scorsese.

'De Niro, who deservedly won an Oscar for his stunning performance completely convinces the viewer of the authenticity of his portrayal but fails to promote any sympathy for the character,' said Chris Greyvenstein in *Boxing World* magazine.

'I don't think *Raging Bull* was remotely equalled in the 1980s for its blending of performance, photography, music and editing,' said Mike Clark in *USA Today*. Other respected film critics like Gene Siskel, Roger Ebert and Richard Shickel agreed, and both *American Film* and *Premiere* magazines declared *Raging Bull* the decade's number one movie.

'How often do you find out so much about a man's life in one film?' asked Ebert. 'It's such a compelling psychological portrait. Movies like this make *Batman* look almost transparent.'

Well, yes and no.

Yes, the film was a critically acclaimed success. But no, the man it portrayed later had second thoughts about its true worth. LaMotta claimed afterwards that the movie not only misrepresented his life, but showed him trying to play comedy very badly. 'I want people to know I ain't that bad,' LaMotta told me in 1988. 'I'm still trying to get them to do a sequel to put things right.'

Fat chance. The film portrayed LaMotta as a tinpot hoodlum and now that it has become an icon of sorts, that's the way it is going to stay.

MUSIC

It is surprising how many fighters have thought of themselves as singers. Among the more notable were Sugar Ray Robinson, Lionel Rose, Joe Frazier and Larry Holmes. Robinson, the former world welterweight and middleweight champion, even travelled to Paris in the 1950s to do a song-and-dance number at a night club in the French capital. Fortunately, Robinson later went back to doing what he did best – boxing.

However, former WBC strawweight champion Napa Kiatwanchai actually gave up the chance to regain the world title in 1990 to concentrate on a singing career. Smart Payakarun, another Thai boxer with movie-star looks, became a popular singer in his homeland after losing his WBC junior featherweight title in 1988.

Others have done the odd recording. British junior lightweight Jim McDonnell made a record entitled 'Feel No Pain' in 1990, while former world bantamweight champion Lionel Rose put out a record called 'I Thank You' that sold over 50,000 copies in Australia. Barry McGuigan, a former WBA featherweight champion, sang 'Somebody To Call My Girl' on BBC television in 1987, and two boxing songs entitled 'Barry Michael' and 'The Ballad of Dave Sands' were marketed in Australia on a country and western label in the 1980s.

Both 'The Kid's Last Fight', based on the famous boxing poem, and 'Eye of the Tiger', from the popular *Rocky* movies, became worldwide hits when they were released in the 1940s and 1970s respectively. And nor is it generally known that before he turned to writing music, Frederick Loewe of *Brigadoon*, *My Fair Lady* and *Camelot* fame tried his hand at professional boxing. Luckily for the world of music, Loewe decided to stick to writing melodies.

There is even an opera with a boxing theme. Commissioned by the Swedish Royal Opera House in 1990, novelist Torbjorn Savfe wrote the libretto for an opera based on the boxing career of popular Swedish heavyweight Harry Persson, who went to the United States in 1926 in the hope of winning the world title. 'He was the victim of con tricks,' says Savfe.

Balladeer Bob Dylan gave American middleweight Rubin Carter a touch of immortality when he described Carter's plight – the boxer was serving three life sentences for three murders he did not commit – in the hit song 'Hurricane' in 1975.

Rob Stoner, who was the bass player and arranger for the hit song, released an album of his own in 1980 called *Patriotic Duty*. One of the songs on the album was entitled 'What Round Is This?' with the following lyrics:

> Take me to a neutral corner baby
> Don't count me out
> I might be dizzy
> But I know just what I'm talking about
>
> Moving to the champ's tax bracket
> Wasn't my main concern
> All I ever wanted from you, baby
> Was a chance to take my turn
>
> Somebody tell me what round this is
> Will it ever be over with?
> You can knock me out
> 'Cause you know what love's about

Several years later rock singer Warren Zevon released an album that included an opus called 'Boom Boom Mancini' (about you know what, and you know who).

Seven years after making his debut as a singer in the Rainbow Room in New York, Joe Frazier joined Larry Holmes on the stage of the Copa Room at the Sands Hotel in Atlantic City in 1987 in what the hotel billed as 'The Battle of the Singing Heavyweight Champs'.

Holmes took the opportunity to protest in song about the loss of his IBF heavyweight title to Michael Spinks in 1986. The lyrics of the rap song went something like this:

> I trained real hard to do the job,
> Then beat the man and I got robbed.
> Yeah, won that fight.
>
> Everybody knows I beat Spinks,
> Everybody knows boxing stinks.
> Yeah, won that fight.

NO CONTEST

There was a time when a 'no contest' meant exactly that, either because the referee had decided to pull the plug as neither contestant was honestly trying, or because the circumstances were such that the fight couldn't possibly continue. Not any more. Nowadays the term has been widened to include all manner of decisions.

A case in point was the IBF bantamweight title fight between defending champion Orlando Canizales and South African challenger Derrick Whiteboy in Houston, Texas, on 20 June 1993. Referee Bobby Gonzales stopped the fight in the third round and declared it a 'no contest' when a clash of heads opened a severe cut on the champion's left eye. Later the decision was changed to 'no decision', but a technical draw might have been more appropriate.

Even more perplexing was the decision of the New Jersey State Athletic Commission to declare the heavyweight fight between

Riddick Bowe and Buster Mathis Jr a 'no contest' after Bowe had struck Mathis with a right to the jaw while Mathis was in a half-kneeling position on the canvas.

It happened in the fourth round of their fight in Atlantic City on 13 August 1994. At first it looked as though referee Arthur Mercante had decided to disqualify Bowe for committing a foul, but Commission chairman Larry Hazzard entered the ring before Mercante rendered a decision and after much discussion the fight was declared a 'no contest'. How or why remains a mystery.

And yet Rule 346 of the California State Athletic Commission clearly describes the circumstances under which a fight can be declared a 'no contest':

> ... where the referee decides that the contestants are not honestly competing, that the knockdown is a 'dive', or the foul a prearranged termination of the bout, he shall not finish the knockdown count or disqualify for fouling or render a decision, but shall stop the bout not later than before the end of the last round and order purses of both boxers held pending investigation and disposition of the funds by the commission. The announcer or referee shall inform the audience that no decision has been rendered.

NO-FOUL RULE

Even today, there are those who insist that it was hardly sporting to legalize a punch below the belt. The British still cannot accept the idea. 'We do not have such a rule in British boxing and, to the best of our knowledge, we do not intend to bring one in,' said John Morris, general secretary of the British Boxing Board of Control, when asked to clarify the position.

And yet the introduction of the no-foul rule by the New York State Athletic Commission in 1930 was a life-saver for boxing. The 'foul' epidemic had reached a peak. Fighters were falling over themselves to win the easy way. Others were deliberately hitting low to lose their fights and win huge bets for themselves and their gambling friends.

The last straw came on the night of 12 June 1930 when Max Schmeling won the world heavyweight title while lying on the canvas in the fourth round of his championship fight with Jack Sharkey in New York.

'Schmeling was writhing in pain, helpless, incapacitated by an illegal punch, and had to be carried to his corner,' James P Dawson reported in the *New York Times*. 'Sharkey was signalled quickly to his corner in the uproar, and for the minute's rest between rounds the confusion held sway.'

Referee Jim Crowley was in a quandary. Neither he nor judge

Max Schmeling is the only heavyweight to win the world title on a foul.

Charles F Mathison had seen the blow. But judge Harold Barnes had – and it was Barnes who confirmed that the punch was low.

Schmeling became the first man to win the world heavyweight title on a foul and the New York State Athletic Commission moved quickly to make sure that he would be the last. Less than three weeks later the NYSAC adopted the no-foul rule.

Discrediting the idea that fouls had become the rule rather than the exception, New York chairman James A Farley disclosed at a press conference that of 1,500 matches held in the state during the first six months of 1930, only 22 had ended in fouls. Even so, the spate of disqualifications in major fights had threatened the very future of boxing in the United States and clearly something had to be done.

Fortunately, a man called Taylor, inevitably nicknamed 'Foulproof Taylor' by the sportswriters of the time, had already come up with a solution to the problem. Taylor had perfected a foul-proof cup, made in his Brooklyn cellar of sponge rubber and aluminium, which he claimed would protect a man against any low blow.

Mind you, when Taylor first exhibited his protector he was dismissed as something of a mental case. Dressed in a white sweater across which was written 'Foulproof Taylor', the proud inventor had picketed the offices of the boxing commission and sports editors without much success.

It took the Sharkey–Schmeling fight to convince the sceptics that Taylor was on to a good thing. Lew Eskin, the well-known American referee and former editor of *Boxing Illustrated*, remembers meeting Taylor when he was a young man hanging around Stillman's Gym in New York.

'He was a small grey-haired man, a bantamweight at best, and he used to challenge the biggest heavyweights to hit him in the groin,' Eskin recalled in 1982. 'I never ever saw him flinch. And while I never saw it myself, it was also said that he allowed himself to be kicked and hit with a baseball bat without any ill effect.'

The first world championship fight to be fought under the no-foul rule took place at the Yankee Stadium in New York on 17 July 1930 when Al Singer knocked out Sammy Mandell in the first round to win the lightweight title.

Most countries where boxing is practised around the world now recognize the rule – Britain is perhaps the only exception – and all the world sanctioning bodies have incorporated the no-foul rule into their rules and regulations governing championship fights.

This is how Rule 4 of the World Boxing Association reads:

4.1 It is expressly understood that a World Championship contest is not to be terminated by a low-blow, as the protector that must be used by both contestants is sufficient protection to withstand any so-called low-blow which might incapacitate any of the contestants.

4.2 If one of the contestants shall fall to the ring floor or otherwise indicate an unwillingness to continue because of a claim of a low-blow foul, the contest shall be terminated and the Referee shall award the contest to his opponent.

In case of an accidental foul so determined by the Referee, he shall determine whether the boxer who has been fouled can continue or not. If his chances have not been seriously jeopardized as a result of the foul the Referee may order the bout continued after an interval of not more than five (5) minutes' rest.

4.3 Any contestant who deliberately fouls his opponent during a contest will be penalized with loss of points or disqualified depending upon the severity or harmlessness of the foul and its effect upon the opponent.

So technically it is still possible for a fight to end in a disqualification even in the United States, but the last attempt to win a world title fight because of a low-blow resulted in the referee ruling against the boxer who claimed he had been fouled. Jorge Fernandez claimed Emile Griffith had hit him low in the ninth round of their world welterweight title fight in Las Vegas in 1962. Fernandez was given five minutes in which to recover but when he still refused to continue the fight, Griffith was declared the winner by a knockout.

Advertisement for the original Taylor Foulproof Cup which 'brought about the no foul rule' in 1930.

OFFICIALS

Once, the only official who really mattered in boxing was the referee. Under London Prize Ring Rules there was also a place for umpires and whips, but only the referee controlled the fight. Later, when the Queensberry Rules were adopted, timekeepers gained in importance but it was not until the 1920s that judges became a familiar sight around the ringside.

The first world heavyweight championship fight in which judges were appointed was between Jess Willard and Jack Dempsey at Bay View Park Arena, Toledo, Ohio, on 4 July 1919. Promoter Tex Rickard and Major A Drexel Biddle, chairman of the Navy and Civilian Boxing Board of Control, were chosen to act as the judges.

However, in the event the vote of the judges differed, the contract called for referee Ollie Pecord to decide the winner. Willard retired in his corner at the end of the third round.

In time the number of judges was increased from two to three and the referee became a non-scoring official.

First woman to judge a world heavyweight championship fight was Eva Shain, who was later inducted into the New Jersey Boxing Hall of Fame. Shain was appointed to judge the heavyweight title fight between Muhammad Ali and Earnie Shavers in Madison Square Garden, New York, on 29 September 1977.

Sixteen years later three women – Patricia Jarman, Sheila Hormon-Martin and Eugenie Williams – were appointed to judge the IBF heavyweight championship fight between Riddick Bowe and Jesse Ferguson in Washington, DC. Bowe saved the ladies from any embarrassment by knocking out Ferguson in the second round.

Americans Tony and Barbara Perez made history as the first husband and wife to officiate in a world title fight when Tony was appointed to referee and Barbara to judge the World Boxing Council bantamweight title bout between Byun Jung-Il and Yasuei Yakushiji in Nagoya, Japan, on 23 December 1993. Yakushiji took the title on a split decision when Barbara Perez scored the fight in his favour by 115–113. The two Mexican judges working with Ms Perez disagreed with each other. Guillermo Ayon had Jung-Il in front by 115–113 while Alberto Barahona scored it for Yakushiji by 116–115.

A woman also became one of the first judges to be attacked at the ringside by a boxer in Michigan when junior lightweight J L Ivey struck boxing judge Sue Denton in the face after she voted against him in his fight with Jose Vidal Concepcion in Detroit in 1986.

'He came to the side of the ring, stuck his head through the rope strands and hit her [Denton] in the face,' commission chairman Dr Stuart Kirschenbaum told the *Detroit Free Press*.

Ivey went into a rage after Judges Denton and Rosemary Grable both scored the fight for Concepcion 96–94. Judge Jim Homanian split the decision, giving the fight to Ivey by the same score. Ivey claimed that Denton scored the fight against him because he was black and because she did not like fighters from the Kronk Gym.

Ivey later issued a formal letter of apology to Mrs Denton but the lady judge filed assault and battery charges against the boxer. 'I don't intend to let it go,' Denton said. 'I can take the verbal abuse, but getting slapped or poked at is another matter. What happens next time when an official makes a decision and a fighter, possibly a heavyweight, doesn't like it and comes after you?'

Judges seldom admit they were wrong but Dalby Shirley of Las Vegas did exactly that after watching a videotape of the WBC super lightweight title fight between Frankie Randall and Julio Cesar Chavez four months after the Mexican had been awarded a technical win in the eighth round. The fight had been stopped when Chavez suffered a bad cut over the right eye as a result of an accidental head butt.

On checking the scorecards in terms of the technical decision rule, it transpired that Chavez was three points ahead on the card of Mexican judge Rey Solis, one point ahead on the card of Shirley, and one point behind on the scorecard of judge Tamotsu Tomihara of Hawaii. Had Shirley given the eighth round to Randall, as he later said he should have, the fight would have been declared a draw and Randall would have retained his title.

Shirley admitted his mistake when the Nevada State Athletic Commission held a seminar for officials and showed the eighth round of the Chavez–Randall fight as part of the exercise. 'I screwed it up,' Shirley later told the Las Vegas *Review-Journal.*

Two other officials who 'screwed it up' but never admitted their mistake were South African timekeepers Brown Mogotsi and Blackie Swart.

Timekeepers, by and large, are the forgotten men of boxing. They ring the bell to start a round and strike a gong to end it. Occasionally they are instructed to put their clock on hold while the referee takes time out, but mostly their world consists of three minutes with a one-minute break.

Sometimes, however, things can go horribly wrong as Mogotsi and Swart discovered in the eighth round of the WBA world heavyweight title fight between Gerrie Coetzee and Greg Page at Sun City in December 1984. Coetzee was counted out after the round had gone three minutes and 50 seconds. The defending champion should have been sitting on his stool, enjoying the minute rest period when he lost his title on a knockout. The Coetzee camp's objections were

This knockout sequence shows Gerrie Coetzee lying flat on his back after being dropped by Greg Page in the eighth round at Sun City in December 1984. Coetzee should have been sitting on his stool, enjoying the minute rest between rounds, when he was counted out.

ignored by the WBA.

Another bugbear of boxing is the long count. Both before and after the infamous 'long count' in the fight for the heavyweight championship of the world between Jack Dempsey and Gene Tunney in Chicago in September 1927, other boxers have made similar claims.

One of the last to attempt such a scam was Mike Tyson, after he was knocked out in the tenth round by Buster Douglas in their world heavyweight championship fight in Tokyo, in February 1990. With the support of Don King and José Sulaiman, Tyson insisted that he was the victim of a long count. Tyson's claim was evidently based on the fact that after he dropped Douglas in the eighth round, referee Octavio Meyran called 'one' at Japanese timekeeper Riichi Hirano's count of 'three'.

Lew Eskin, the well-known American referee, explained why Tyson's claim was spurious in the April 1990 issue of *Boxing World* magazine. 'The count by the timekeeper is NOT the official count,' Eskin pointed out, and added: 'I've often been a knockdown timekeeper and it is then my job to start counting as soon as a man goes down. Many times the referee will rule it a slip and wave the count off. A competent referee will pick up the count if he wants to ... or make his own count.'

That, in fact, is what referee Dave Barry did when Dempsey dropped Tunney in the seventh round of their rematch. Barry delayed starting his count until Dempsey had moved to a neutral corner in accordance with the rules. The film of the fight confirmed that Tunney got the benefit of a few extra seconds on the canvas (14 altogether).

'When the fight was over, and ever after, there was never a peep out of Jack Dempsey. *He* knew who was to blame for the long count,' Paul Gallico, the then sports editor of the New York *Daily News*, wrote afterwards.

In 1992, Visual-Audio Counting Systems, an American electronics company, invented a device that promised to take the controversy out of all future long counts. The idea was to erect two electronic display monitors on the ring posts of neutral corners, and when a boxer was knocked down, a ringside official would press a button.

Right: Buster Douglas traps Mike Tyson against the ropes during their world heavyweight title fight in Tokyo in 1990.

Below: Jack Dempsey drops Gene Tunney for the famous 'long count' in Chicago in September 1927. Referee Dave Barry refused to start the count until Dempsey went to a neutral corner.

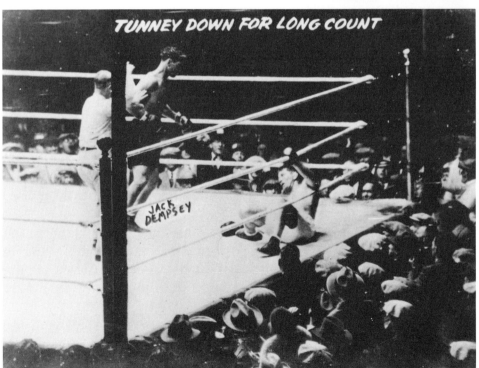

Simultaneously, a corresponding voice would start to call out the count through the public address system. When the fallen fighter had risen, the button would again be pressed to allow both the referee and the fans an opportunity to see the time that had elapsed.

It seemed like a good idea at the time ... but evidently nobody has yet bothered to try it.

ORIGINS

Boxing was born in Africa – amid the rolling hills, lush valleys and mountain streams of Ethiopia – more than 8,000 years ago. In the beginning it was merely a pastime, later it became a spectacle and later still the ancient Ethiopians regarded it as an athletic exercise.

When the Egyptians invaded the Nubian region in 4500 BC their soldiers learned the art of boxing from the local inhabitants, and took the sport back to Egypt where it became very popular. Even Egyptian pharaohs attended some of the competitions.

From Egypt, boxing spread to other countries in the region, including Greece (where it became a part of Greek mythology), eastwards to Mesopotamia (now known as Iraq, capital Baghdad) and northwards to Rome. By 688 BC, Onomastos had become the first boxing man to fight his way to the championship in the 23rd Olympiad.

Boxing died in the Dark Ages only to resurface in England in the seventeenth century. The first record of a bareknuckle fight was in 1716, the year James Figg issued his famous calling card announcing that he taught boxing. Figg also claimed that he was the champion of England.

Boxing in the United States began among the slaves of the southern states early in the nineteenth century and spread gradually northwards. The first fight on record between white men occurred in 1816. It was only in the 1850s that boxing began to gain public support.

Besides England, one of the earliest European countries to accept boxing as a sport was Italy. In 1731, the Earl of Bath, who was in Venice at the time, wrote to John Broughton describing how an Italian boxer named Tito Alberto Di Carni had knocked out three opponents, one after the other. Three years later Di Carni visited London where he went down to defeat at the hands of Bob Whitaker.

Boxing was slower to spread to other European countries. La Savate, the forerunner of Muay Thai and kickboxing, can be traced back to 1854 in France. Boxing as we know it, however, did not start there until 1900. Germany's first recorded fist-fight took place in Hamburg in 1899 but the sport was suppressed until after the First World War.

Boxing in Spain also did not start until after the First World War but the sport began in Denmark in 1889, in Belgium in 1910, in Norway and Sweden in 1920 and in Finland and Switzerland in 1935.

Yoshio Shirai became the first Japanese boxer to win a world championship when he beat Dado Marino for the flyweight title in 1952.

Boxing in the Far East started in the Philippines. The first great Asian boxer was Francisco Guilledo, who boxed under the name of Pancho Villa. Born on the Philippine island of Iloilo in August 1901, Villa was crowned American flyweight champion when he knocked out Johnny Buff in 11 rounds in 1922. A year later he knocked out Jimmy Wilde in a sensational fight at the Polo Grounds in New York to win the world title.

Japan entered the fistic world in the 1920s. However, the Japan Boxing Commission was only established in 1952, the year in which Yoshio Shirai became the first Japanese boxer to win a world title by outpointing Dado Marino in Tokyo for the flyweight crown.

Korean boxing champions can be traced back to 1946 but western-style boxing still runs second to Muay Thai (traditional Siamese kickboxing) in Thailand.

PHANTOM FIGHTS

Astrologers may tell you the collapse of the world heavyweight title fight between Gerrie Coetzee and Larry Holmes in Las Vegas, Nevada, in June 1984 was written in the stars. Bankers will tell you it was written in the balance sheet.

Both have a point. Despite its superfight tag, the Coetzee–Holmes fight was destined to be a financial flop from the moment the promoters foolishly decided to pay the boxers and their handlers exorbitant purse moneys. This was because Coetzee and Holmes both lacked charisma and neither had the magic to make the turnstiles click.

Somehow the promoters overlooked the fact that even Kallie Knoetze could outdraw Coetzee in South Africa, and that just about everybody was outdrawing Holmes at the gate in the United States.

But this was not the first big fight to run into trouble. Boxing history is full of them. Some never took place at all, while others were delayed for several years before the fighters eventually climbed into a ring. A classic example was the world heavyweight title fight between James J Corbett and Bob Fitzsimmons. Corbett first signed to defend his title against Fitzsimmons at a meeting in the *New York Herald* building on 11 October 1894.

However, it was not until nearly three years later (17 March 1897) that the two men climbed into an outdoor ring in Carson City, Nevada, to contest the title. In the years between, three serious attempts were made to stage the fight, all without success.

'The biggest offer was made by a promoter named Dan Stuart, who at once started to build a big arena in Dallas,' Corbett later recalled. 'Everything was breezing along nicely when we had trouble from an unexpected quarter.

'Before Stuart had sent in his offer for the fight, he had seen his political connections and also the governor, who assured him that everything was all right and to go ahead. But after the promoter had spent a fortune on the big arena, and interest in the fight had been worked up to the highest pitch, the governor came out and declared we could not fight in Texas.'

The next offer to promote the fight came from the Hot Springs Athletic Club in Arkansas. But unlike the governor of Texas, the chief executive of Arkansas came right out at the start and refused to allow the fight in his state.

Corbett was so disgusted he announced his retirement from the ring and presented the championship to Peter Maher. But a purse of $15,000 and a side bet of $5,000 were enough to lure him back in 1897. This time there were no hitches and the fight took place in front of a motley crowd of cowboys and crooks (Jesse James was reportedly at the ringside). Fitzsimmons won on a knockout in the 14th round.

Another celebrated fight that took years to put together was the return bout between Joe Louis and Billy Conn. Louis knocked out Conn in a thrilling fight in June 1941 but before promoter Mike Jacobs could arrange a return bout the United States entered the Second World War. Moreover, both Louis and Conn joined the armed forces.

Early in 1942 the US Army decided to let Louis and Conn fight for the heavyweight championship in New York, with Army Relief getting all the proceeds. A Sports Writers' Committee was formed to supervise the fight and Mike Jacobs was drafted as the nominal promoter, but supposedly without any financial interest.

The fight ran into trouble when the boxers' connections served notice that new arrangements would have to be made to take care of the fighters' indebtedness, amounting to $134,000. This demand did not sit well with the US Army, and the secretary of war, Henry L Stimson, ordered the fight to be cancelled and the two soldiers back to their military duties.

Nat Fleischer, the then editor of *The Ring* magazine, described the collapse of the fight as 'the greatest fiasco in the history of boxing'. Four years later Louis and Conn met in a much publicized fight at Yankee Stadium, New York, but both were past their prime and Louis won a boring bout on a knockout in the eighth round.

At least the fight did eventually take place, which is more than can be said for the much talked-about fight between Jack Dempsey and Harry Wills, possibly the best black heavyweight of the time.

Dempsey has been accused of ducking Wills but the truth is that racial prejudice killed the bout, and this despite the fact that both men actually signed contracts and promoter Tex Rickard even went as far as to print tickets for the non-event. Wills was the best black heavyweight of the era but back in the 1920s black was not considered beautiful – especially in heavyweight boxing.

'Wills was mostly the victim of bigotry,' Dempsey said years later. 'He was gypped out of his crack at the title because people with a lot of money tied up in boxing thought a fight against me, if it went wrong, might kill the business.

'People of importance still worried about "white supremacy", race riots, the Negro vote – which might swing somewhere else if I flattened Wills – and things like that.'

Rickard was against the fight because of the criticism he had received for promoting the Johnson–Jeffries fight years before. William Muldoon, chairman of the New York State Athletic Commission, was against it because he thought it might end up in a race riot, regardless of who won.

The most serious attempt to stage the fight was made by Floyd

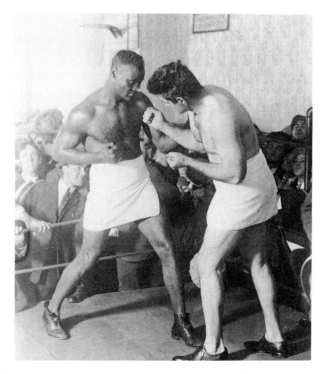

Harry Wills (left) and Luis Angel Firpo pose before their heavyweight fight in 1924. Racial prejudice killed a proposed fight between Wills and world champion Jack Dempsey.

Fitzsimmons. He invited Dempsey and Wills to South Bend, Indiana, to sign contracts. Amid great publicity Wills signed for a down payment of $50,000 while Dempsey was supposedly to get $300,000 with the balance of one million later.

Dempsey always insisted that Wills was made for him. 'I could always lick those big slow guys,' he said. 'I personally never ducked him. I thought the fight should take place. Why the hell shouldn't I have fought him? I was champion of the world.'

Perhaps the weirdest phantom fight of all was the proposed heavyweight championship bout between defending champion Jim Braddock and former champion Max Schmeling. Madison Square Garden held a signed contract for the fight, which was scheduled to take place on 3 June 1937.

Promoter Mike Jacobs wanted Braddock to defend the title against Joe Louis instead, and Joe Gould, Braddock's manager, skilfully used the political climate of the time to launch a propaganda campaign against giving Schmeling a title shot. And when a New Jersey judge, named Guy L Fake, ruled in favour of Braddock over the contract he had signed with Madison Square Garden, Jacobs matched the champion against Louis in Chicago.

In a strange charade, the New York State Athletic Commission went ahead with the weigh-in ceremony for the fight. Of course, only Schmeling weighed-in. But Schmeling's connections used the charade to persuade the German Boxing Commission, the French Boxing Federation and the British Boxing Board of Control to recognize Max as the true world champion.

POETRY

The men who went down fighting
Were gamesters to the core,
And kept unchanged the lustre
Of laurels that they wore;
Each passed with pride unbroken
From out a champion's place,
True to the Prize Ring's slogan -
'Defeat is not disgrace!'

So from time immemorial
Men fell on stricken fields,
Red with the blood of heroes
The strain that never yields;
So Rome's fierce gladiators
Shrilling their battle-cry,
Made grim salute to Caesar
Content to do or die!

Arthur Thompson (1941)

The first heavyweight champion of the world to show a genuine interest in literature was considered something of an oddball because of it by the American media. Unable to come to terms with a fighter who read the classics and could quote poetry, the boxing writers of the time dismissed him as an enigma of the ring.

When Gene Tunney retired as undefeated world champion in 1928 to marry Andrew Carnegie heiress Polly Lauder, many in the boxing business were secretly glad to see the back of him. They envied his personal friendship with literary giant George Bernard Shaw, they begrudged him his greatness for beating Jack Dempsey, and they disliked him as a man who often talked down to the boxing writers of his time. Nor did it help when Tunney later went on to lecture at Yale University on *Troilus and Cressida*.

And yet the first boxing story ever written was as a poem. Homer was its author and you will find it in the *Iliad*. Virgil wrote an even

Gene Tunney greets James J Jeffries while preparing to challenge Jack Dempsey for the world heavyweight title in 1926. Tunney was the first champion to show a genuine interest in literature.

longer piece in the *Aeneid*, telling in verse how an old boxing champion made a .comeback. Irish bard Thomas Moore penned poetry with a boxing background in the nineteenth century, as did John Hamilton Reynolds – a protégé of Byron – in his book *The Fancy*, published in 1820.

The first truly international fight between Tom Sayers, champion of England, and John C Heenan, champion of America, at Farnborough, on 17 April 1860, inspired William Makepeace Thackeray to write 'A Lay of Ancient London', a poem in which he changed the names of the prize-fighters to Sayerius and Heenanus.

Thirty-nine years later, the celebrated poet-troubadour Vachel Lindsay wrote 'John L Sullivan, the Boston Strong Boy', a piece of poetry (and song) that recounted the last bareknuckle heavyweight championship fight between Sullivan and Jake Kilrain in Richburg, Mississippi, on 8 July 1889.

Arguably the most famous boxing poem of all time was written by a lawyer. M J McMahon was so disturbed by the neglect of the grave of middleweight Jack Dempsey (1862-95) that he wrote a poem entitled 'The Nonpareil's Grave' and then circulated a thousand copies of it anonymously. One of the copies of the poem reached the offices of the *Portland Oregonian*, which printed it on 10 December 1899.

There were five stanzas altogether, the first of which read as follows:

> Far out in the wilds of Oregon,
> On a lonely mountain side,
> Where Columbia's mighty waters,
> Roll down to the ocean tide;
> Where the giant fir and cedar
> Are imaged in the wave,
> O'ergrown with firs and lichens,
> I found Jack Dempsey's grave.

The poem pricked the conscience of many in the sport and a public subscription drive resulted in an imposing monument being erected on Dempsey's grave in Mount Calvary Cemetery in Portland, Oregon, in 1904.

Another famous boxing poem, 'The Kid's Last Fight', was also written anonymously (the author has never been named) and besides being a vaudeville favourite before the turn of the century, was the basis for a hit song by Frankie Laine in the 1950s. The poem tells the poignant tale of a ring death, with simple yet moving words. Consider the last three stanzas:

> The mob kept tellin' me to land,
> And callin' things I couldn't stand;
> I stepped in close and smashed his chin,
> The Kid fell hard; he was all in.

> I carried him into his chair,
> And tried to bring him to for fair,
> I rubbed his wrists, done everything,
> A doctor climbed into the ring.

> And I was scared as I could be,
> The Kid was starin' and couldn't see;
> The doctor turned and shook his head,
> I looked again – the Kid was dead!

POSTERS

The practice of using boxing posters to advertise fights is older than many in the sport suspect. There is evidence that posters were being used as long ago as AD 63, when the city of Pompeii was destroyed by an eruption of Vesuvius – and perhaps even earlier.

When archaeologists uncovered the Colosseum, where boxing contests in Pompeii had been held from about 300 BC, they discovered wonderfully preserved boxing posters on the outer walls of some of the buildings.

'The gladiatorial troupe of Suettius Curuis, the Aedile, will fight at Pompeii on the last day of May,' one read. 'There will be a chase of field beasts, and awnings to protect spectators from the sun.'

Until the 1920s, posters were produced in small quantities and few have survived. But from the 1930s until the 1970s, many fights –

particularly in the New York area – were advertised on cardboard posters printed in yellow, black and red. The 1980s even saw billboards being used for the purpose.

And yet the production of posters has not been without problems. Many of the bouts advertised turned out to be phantom fights – Jack Johnson *vs* Bombardier Billy Wells in London in 1911, Jack Dempsey *vs* Harry Wills in Jersey City in 1924, Larry Holmes *vs* Gerrie Coetzee in Las Vegas in 1984, among them – and a poster was even printed advertising a 'Grand Boxing Carnival' in the Recreation Hall of the Dayatalawa prisoner-of-war camp in Ceylon during the war between the British and the South African Boers in 1902.

Don King unwittingly encountered a political problem when he produced two sets of posters for the world heavyweight title fight between Muhammad Ali and George Foreman in Kinshasa, Zaire, in October 1974.

King called the fight 'The Rumble in the Jungle', which met with the approval of President Mobutu, but when he also produced posters proclaiming 'From the Slave Ship to the Championship!' Mobutu ordered that they be burned.

The production of boxing posters is now considered so important as a marketing tool that they are no longer left in the hands of the naive. Among the top artists commissioned to paint boxing posters since the 1970s are Leroy Neiman and Luigi Castiglioni. Both men produced original work worthy of the most discriminating art lover.

Not only did Neiman paint posters for big fights like Ali–Frazier, Ali–Foreman, Ali–Spinks, Ali–Holmes and Cooney–Holmes, he also produced original work for special presentations such as 'A Night at the Theater with Muhammad Ali' (Auditorium Theater, Congress Park, Chicago, 2 December 1977), 'A Tribute to Joe Louis (Joe Louis Arena, Detroit, 12 June 1981) and 'America Honors the Heavyweight Champions' (Theater for the Performing Arts, Aladdin Hotel, Las Vegas, 19 May 1977).

Best of all is that Neiman is a boxing fan and a great admirer of Muhammad Ali. 'Ali's greatest achievement, in my mind, wasn't that he won the crown three times, but that he did the same act for 20 years and never bored us,' Neiman said in 1983.

Luigi Castiglioni was discovered as an artist of exceptional talent

Abstract paintings like this work of Muhammad Ali by Leroy Neiman often make stunning fight posters.

Leroy Neiman has been ringside for most of the big heavyweight fights since the 1970s. Neiman showed remarkable deftness in capturing Mike Tyson's prowess while knocking out Frank Bruno in 1989.

by European boxing promoter Rodolfo Sabatini in 1972 and both Sabatini and Charles Michaelis (manager of the Palais Des Sports in Paris) were quick to commission him to paint boxing posters. In the words of André Parinaud, founder of the French National Academy of Arts, '... quality is his gift.'

Of the 50 or more posters Castiglioni has painted, arguably the most sought-after is the one commissioned by Top Rank in 1976 for the third fight between Muhammad Ali and Ken Norton. It features a 'wide-mouth' Ali head protruding out of an upright boxing glove, staring across at a profiled Ken Norton on a similar glove design. The heads are featured over a field of trees. Actually, using a glove as a head has almost become a Castiglioni trademark.

For the French middleweight title fight between Jean-Claude Bouttier and Max Cohen in Paris in 1974, Castiglioni featured a 'rooster head' protruding from a horizontal boxing glove. Pure surrealism, but stunningly effective! Gloves were also used for the poster of the Monzon–Valdes fight in 1977 (Carlos Monzon's last fight).

In commemoration of the 80th birthday of the famous French boxer Georges Carpentier, Castiglioni was commissioned to paint a portrait. What emerged was a smiling Carpentier head, peering through a mist of clouds, giving the French hero a ghostlike appearance as he gazed out over the French countryside.

PROGRAMMES

Boxing programmes first became popular in the late nineteenth century. The practice of publishing special programmes for big fights soon spread throughout the world and became so profitable that leading artists were often commissioned to prepare illustrations for the covers.

Top promoters, such as Don King, Frank Warren, Bob Arum and Dan Duva, have made the production of programmes an art form, often in collaboration with programme specialists like Jay Seidman.

Many programmes have become collectors' items, as, for example, the previously unknown Sullivan–Corbett programme from 1892 which sold for more than $20,000 at an auction in San Francisco in 1992. Others in demand include the programmes produced for the fights between Dempsey and Carpentier (1921), Dempsey and Tunney (1926 and 1927), Louis and Schmeling (1936 and 1938) and Marciano and Walcott (1952 and 1953).

The trend today is to produce more copies of the programme than could possibly be sold at the fight, with a view to marketing the balance to collectors afterwards. There is also a tendency to give big fights marketable titles such as 'Unfinished Business', 'Star Spangled Glory', 'Sudden Impact', 'The Rumble in the Jungle' and 'Thrilla in Manila'.

The practice of inserting a list of the fights in a boxing magazine as a free giveaway first started during the heyday of *The Ring* magazine in the 1930s. The benefits are obvious. The promoter is able to offer his patrons a classy production while the fans get a complete list of the fights they are about to see plus the latest news and views from the world of boxing.

PROMOTERS

Without them the chances are that even the most talented of boxers would wallow in obscurity. Promoters are the people who make the world of boxing go around. And yet you can count the number of truly great boxing promoters on the fingers of one hand.

The giants of boxing promotion come quickly to mind: Tex Rickard, Mike Jacobs, Jim Norris, Don King. Surprisingly few, considering the thousands of men who fight for a living, or the countless number of tournaments that are staged around the world each year.

Well, that's where the *other* promoters – not necessarily the Gullivers of the game – come into the picture. Among them are men like Bob Arum, Dan Duva, Cedric Kushner, Frank Warren, Barry Hearn, Don Chargin, Wilfried Sauerland, Mickey Duff, Rodney Berman and the Acaries brothers of France. In the past, this list would also have included promoters like Jeff Dickson, George Parnassus, Jack Solomons, Hugh D McIntosh, Chris Dundee, Sydney Hulls, Aileen Eaton and Rodolfo Sabatini.

They come from a variety of backgrounds. Rickard was a professional gambler. 'The fundamental rock on which his success was grounded was courage in taking chances which the average gambler would have side-stepped, as well as an ability to gauge public desires, and a matchless flair for the employment of colorful, far-reaching ballyhoo,' Dan Daniel, the American sportswriter, wrote 11 years after Rickard's death in January 1929.

Rickard had the vision and gambler's good fortune to bring million-dollar gates to boxing, but he also had a great heavyweight champion to work with in Jack Dempsey.

American promoter Mike Jacobs and badly battered British heavyweight Tommy Farr after Farr's fight with Joe Louis in 1937.

Jacobs was a New York concessionaire and ticket scalper who was also something of a workaholic. 'Jacobs does all his business when most of the boys in the fight racket are either just going home or climbing out of the covers,' New York publicist Francis Albertanti said in 1936. 'Put a ticket in his hand and Mike could squeeze three times as much money out of it as anybody else,' an associate said after Jacobs died of a heart attack in 1952.

Jacobs also had his trump card in Joe Louis, the legendary 'Brown Bomber', who ruled the heavyweight division with an iron fist for more than 11 years.

Norris was a millionaire industrialist whose monopoly of the sport in the 1950s, through his International Boxing Club, was finally broken by the United States government in 1957. Like Rickard and Jacobs before him, Norris had a top drawcard in heavyweight champion Rocky Marciano.

With Rickard, Jacobs and Norris all dead, Don King can safely be described as the world's greatest living promoter. Or can he? 'King polluted everything he touched, from *Ring* magazine (1977 version, which produced phoney ratings for the scandal-ridden ABC tournament) to Donald Trump,' Michael Katz wrote in the New York *Daily News* in July 1994.

An ex-convict who once ran a numbers racket in Cleveland and kicked a man to death, King has since received a pardon from Ohio governor James Rhodes. Even so, few in the American media are prepared to accept him as the 'world's greatest promoter'. And yet, no one is more deserving of the title.

Consider his achievements. King's promotions are truly international; his accomplishments unparalleled in the history of the sport. King has promoted more than 350 world title fights, was the promoter of the Mexico City tournament that set a new world record for paid attendance, and was the man who gave us such momentous heavyweight fights as 'The Rumble in the Jungle' and the 'Thrilla in Manila'.

The World Boxing Council has no reservations. 'These facts and countless others qualify Don King as the most outstanding promoter of all time,' the Council declared in 1994. And despite the cosy relationship that exists between WBC president José Sulaiman and

Left: Don King, arguably the greatest boxing promoter in the world today. Right: Bob Arum, a one-time attorney in the Kennedy administration, who decided to try his hand at promoting fights.

King, the WBC may well be right.

What of the others? Arum was a one-time US attorney in the Kennedy administration, who after spreading his wings wide in international boxing, now concentrates on promoting the sport in the United States. Duva also had a legal background but as the son of Lou Duva, the famous American trainer, was well-schooled in the ways of the sport.

If your idea of a boxing promoter is a fellow who chews a fat cigar, carries a half-jack in his back pocket, and talks out of the side of his mouth, the chances are you have been watching too many movies. King, Arum, Duva and South African-born Cedric Kushner are none of these things.

'I like to think of myself as a businessman, first and foremost,' Kushner says. 'The fact that my business is boxing is neither here nor there; it used to be rock concerts and ticket scalping.'

Kushner admits he learned about boxing the hard way from two of the best teachers in the business – Bob Arum and Don King. 'There's little difference between them,' he says. 'One happens to be of the Jewish persuasion and the other has a dark skin, otherwise you could never tell them apart.'

Kushner describes Arum as a businessman. 'At least he returns your phone calls and he doesn't play mind games,' he says. 'For the most part, Bob is truly interested in what deals can be done. King is less of a bottom-line man. If he has a fault, it's a tendency to waste money on lavish promotions for no good reason. King also likes to pose as a concerned citizen, but the truth is Don is concerned with only one colour – and that's the colour of money.'

Can *any* boxing promotion be too lavish? British promoter Jack Solomons, a fishmonger who started out as a manager and club promoter before becoming a force to be reckoned with in world boxing, evidently thought not.

'A Solomons promotion was something special – even his enemies agreed,' Reg Gutteridge wrote in the April 1980 issue of *The Ring* magazine. 'He would change dinner jacket from white to midnight blue or tartan as the sun dimmed at an open air show. His cigar was as much a part of the fight scene as the Lonsdale Belt. And he punctuated his speech with colourful Solomonesque expressions like "We tame lions". With a bit more shyness he could have been an extrovert.'

PUNCHES

Ask a dozen experts to name the most effective punch in boxing and the chances are you will get a dozen different answers – and this despite the fact that there are fewer than six basic blows. Mind you, there are countless variations and down the years these punches have been given all kinds of exotic names.

Among the best remembered are the solar plexus punch with which Bob Fitzsimmons knocked out James J Corbett in 1897, and Kid McCoy's corkscrew punch, which was delivered with the left hand and landed with the twist of the wrist. Others, like the rabbit punch, the kidney punch and the pivot blow, have long since been banned from the sport but there was a time when they were freely used in big fights.

We all know that boxing technique has changed over the years but a survey carried out several years ago by *Boxing World*, the South African monthly, among managers, trainers and boxers confirmed that the left hook – or the hook off the jab – is generally considered the most effective punch in boxing today.

Others have felt just as strongly about other blows in the past and some boxers have even been credited with inventing punches of their own. But since most of these blows were being used long before their time it would be more truthful to say that they popularized the punches rather than invented them.

For example, the only thing new about the punch Fitzsimmons used to knock out Corbett was the name. And yet, thanks to Bob Davis, an enterprising reporter for the *New York Journal*, Fitz was credited with having invented a new punch.

Davis was returning by train to San Francisco after covering the fight in Carson City when he overheard two doctors discussing the bout. The conversation took a professional turn and one of the doctors spoke at length about the nervous shock to the system produced by striking the solar plexus. Davis liked the term and promptly reported that not only had a new heavyweight champion been crowned in Carson City, but a new blow – the 'solar plexus' – had been discovered and used with deadly effect.

In fact, the punch was nothing more than a straight left to the pit of the stomach. 'A bloomin' good belly clout,' was how Fitzsimmons described it. But that was before the newspapers lauded him for having studied anatomy and for making his target a weak spot in the human body then largely unknown to the average fight fan.

'As this made Bob look like a pretty smart fellow, the new champ stood for the printed statements complacently, quite undisturbed by the fact that, until he saw the words in the newspapers, he never knew that he, Corbett, or anyone else, rejoiced in the possession of a solar plexus,' said George T Pardy, the veteran boxing writer, years later.

Even so, the idea quickly caught on and before long several boxers had claimed the discovery of new punches. Among these were the scissor punch, the corkscrew punch, the kidney punch, the rabbit punch, the pivot blow and even the six-inch punch. Most were largely a figment of the imagination of the boxer or his manager and none was new, but some – like the kidney punch, the rabbit punch and the pivot blow – were so deadly that they were banned.

It was Gus Ruhlin who supposedly invented the scissors punch. Ruhlin, who failed in a bid to win the world heavyweight title from Jim Jeffries in 1901, can thank his manager Billy Madden for his notoriety. It was Madden who dreamed up the idea of the new punch, even going as far as to have an artist draw a diagram of the scissor style of attack, which was published in all the papers.

The punch, however, was nothing more than a left to the ribs followed by a right to the jaw – one blow coming right on top of the other and nowadays invariably referred to as a combination – but in the eyes of Mr Madden it resembled the shutting down of two blades of a pair of scissors, and hence the name.

Kid McCoy had far more success with his corkscrew punch, but strangely enough it was not until he fought Ruhlin in 1898 that the blow brought him fame. McCoy had been practising the punch for years and had actually knocked out Tommy Ryan with it for the welterweight title two years before.

The Kid was a cruel man who delighted in cutting up his opponents. He had a habit of twisting his upper lip into a sneer of contempt the moment the bell rang. The corkscrew punch was really a left hook, delivered from a high, outside position.

'As McCoy's fist neared his objective, whether to the jaw or the body, he would turn his wrist suddenly so that his fist actually turned within a half circle,' said Nat Fleischer, the American boxing historian. 'It was this twisting, corkscrew-like turn of the fist which gave it such crushing leverage as it made contact.'

McCoy made a fortune specializing in the punch. He seemed to revel in cutting up a victim. He wanted the blows to rip and tear flesh and that is usually what they did.

George Dawson, the crack Australian welterweight who made his name before the turn of the century, is generally credited with having introduced the kidney punch into American rings. But it would be far more correct to say that Dawson popularized the

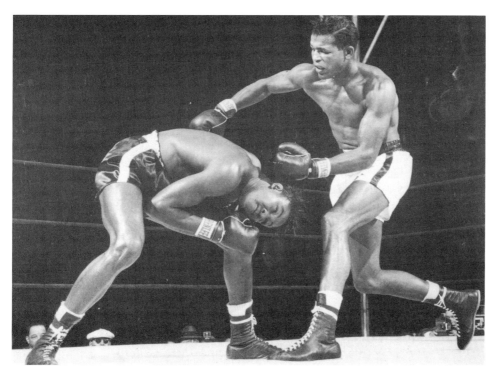

Sugar Ray Robinson strikes Kid Gavilan with a right to the kidneys in their world welterweight title fight in 1949. Gavilan was famous for his bolo punch.

punch because it was freely used all through the 1880s and 1890s, when glove fighting took the place of bare knuckles. Tommy Ryan, the old welterweight champion, was one of its best exponents.

'When Ryan got that punch home, you could see the other fellow's legs first stiffen, and then go limp under him,' Jack Curly, the famous American manager and promoter, later recalled. 'I never saw another fighter who could use the kidney punch with such tremendous effect. It isn't nearly so spectacular a blow to watch as a hook or swing to the jaw. But, man, it's as deadly as the venom of a poisonous snake!'

The punch was first barred in New York when the Frawley Law came into effect in 1911 and today it is banned throughout the world. Even so, you can still see it being used on the odd occasion.

There was a howl of protest by Germany when Joe Louis almost paralysed Max Schmeling with a vicious blow to the kidneys in their return fight in New York in 1938. And as recently as 1951, Sugar Ray Robinson was disqualified for using the punch against Gerhard Hecht in Berlin. (The result was later changed to 'no decision'.)

The rabbit punch – a blow delivered to the back of the neck – was so named because it was an adaptation of the way in which rabbits taken in a snare were killed by the finder. The blow, once freely used in ring battles before the turn of the century, is now banned throughout the world.

Old-timers will tell you that more than one ring death occurred through the use of the punch, but it was not until Jack Dempsey nearly killed Bill Brennan with rabbit punches in 1920 that the New York State Athletic Commission took steps to have the blow banned. Dempsey's free use of the punch left Brennan partially paralysed and confined to a hospital bed for more than two weeks after their fight.

As a young lad I recall writing to Nat Fleischer, the then editor of *The Ring* magazine, to complain about the use of rabbit punches by Freddie Mills in his fight with Johnny Ralph in Johannesburg in 1948.

'The rabbit punch, the same as a kidney blow, is not a foul when landed while the action is on,' Fleischer replied. 'They are fouls only when landed on an opponent while holding him with one hand and battering away with the other or while striking the opponent from behind, in which case it may be regarded as an intentional punch. So long as the action is free no foul is involved and judging by your letter, Mills was not guilty at any time of intentional fouling. It was up to Ralph to defend himself.'

Also banned but occasionally seen today is the pivot blow, a back-handed swing with the boxer pivoting on his heel. The punch was barred by universal consent after George La Blanche knocked out 'Nonpareil' Jack Dempsey with it in August 1890.

'Had the victim been anyone but "Nonpareil" Jack, it is probable that the pivot blow would not have excited such general condemnation,' wrote A D Phillips, the doyen of American boxing scribes, in 1938. 'Many a boxer had been pivoted into temporary oblivion, without any action being taken toward outlawing the blow. But Dempsey was such a hero in the eyes of the ring patrons, that both promoters and public were bound to show their detestation of the punch that brought him misfortune, and they acted accordingly.'

Old-timers claim that the pivot blow was no more brutal or inhuman than many others, but there was no doubt about its spine-chilling effect when it landed squarely on target. Even so, good judgement was required in using it because if the 'pivoteer' happened to miss, he was left wide open to a counter punch.

Another blow that is seldom seen today, although perfectly legal, is the bolo punch. So named because the action is similar to that adopted by workers in sugar plantations when cutting cane with a bolo knife, the punch is brought up almost from the floor. Ceferino Garcia, the former world middleweight champion from the Philippines, is generally credited with having made the punch popular in the 1930s but others like Kid Gavilan and Ike Williams actually used it to even better effect.

British boxing fans still talk about the night in 1946 when Williams used a bolo punch to knock out Ronnie James in a world lightweight title fight in Cardiff. Williams unleashed the blow in the ninth round. 'Nobody in the stadium had ever seen a blow like it before,' recalls O F Snelling, the British boxing historian. 'James got up only to go down again and again from similar deliveries to the self-same spot.'

The following day British fans learned from their newspapers that they had witnessed the dreaded bolo punch, a blow seldom seen in British rings before or since.

More frequently seen is the uppercut. A great match-winning punch, and one that excites the crowd even when it misses, the blow must be timed to the split second to be really effective. The master of the uppercut was Jack Johnson, the legendary world heavyweight champion. Considered one of the greatest defensive boxers of all time, Johnson won numerous fights with his uppercuts, but none was more spectacular than his knockout of Stanley Ketchel in 1909.

Ketchel dropped Johnson with a savage right to the jaw in the 12th round, but Johnson's massive frame had scarcely struck the floor when it bounced back to drive a powerful uppercut to Ketchel's mouth. Ketchel's feet left the canvas under the impact of the blow. He turned a half somersault in the air, fell heavily, and collapsed in a heap.

A picture-perfect right cross from Alfredo Evangelista swivels the head of Renaldo Snipes during their heavyweight fight in 1983.

Jess Willard, the man who beat Johnson for the heavyweight title, was often described as being bone-lazy. He had a lethargic temperament, hated training, and was given to loafing in the ring in a way that drove his backers frantic.

But if there was one thing the big fellow could do well, it was to throw an uppercut. Willard lifted Soldier Kearns clean off his feet and hurled him across the ring with an uppercut in 1912, and a year later he used a terrific right uppercut to knock out Bull Young. Unfortunately, Young failed to regain consciousness and died a few hours later from what was diagnosed as a broken neck.

Many attempts have been made to measure the power of a punch. In 1987, Barry French, a self-employed American broker of scientific instruments, invented what amounted to a punch-measuring machine for boxers. French calculated the force of a punch to the number of pounds it represents when it hits a surface.

'The average amateur heavyweight delivers 152 to 200 pounds of force per punch,' he said. 'A guy off the street would deliver 100. A professional heavyweight, 200 to 400 pounds.'

French planned to offer his device, which he later called Punch Impact, to American television networks. Madison Square Garden TV used it during a telecast in May 1990 but little has been heard of it since.

RACISM

John L Sullivan, the last bareknuckle heavyweight champion, did it before the turn of the century. Jack Dempsey, the legendary 'Manassa Mauler', did it when it was still fashionable in the 1920s. And Larry Holmes, the then World Boxing Council heavyweight champion, did it in the 1980s.

But while many may have considered the reasons advanced by

Holmes as more specious than those of Sullivan and Dempsey, the bottom line was still racism. Sullivan and Dempsey drew the colour line against black fighters at a time when it was considered the prudent thing to do. Holmes at first drew the line against Gerrie Coetzee not because of his colour, but because of his nationality.

'I'll never fight him,' Holmes said in the early 1980s. 'Nothing personal, you understand. I just don't want to get involved with the racism.' In the event, Holmes did sign to fight Coetzee in Las Vegas in June 1984 but the fight fell through when the promoters pulled the plug for financial reasons.

Sullivan and Dempsey were less yielding. Sullivan, who openly boasted that he 'could lick any son of a bitch in the land', publicly refused to fight Peter Jackson, the great black heavyweight from Jamaica, in the 1890s. 'I will not fight a Negro,' John L declared. 'I never have and I never will.'

And the day after he had knocked out Jess Willard to win the world heavyweight title on 4 July 1919 Dempsey made his own position in regard to mixed fights quite clear.

Under the headline 'Dempsey Will Meet Only White Boxers', the *New York Times* published the following report from Toledo, Ohio: 'In the first statement he has made since becoming the heavyweight champion of the world, Jack Dempsey announced today that he would draw the color line. He will pay no attention to Negro challengers, but will defend his title against any white heavyweights as the occasion demands.'

After five years as champion, Dempsey evidently changed his mind and signed to defend the championship against black challenger Harry Wills in Benton Harbor, Michigan. The fight, however, never took place.

Despite the apprehension of Holmes, Coetzee enjoyed excellent press in the United States when he won the World Boxing Association heavyweight title in September 1983. Other foreign heavyweights to win the title – like Max Schmeling of Germany, Primo Carnera of Italy and Ingemar Johansson of Sweden – were less fortunate. The American media were openly hostile to both Schmeling and Carnera and treated Johansson more like a diversion than a world champion.

The fact that Carnera was managed by known gangsters and Schmeling was closely associated with Nazi Germany did not help their cause. But even Johansson, whose biggest 'crime' was being disqualified in the finals of the 1952 Olympic Games and having his girlfriend share his training quarters before the first Patterson fight in 1959, failed to break the ice.

Hitler and Mussolini were the crosses Schmeling and Carnera had to bear back in the 1930s, just as the South African government's apartheid policy was a cross Coetzee had to carry in the 1980s. But whereas Schmeling dined with Der Führer and Carnera performed for Il Duce, Coetzee wisely turned his back on racism.

Dick Young, boxing writer for the *New York Post*, was impressed. 'I'm not saying Gerrie Coetzee, world heavyweight champ, makes South Africa morally antiseptic. Soweto stinks. The fact that a man, because of his skin, must carry an ID, stinks. But it will change, it is changing, and men like Gerrie Coetzee will help,' Young wrote in the *Post*.

And when Roy Innis, national chairman of the Congress of Racial Equality, made the heavyweight title a platform on which to sound his political views on apartheid, Dave Bontempo of the Atlantic City *Press* came right back to shoot him down in flames. Innis had implored WBC champion Larry Holmes to unify the title against Coetzee because he claimed the heavyweight title was symbolic for black people. 'Competition instils racial pride,' said Innis, 'something to shoot for. It's kind of a healthy racial rivalry.'

'What?' Bontempo asked. 'Why not coin the phrase "healthy nuclear holocaust"? We're not talking about neighborhood versus neighborhood, city versus city. This so-called "healthy rivalry" produced rioting in the streets only a few years ago. Today, both sides still carry deep-seated resentment, despite progressive attempts for integration. Race relations remain a slow, delicate process.'

Few writers were prepared to go to bat for Schmeling and Carnera in the 1930s. Carnera was a tragic figure at the best of times, but when he returned to Italy after winning the world title from Jack Sharkey in 1933, he quickly became a pawn of Italian dictator Benito Mussolini. Not only did Mussolini order a specially tailored uniform of the blackshirt fascists for the world champion, but photographs of Carnera smartly delivering the fascist salute went to newspapers

Larry Holmes, the former WBC and IBF heavyweight champion, refused to fight Gerrie Coetzee because 'I just don't want to get involved with the racism.'

around the world.

And then, with Il Duce on hand to lend encouragement, Carnera defended his newly won title against Spaniard Paulino Uzcudin in Rome.

Not surprisingly, the Carnera–Louis fight in 1935 became to some degree a contest between a representative of fascist Italy and an

American of African descent. At least one college professor went on record as saying that defeat of Carnera by Louis 'might cause Mussolini to take the final steps to punish Ethiopia'.

Max Schmeling was in an even worse predicament. 'What can you do if your prime minister or president invites you to tea? Of course you must accept,' Schmeling told me in 1980. This was Schmeling's way of explaining the weekend he spent at Berchtesgaden with Adolf Hitler and his Nazi cohorts in 1936 following his sensational victory over Joe Louis at Yankee Stadium in New York.

That visit was to cost Schmeling dearly. When Schmeling met Louis in a rematch two years later he was openly branded a Nazi by the American media. In a two-part piece for the *Saturday Evening Post*, Paul Gallico, in describing Schmeling's home, noted a basket of flowers with a red swastika ribbon, sent by Adolf Hitler to Anny Ondra (Max's wife) and a photograph of Der Führer with a personal inscription hung over a trophy case.

Max Schmeling explains why he spent a weekend at Berchtesgaden with Adolf Hitler in 1936.

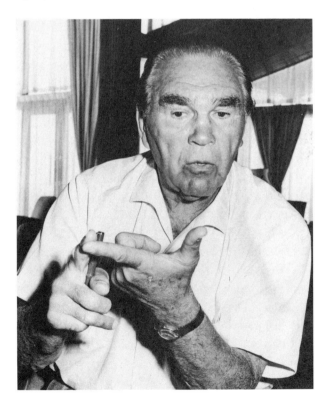

'The atmosphere between Germany and America was very bad in 1938,' Schmeling reminded me as he recalled the past. 'There were pickets in front of my hotel every day and when I walked from the dressing room to the ring at Yankee Stadium, the crowd threw things at me and called me dirty names.'

Schmeling claimed he found it almost impossible to keep his mind on the fight and admitted that he was still badly shaken by the reception of the crowd when the bell rang. 'To be honest, on that night nobody would have beaten Louis,' he said. 'They poisoned his mind against me and he fought like an animal. I never had a chance.'

While Jack Johnson was the first black man to win the heavyweight championship of the world, the first black men to challenge for the championship were Bill Richmond and Tom Molineaux. Both were beaten by Tom Cribb – Richmond after one hour and 30 minutes of terrific fighting, and Molineaux in 33 rounds under London Prize Ring Rules.

And while Johnson thumbed his nose at the establishment by cavorting with white women after he beat Tommy Burns in Sydney in 1908 – the US Congress later passed the Mann Act to force him into exile – the racist tone of both the Australian and American press in reporting the fight inflamed public opinion and resulted in race riots across the United States.

Jack London's emotional report from the ringside for the *New York Herald* did little to placate white resentment, but as Randy Roberts pointed out in his book *Papa Jack* in 1983, the Australian media was even more irresponsible. *Fairplay*, the brewery trades weekly, called Johnson 'a huge primordial ape', while the *Bulletin*'s cartoons likened him to a shaven-headed reptile. And by far the most racist reporter at the ringside was Randolph Bedford, who used descriptive terms like 'the white beauty' and 'the black unloveliness'.

The naked racism encouraged Americans to search for a white heavyweight hope capable of beating Johnson. This in turn resulted in the deplorable White Hope Era of boxing, which came to an end on 5 April 1915 when Jess Willard knocked out Johnson in the 26th round in Havana. 'Now mebbe de'll let me alone,' Johnson said afterwards.

Fat chance! For the next 20 years Johnson was blamed for having

Jack Johnson thumbed his nose at the Establishment when he became heavyweight champion of the world in 1908. Below:Johnson knocks out Jim Jeffries in the 15th round in the fight that triggered race riots all over America in 1910.

made it virtually impossible for another black man to challenge for the heavyweight championship of the world. Against all odds, Joe Louis was given a title shot at Jim Braddock in 1937 and when Joe won on a knockout in the eighth round, the so-called 'gentlemen's agreement' between boxing men, designed to keep another black from winning the richest prize in sport, was broken for ever.

'How important was Joe?' Dick Edwards, a veteran black sportswriter for the *New Age Press*, asked in 1987. 'If Joe hadn't won that title, I don't know if we'd have ever gotten out of the jailhouse.'

Even so, boxing remained segregated in some of the southern states of America until the late 1940s, which was about the time that the colour bar in British boxing was also lifted. Dick Turpin celebrated the belated change in the rules by beating Vince Hawkins over 15 rounds at the Aston Villa football ground on 28 June 1948 to win the British middleweight title.

Forty years later there were still allegations of racism in British boxing and Channel 4's *Black Bag: The New Gladiators* highlighted claims that the British Boxing Board of Control was reluctant to allow black athletes to become involved in the administration of the sport.

'The colour issue is an important question in boxing, but it's never been that big a thing and, in my opinion, over the next ten years there will be many changes in the sport,' John Morris, General Secretary of the Board, told *Boxing Monthly* magazine.

South Africa, regarded by many as the most racist country in the world, had already removed all the racial barriers in boxing. First, by approving the world light heavyweight title fight between Bob Foster and Pierre Fourie in Johannesburg in December 1973, then by permitting multi-national tournaments in 1974, and finally by legalizing mixed bouts between black and white South Africans in 1977. An age where black is beautiful had finally dawned.

The transition was surprisingly easy but not without the odd hiccup. There was natural indignation when José Sulaiman, president of the World Boxing Council, called for South Africans to be barred from international competition in 1981. In the event, Sulaiman had to settle for a United Nations blacklist, applicable to all sportsmen who competed in South Africa while the country was under the apartheid regime.

Floyd Patterson, the former heavyweight champion of the world and a New York State boxing commissioner, was in the Republic at the time. Asked to comment, Patterson told *Boxing World* magazine that he supported change – but without the threats.

'Why is it that the word "black" so often has bad vibes?' Patterson asked. 'There are the words "blackmail" and "blacklist". Why not call them "whitemail" and "whitelist"? But to answer your question, as a former sportsman and a current sports administrator, I don't believe that politics should enter the sporting arena and I'm not in favour of political pressure being exerted on any athlete.'

RADIO

First it was the printed word that helped to make boxing popular and accepted as a legitimate sport. Then it was radio that carried the excitement of a fight into millions of homes. And now it is television that has given viewers around the world a ringside seat at many of the biggest fights of all time.

And yet, when radio was first used to broadcast fights in the early 1920s, many in boxing felt it would ultimately hurt the sport by keeping the fans away from fights. With hindsight we now know that it took the advent of television to reduce live attendances. Radio not only stimulated interest in the sport, it added to boxing's mystique.

The medium was first used at a boxing match in the United States in 1919 when Jack Dempsey knocked out Jess Willard in the third round to win the world heavyweight title at Toledo, Ohio. Reporters telegraphed the result of the fight via radio from the ringside.

But the first radio broadcast of a fight came two years later when Major Andrew White and J O Smith described the world heavyweight title fight between Jack Dempsey and Georges Carpentier at Boyle's Thirty Acres, Jersey City, New Jersey. The date was 2 July 1921 and their commentary was heard in a number of theatres across America.

To test their equipment, which was on loan from the United States Navy, White and Smith started commentating during the last round of a no-decision preliminary bout between Packey O'Gatty and Frankie Burns.

The Dempsey–Carpentier broadcast almost didn't happen. Problems arose when it was discovered that the radio equipment belonged to the US Navy and that special permission was required in order to take it to the arena in Jersey City. Franklin Delano Roosevelt, later to become president of the United States, was the naval officer who finally authorized its use.

Listeners on that hot summer's day were caught up in the excitement of the fight in the fourth round when White yelled: 'The Frenchman is down! The referee is counting – three, four ... Carpentier makes no effort to rise ... six, seven ... he's sinking to the mat ... nine, ten! The fight is over! Jack Dempsey remains heavyweight champion of the world!'

A year later Dempsey himself was at Olympia in London to broadcast the light heavyweight title fight between Carpentier and Ted 'Kid' Lewis via wireless telephone for station 2LO in the United States. Carpentier knocked out Lewis in two minutes 30 seconds of the first round.

Six years after the first ever radio broadcast of a boxing match, 82 radio stations broadcast the second fight between Dempsey and Gene Tunney in Chicago in September 1927. But the first bout to be broadcast worldwide on radio was the heavyweight title fight between Max Baer and Primo Carnera in June 1934. NBC carried the broadcast, which was sponsored by the B F Goodrich Company of America.

The first of the once famous Gillette *Cavalcade of Sport* broadcasts came a year later when Baer defended the heavyweight title against Jim Braddock. Baer had become well known on radio in America for his coast-to-coast serials, *Taxi* and *Lucky Smith*, and the champion's popularity on the airwaves went a long way towards making the

EMPSEY KAYO'S
CARPENTIER, 4TH ROUND
BOYLE'S THIRTY ACRES
JERSEY CITY N.J.
JULY 2, 1921

Above: in the first fight to be broadcast on radio, from Jersey City on 2 July 1921, Jack Dempsey knocked out Georges Carpentier.

Right: The end of the heavy-weight championship fight between James J Braddock (left) and Max Baer in 1935. The fight was the first in the once famous Gillette *Cavalcade of Sport* broadcasts in America.

Braddock fight a viable economic proposition.

After Andrew White had started the ball rolling with his Dempsey–Carpentier broadcast in 1921, a host of other men made names for themselves as radio commentators in the US, including Graham McNamee, Ted Husing, Bill Stern, Sam Taub, Clem McCarthy and Don Dunphy.

A noted boxing expert and former newspaperman, Taub was posthumously inducted into the Boxing Hall of Fame in Canastota, New York, in 1994. The American had a quick delivery and a flair for dramatics as a commentator and broadcast more than 7,000 fights during the 1920s, 1930s and 1940s. His radio programme *The Hour of Champions* ran every Sunday in the United States for 24 years.

In June 1934, the National Broadcasting Company attempted an experiment. George Hicks was assigned to interview Primo Carnera in his dressing room following the champion's defence of his world heavyweight title against Max Baer in Long Island.

It turned out to be an idea whose time had not quite come. Not only did Carnera return to his dressing room as an ex-champion (Baer knocked him out in the 11th round), Primo was hardly in the mood to be interviewed. And then, after much coaxing, when the big fellow finally agreed to talk, he broke down and cried.

Somebody at Radio City, however, had already pulled the plug on the broadcast and Hicks later recalled how he could hear Graham McNamee at the ringside screaming into his microphone: 'For Christ's sake! Get this on the air! It's great! Primo Carnera is crying!'

Boxing broadcasts had clearly come of age and to underline their popularity Mike Jacobs, who was then promoting fights at the Hippodrome in New York, signed an 18-week contract with Adams Hats in 1937 for a series of broadcasts on station WHN. It was the first paid radio sponsorship for boxing.

Arguably the best British boxing commentary team at the time was that of Raymond Glendenning and W Barrington Dalby, a former Grade A referee who worked as a boxing commentator for the BBC for more than 25 years.

Glendenning handled the blow-by-blow descriptions and Dalby provided the inter-round summaries. Between them they almost became an institution on the BBC, having started in the days when

LOU NOVA 202½ versus JOE LOUIS 202½
WORLD HEAVYWEIGHT TITLE FIGHT, 60,875 FANS
POLO GROUNDS, NEW YORK, SEPT. 29, 1941
LOUIS BY TKO 6th. ROUND
NATIONS BIGGEST RADIO AUDIENCE.

The world heavyweight title fight between Lou Nova and Joe Louis at the Polo Grounds, New York in 1941 was estimated to have had the biggest radio audience in the United States.

boxing commentators sat in glass-fronted boxes, which were placed behind the last row at the ringside. 'They were dreadful places to work in,' Dalby later recalled.

Choice of the correct word is absolutely essential in broadcasting as Dalby discovered to his cost after a slip of the tongue got Glendenning and himself in hot water with the press following the first fight between Sugar Ray Robinson and Randolph Turpin at Earls Court, London, in July 1951.

At the end of the 14th round, Dalby told listeners: 'If Turpin can stage a really grandstand finish in this round, I think he may well snatch the verdict.' The word Dalby meant to use was 'clinch' not 'snatch'. It made a world of difference because it implied that the fight was closer than it was.

The British press had a ball as they toasted Turpin for his magnificent victory and roasted the BBC commentators for doubting Turpin's ability. At least one Sunday newspaper claimed that the commentators were incompetent and suggested that they should be sacked.

Such was the price men had to pay for being boxing commentators in the days when radio was king.

RATINGS

The idea of rating fighters originated in American football. And if that surprises you, stand by for yet another shock: the very first boxing ratings were published not under the name of the man who conceived them, but under the name of one of the greatest promoters of all time.

Rating fighters was the brainchild of Nat Fleischer, the then editor and publisher of *The Ring* magazine. Fleischer borrowed the idea from Walter Camp, who had initiated the custom of ranking All-American football players.

But when Fleischer decided to publish the first ratings in the February 1925 issue of *The Ring*, he asked promoter Tex Rickard to put his name to the list to give it credibility (much in the same way that John Graham Chambers asked the eighth Marquess of Queensberry to sponsor the Queensberry Rules in 1867.

Fleischer later explained in his book *Fifty Years at Ringside* why he chose Rickard to do the job. 'The fabulous Tex was in his heyday then, and following the announcement that he was to make a selection of the world's ranking boxers, his ratings were awaited with tremendous interest,' Fleischer wrote.

The ratings caused worldwide comment and became a regular

feature in the magazine. Rickard continued to make the choices for a number of years, but after his death in 1929, Fleischer invited Jack Dempsey to make the selections. However, Dempsey suffered from the same shortcomings as his predecessor – a reluctance to take the lighter division boxers seriously – and lasted only one year.

Tom McArdle, then matchmaker at Madison Square Garden, succeeded Dempsey and compiled the ratings until 1933 when Fleischer inaugurated a system of rating boxers on the basis of a poll conducted among *The Ring* correspondents throughout the world.

The Ring set the benchmark for good ratings but when the National Boxing Association started to issue its own official list on a semi-annual basis, things immediately began to go wrong. The 1935 NBA ratings listed Black Bill, who had died two years previously, as the head of the bantamweight contenders, and Ernie Schaaf, who likewise had passed away many months before, as No 3 among the heavyweights.

Left: Tex Rickard (seen here with Jack Dempsey) agreed to put his name on the very first ratings published in *Ring* magazine. *Right:* Ratings were the brainchild of Nat Fleischer, a dandy American who had an astonishing influence on the fight game.

A glance at the official rating lists currently being issued by the World Boxing Association, World Boxing Council, International Boxing Federation, World Boxing Organization and any of the other so-called sanctioning bodies confirms the suspicion that little has changed. The ratings are often an insult to the intelligence of boxing fans everywhere.

I once asked Bobby Lee, the then president of the WBA, how his organization compiled its official ratings. 'I tell you, sir, you can have ratings and ratings and I don't care what you do you'll always have an argument,' Lee said.

'The system adopted by the WBA is that we have rating committee people in various parts of the world, and it's their job to send to us the results of all fights that they may have. Then the chairman gets together with a couple of his people and they look at the results and they come out with the ratings.

'Of course, it's difficult because the chairman is in Hawaii and we have a member in Japan, a member in the Philippines and a member in the Argentine. So all he can do is take all of the results and look at it and say, "Okay, this fellow lost and this fellow won" and try to make a rating like that.

'But I've said it before and I'll say it again, that even if Jesus Christ was rating the fighters somebody would have a complaint.'

Everybody, it seems, has a complaint and largely because the official ratings issued by these organizations determine whether or not a boxer will get a title shot. The concept came in for strong criticism from the International Boxing Writers' Association, a New York-based body, in 1982 .

'The WBA and WBC make no pretences,' the IBWA declared in their newsletter *Center Ring*. 'They rate the fighters they are promoting in title fights, almost at whim. They are at cross-purposes. It's a clique of promoters determined to advance their own interests, and who oppose anything that's not in their interest.'

Told by the *Financial Mail*, a South African business magazine, that there were accusations that ratings are rigged, American promoter Bob Arum said: 'People don't understand how either I, or the ratings, work.

'I take a promising boxer, build him up, talk to the people in the business and they send letters of recommendation. I am happy if I slot my fighter into ninth or tenth position and from there he fights it out with the other champs. It is called planting. You plant a tree and through nutrition it grows. I am not the only promoter doing it.

'This is not manipulation, it is marketing – as one would find in any other business.'

Sandy Johnson, secretary of the Nevada State Athletic Commission, put the whole question of ratings into perspective in 1993. 'If there weren't any alphabet groups in boxing, it wouldn't make any difference to us,' she said. 'We'd sanction the fights anyway because the public knows who's who if they are interested in boxing. We approve bouts on fighters' records and merits. The various ratings mean nothing. They're usually garbage anyway.'

RECORDS

Few sports have been as carefully documented as boxing. Pierce Egan, boxing's first truly great historian, set the standard when he published *Boxiana* in 1818 and few can complain about the quality.

Admittedly, the first known record book – *Fistiana and Boxiana, the Oracle of the Prize Ring* – was only published in America in 1841 but others soon followed and, by and large, the sport has been well served by its record-keepers and statisticians.

Fistiana and Boxiana appeared regularly until 1869 and was followed by the *New York Clipper Annual*, which lasted until 1901. But boxing record books really only came of age when Richard K Fox, publisher of the *Police Gazette*, produced a record book in January 1896. The book listed the records of 45 prominent boxers, plus a list of champions, collection of fistic facts and biographies of leading fighters. Fox published the annual until a fire destroyed the *Police Gazette* office and all the records in 1918.

Other record books, which also made their appearance before the turn of the century, were *Little Fistiana* in 1880, F K Lanpher's *Ring Records* in 1888, the *Champions Pocket Book Sports Annual* in 1889, and Nelse Innes's *Boxing Records* which was first published in Boston, in 1895. Innes, the then sports editor of the *Boston Herald*, produced the pocket-sized book in conjunction with Don Saunders, a sportswriter for the *Boston Globe*.

Veteran promoter and newspaperman Tom Andrews published his *Ring Battles of the Century* in 1903 and continued on an annual basis until 1937. The Everlast Sports Equipment Company published a record book in 1922 that appeared regularly for fifteen years. The final 1937 edition had no connection with the original owners. Eddie Borden was granted permission to use the name, but ceased publication after one edition.

In 1930, the *Post Boxing Record* book made its first appearance. Edited by John L Romano, the pocket-sized booklet was able to call upon many of the top American sportswriters as contributors. An advertisement for the 1935 edition claimed that 'all records are complete, more than 300 in all. You do not have to refer to old, outdated copies to find out the date a fight took place or a championship changed hands. The *Post Boxing Record* gives you all the necessary information and goes back to 1881.'

But by far the most famous boxing record book to be published in the United States was *The Ring Boxing Encyclopedia and Record Book*. It first appeared as a paper-bound book limited to 250 copies in 1942. Editor and publisher Nat Fleischer was so pleased with the international interest it provoked that he quickly got out another 750 copies in a hard cover.

It was never Fleischer's intention to produce the book on an annual basis, as can be gleaned from the remarks he made in the 1943 edition. 'What about the future? Is there to be a new edition of this book every year?' Fleischer asked in his introduction. 'I can say only that it is my plan to get out an All-British Empire Record Book. Whether this will be a separate volume or a supplement to the main edition, I will decide when we reach that point.

'In the meantime, the future of this all-time *Ring Record Book* rests with the war. We are going to win. That is certain. But it may not be over within the year, and in consequence, raises issues which I am not able to determine now.'

The last edition of the book appeared in 1987, an incredible run of 45 years, and was edited by Herbert G Goldman.

Boxing records have since become an essential part of the sport and in keeping with modern communication trends, the *Boxing Record Book* – published by Fight Fax Inc of Sicklerville, New Jersey and edited by Phill Marder – provides a service no other record book ever has. Updated records are available upon request for a small fee and can be faxed anywhere in the world.

Europe lagged behind America when it came to the publication of boxing record books. The British daily *Sporting Life* issued a boxing record book in 1909 and again in 1921, while *Boxing*, the British weekly, also produced record books in 1914 and 1921. Victor Breyer, a Paris journalist and boxing referee, published *Annuaire Du Ring*, a record book mainly devoted to French boxers, from 1909 until 1939.

The *Post Boxing Record* book was first published in 1930 and was one of the most popular record books of the 1930s, while *The Ring Boxing Encyclopedia and Record Book* had the longest life of any boxing record book yet published.

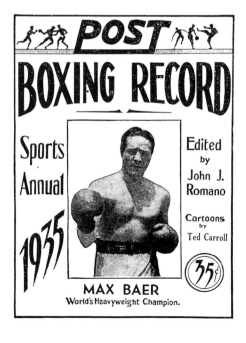

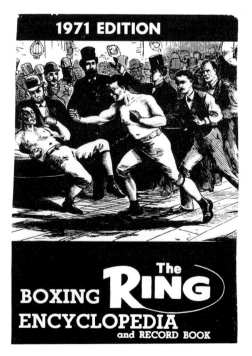

The *Boxing News Annual* came on the market for the first time in 1944 and continued until 1985. The handsomely produced *Pugilato* was first published by Giuseppe Ballarati in Rome in 1972 and was produced annually until his death in 1995. Also worth mentioning is the *British Boxing Yearbook*, founded by Barry J Hugman in 1984, which changed its name to the *British Boxing Board of Control Yearbook* in 1993.

The newest record book to come on the market is the *British Boxing Records* compiled by Bob Mee. The large-format book first made an appearance in 1993 and looks set for a successful run. Mee admitted in the 1995 edition that he was still looking at ways of dividing two- and three-minute round fights in the records. 'The danger is that we make a fight record seem more complicated than it is,' Mee wrote in his introduction.

The style in which fight results are recorded has been the biggest problem facing publishers of boxing record books since *Fistiana and Boxiana* was first issued in 1841.

Nat Fleischer always insisted that there was no such thing as a 'technical knockout' and all inside the distance wins or losses (except for disqualifications) were listed as knockouts in *The Ring Record Book*. Herb Goldman changed the policy with the publication of the 1986–7 edition. Goldman not only recognized technical knockouts for the first time but also accepted some of the 'newspaper decisions' rendered during the no-decision days of American boxing.

Phill Marder of Fight Fax has adopted an even more belligerent stance than Fleischer by refusing to accept the results of fights held in those American states without a boxing commission. Marder lists such fights in his *Boxing Record Book* as 'no contests'.

Incredibly, all the record books show the result of the heavyweight fight between James J Corbett and Peter Jackson at the California Athletic Club in 1891 as a draw over 61 rounds, even though referee Hiram Cook declared it a 'no contest'. And until it ceased publication in 1985, the *Boxing News Annual* insisted on recording the WBC heavyweight title fight between Larry Holmes and Gerry Cooney in 1982 as a win by disqualification for Holmes in the 13th round. All the other record books describe it as a win for the champion by technical knockout.

For many years all the leading record books, including both *Pugilato* and *The Ring Record Book*, recorded the first loss of Julio Cesar Chavez as being by disqualification in one round to Miguel Ruiz in Culiacan, Mexico, on 3 April 1981. This has since been changed to a knockout victory for Chavez, based on confirmation from the local boxing commission in Culiacan that it altered the verdict the following day.

Ramon Felix, manager of Chavez, happened to be a member of the Culiacan commission at the time.

REFEREES

Next to the fighters, the most important man in boxing is the referee. Who says so? The fellows who drew up the rules of boxing, that's who.

It matters not whether you check the London Prize Ring Rules, the Queensberry Rules, the rules and regulations of the World Boxing Association or those of the World Boxing Council. All confirm that only one man has ever been invested with absolute authority in the ring – the referee.

Even the old bareknuckle bruisers realized that somebody had to have the final say. Rule 4 of the London Prize Ring Rules made no bones about the fact that the referee was the man 'to whom all disputes shall be referred, and that the decision of this referee, whatever it may be, shall be final and strictly binding on all parties'.

A couple of hundred years later the WBA has seen fit to confirm that 'the referee shall be the chief official in every Championship contest', while the WBC rules and regulations categorically state that the referee 'has the authority to instruct the head cornermen of their duties and responsibilities during the fight'. Rule 9 of the British

Boxing Board of Control is even more emphatic: 'The Referee's decision shall be final.'

And yet, despite his awesome powers in the ring, the referee is the invisible man of boxing – or should be. Good referees go about their work quietly, almost surreptitiously, and fight fans only become aware of their presence in the ring when things go wrong. The referee is also a man to be respected, even though it has not always been that way.

There was a time when some promoters – notably Hugh D McIntosh and Tex Rickard – even refereed their own fights, and in the early 1920s it was also fashionable for champions to employ their own referees. Worse still, some of the early referees were downright dishonest.

One of the most flagrant examples of ring robbery was the verdict rendered by Wyatt Earp, the famous Western marshal, in the fight between Bob Fitzsimmons and Tom Sharkey in San Francisco in December 1896.

Before the bout Frank Julian, manager of Fitzsimmons, claimed loudly that he had heard on good authority that the outcome had already been fixed by local gamblers and that Sharkey was to win at all costs. The fact that members of the press were not seated at the ringside as usual, but farther back, seemed to lend credibility to Julian's claim.

In any event, when Fitzsimmons drove home a powerful body blow in the eighth round that sent Sharkey to the floor writhing in pain, referee Earp promptly disqualified 'Ruby Robert', asserting that Fitzsimmons had struck Sharkey low.

As the enraged Fitzsimmons turned on the referee, the US marshal drew his gun and ordered him away. Earp may have been a pillar of justice and fair play in Dodge City, but as a boxing referee he left much to be desired.

Mind you, this was not the first time a boxer had attempted to attack the referee – nor was it to be the last. One of the worst such incidents happened at Cologne, Germany, in 1952 when former German middleweight champion Peter Mueller attacked referee Max Pippow in the eighth round of his fight with Hans Stretz, knocking out the referee with vicious blows to the head. To nobody's great

Mike DeCosmo attempts to assist referee Joe Walker as Laurie Buxton looks on. Each accused the other of delivering the knockout blow.

surprise, the German Boxing Association banned Mueller for life.

American referee Joe Walker had even worse luck while officiating in the fight between Mike DeCosmo and Laurie Buxton at the Meadowbrook Bowl in Newark, New Jersey, on 18 May 1948. Walker, who later was to serve as the New Jersey State boxing commissioner, stepped between the boxers at the final bell to call a halt to the fighting and ended out cold on the canvas.

Who delivered the knockout blow remains a mystery. Neither boxer was prepared to accept responsibility. It took quite a while for Walker to recover (he was the sole judge and referee) and to deliver his verdict of a draw.

Perhaps this explains why the men who drew up the London Prize

Ring Rules stipulated in Rule 20 that 'the referee and umpires shall take their positions in front of the centre stake, outside the ropes'.

Even after the Queensberry Rules were drafted in 1865, this strange practice was still strictly adhered to (especially in Britain), and it was not until 1932 that the British Boxing Board of Control made it a rule that fights be refereed from inside the ring.

The Douglas brothers, Johnny and 'Pickles', who were brought up by their father in the tradition of the famous National Sporting Club, were the last British refs to work by remote control. Immaculate in dinner jackets, they sat on chairs close to the ring apron; the embodiment of Corinthian amateurism.

There have, of course, always been good and bad referees. One of the best of the early referees was George Siler of Chicago. Siler started officiating in the bareknuckle days of boxing and was a referee for about 25 years. He refereed thousands of fights and was so honest and so expert that he was invariably the first choice of fighters themselves, especially when a title was at stake.

George Siler, complete with hat, braces and bow-tie, was one of America's top referees at the turn of the century. Here he referees the fight between Tom Sharkey and Jim Jeffries in 1899.

Jay Edson, popular co-ordinator for Top Rank Inc and former referee, proudly poses with actress Bo Derek at Caesars Palace in Las Vegas.

Even so, when Siler was appointed to referee the world heavyweight title fight between James J Corbett and Bob Fitzsimmons in Carson City, Nevada, in 1897, he thought nothing of doubling as chief correspondent for the *Chicago Tribune*.

Such shenanigans would never be tolerated today. Modern controlling bodies are placing more and more emphasis on neutral officials and the names of the referee and judges are seldom announced until just before a fight.

It was lack of control that resulted in Jay Edson not only refereeing and judging the fight between Pete McIntyre and Mike Fisher on the Ali–Berbick undercard in the Bahamas in December 1981, but also playing the role of timekeeper because the official timekeeper had gone home. Edson borrowed a wristwatch from a ringsider to time the rounds.

Referees can make or break a fight, as Joey Curtis proved in the first fight between Mike Weaver and Michael Dokes in Las Vegas in 1982, or cost a champion his title as Carlos Padilla did when he instructed the judges to take a point away from Hector Camacho for attempting to strike Greg Haugen instead of touching gloves in their

When Ruby Goldstein was forced to retire as referee from the 1952 fight between Joey Maxim and Sugar Ray Robinson because of heat exhaustion, Ray Miller (above) took over as third man.

WBO junior welterweight title fight in 1991.

They can also turn a good fight into a great one, as Stan Christodoulou did when he allowed the WBA light heavyweight title fight between Victor Galindez and Richie Kates in Johannesburg in 1976 to continue after a five-minute break. Christodoulou later went on to become the first referee in the world to score a unique grand slam when in December 1991 he completed a lifelong ambition to referee world title fights in each of boxing's 17 weight divisions.

Nor should it ever be forgotten that referees are also human. Ruby Goldstein proved that when he suffered heat exhaustion in a world title fight at Yankee Stadium and had to be replaced by Ray Miller. It happened on 25 June 1952 during a heat wave in New York. (Jesse Abramson, boxing writer for the New York *Herald-Tribune*, reported that the temperature at the ringside was 104°F.)

Sugar Ray Robinson was challenging Joey Maxim for the world light heavyweight title but was literally wilting in the oppressive heat. Goldstein staggered out of the ring at the end of the 10th round and was replaced by Ray Miller as referee. And three rounds later Robinson collapsed on his stool and failed to answer the bell for the 14th round.

It was the first time Robinson was stopped in his career and the irony is that he was comfortably ahead on points on all the official scorecards. The combined scorecards of the two referees had Robinson ahead by seven rounds to four with three even at the time of the stoppage.

RING

No one knows for sure why a boxing ring, which happens to be square, is called a 'ring'. There are several theories, of course, and one of the most popular is that the term originated in Roman days when a contestant declared his challenge by throwing his *cestus* – a leather hand-wrapping, sometimes metal-studded and often caked with blood from previous contests – into a circular arena.

Another theory is that the term originated in the days of George I. King George evidently ordered a piece of ground in Hyde Park to be fenced off and used as a place for 'turn ups', and this eventually became known as the 'ring'.

Whatever its origin, a roped ring is first mentioned in the London Prize Ring Rules of 1838, the first clause of which provided that the ring was to be pitched on turf; that it was to be 24 feet square and that the ropes were to be supported by eight posts.

There was also an outer ring, about a yard in depth. This was reserved for the referee, the umpires (one for each man), the timekeepers, the backers and a few privileged patrons. In the outer ring also were the Whips, tough men armed with whips whose duty it was to keep the spectators from interfering with the fighters.

Such interference was common in the early days of bareknuckle fighting, and one of the most important fights to be terminated because of unruly crowd behaviour was the first ever international heavyweight contest between American champion John C Heenan and British champion Tom Sayers in 1860.

In the 37th round the crowd, most of whom had bet on the Englishman, went wild. Fans clambered inside the ring and some ruffians cut the ropes. Chased by an angry, shouting mob, Heenan managed to escape and the bout was declared a draw.

When the Marquess of Queensberry Rules were drafted in 1865 the 24-foot ring was retained, but it was not until 1892 that a padded ring was used for the first time in a fight between Sammy Kelly and Bob Cunningham at Coney Island, New York.

Many years passed before the importance of ring padding as a safety device was recognized. The National Boxing Association (forerunner of the World Boxing Association) first insisted on approved padding for rings at a convention in Philadelphia in March 1948.

Four years later when the New York State Athletic Commission launched an all-out drive to curb ring deaths and engaged the Cornell Aeronautical Laboratories to investigate the problem, ring padding was again identified as a major cause of head injuries.

The laboratories proved that ring padding should be soft enough to absorb the tremendous blow that occurs when a man's head hits the canvas, but hard enough to prevent the bounce that occurs after a fall. As a result of tests at Cornell Laboratories, several new types of ring padding were produced, but nearly ten years were to pass before the WBA made them mandatory in world championship fights.

WBA regulations are now quite specific on the subject: 'The floor of the ring shall be padded with one inch layer of Ensolite, or the equivalent, placed over a one inch base of building board or other suitable material. The padding shall be covered with canvas, duck, or similar material tightly stretched and laced securely in place under the apron.'

London Prize Ring Rules made provision for only two ropes, but under the Marquess of Queensberry Rules these eventually became three and today the majority of controlling bodies insist on four.

This first became customary following the ring death in March 1963 of Davey Moore, who died while defending his world feather-weight title against Sugar Ramos in Los Angeles. An autopsy proved that Moore's death was caused not by a punch, but by a blow to the back of his skull caused by a snapping ring-rope as he fell.

A month later the New York State Athletic Commission announced that boxing rings with four strands of rope would be tested in a pilot

Rings with four ropes are now commonplace and first became customary following the ring death of Davey Moore in March 1963. This photograph shows Hector Camacho in action against Roque Montoya.

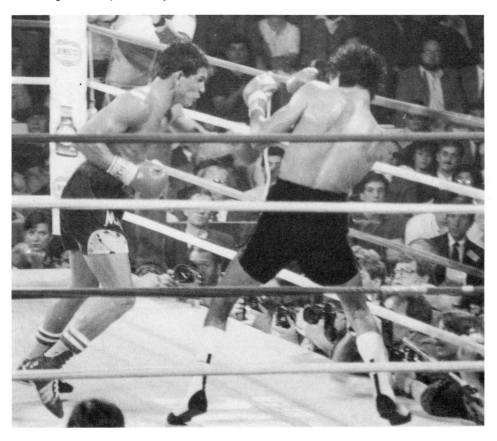

programme to safeguard boxers, and on 8 June 1963 the use of four ropes in all New York rings was adopted.

At the request of the New Jersey State Athletic Commission, the Everlast company tested specially designed ropes for boxing rings in 1984. The ropes were covered with a shock-absorbent foam that had four times the absorbency of floor padding.

Circular rings were first tested in England in 1912, while the practice of using a vertical cord, or string, to tie the ropes together originated in France in the 1930s.

'The boxing innovation – the round ring – is here to stay!' Max Marek declared in 1945. Marek had beaten Joe Louis as an amateur in 1933 and was then chief boxing instructor at the US Navy's Treasure Island training base in California. 'Although it is today considered more or less a novelty, it will in time pass its pioneering stage to become an accepted part of the fight game,' Marek predicted.

The round ring had been built in a San Francisco shipyard a year before and was first demonstrated before workmen on 26 May 1944 when former world middleweight champion Fred Apostoli sparred in an exhibition bout with Vic Grupico. But despite Marek's confident prediction, the circular ring, made of aluminium tubing and covered with heavy velvet cloth, never caught on.

SUGAR RAY ROBINSON

It seems strange that the man regarded by many as the greatest fighter, pound for pound, of all time disliked the sport that made him rich and famous.

'You may find this hard to believe,' Sugar Ray Robinson once said, 'but I've never loved fighting. I really dislike it. I don't believe I watch more than two fights a year, and then it has to be some friend of mine fighting.

'Fighting, to me, seems barbaric. It seems to me like the barbarous

Sugar Ray Robinson, the former world welterweight and middleweight champion, who died in April 1989 at the age of 67.

days when men fought in a pit and people threw money down to them.'

Mind you, Robinson disliked a great many other things besides boxing. As a black man he hated racism, cared little for the boxing establishment of his time, and had a love-hate relationship with Mike Jacobs and Jim Norris, the monopolistic promoters of the 1940s and 1950s. He even had a disdain for the press.

'Few fighters have been as disliked within their profession and by its press as was Robinson while he was struggling to make his way,' said W C Heinz, the great American sportswriter.

But while Robinson may not have been the most popular man in boxing, he earned the respect of just about everyone for his superb skill and marvellous achievements. He held the world welterweight

Sugar Ray and Joe Louis were close friends of long standing.

title for four years and relinquished it undefeated. He was five times middleweight champion of the world. He narrowly missed becoming a triple champion when heat exhaustion forced him to retire at the end of the 13th round against light heavyweight champion Joey Maxim in June 1952.

Robinson boxed for 25 years and fought 22 world championship bouts. He lost only 19 of 201 professional fights and he was never knocked out. He turned pro in 1940 and won 40 fights on the trot before losing to Jake LaMotta in 1943. He won the rematch three weeks later and did not lose again for nine years.

So it came as no surprise that, when Robinson died in April 1989 at the age of 67, newspapers around the world carried lengthy obituaries and lavished praise upon his memory. 'The sweetest style in the whole world,' one headline read. And, sure enough, whenever he climbed into a ring and began flashing those ebony fists, he looked as smooth as silk.

'You can't compare Sugar Ray Leonard with Sugar Ray Robinson,' Jake LaMotta told me a year before Robinson died. 'Sugar Ray Leonard is great for his day but Robinson won the middleweight title five times and fought for 30 years.

'He fought from welterweight to light heavyweight. He fought everybody. Nobody wanted to fight him and nobody wanted to fight me, so we ended up fighting each other.

'He broke my rib, he broke my jaw – but luckily as you can see, he never touched my nose,' LaMotta laughed. 'After the fight he looked into my eyes and said, "Jake, black is beautiful."'

Robinson was always conscious of his colour. When he and Joe Louis boxed exhibitions at US Army camps in the American south during the war years, they were almost always in trouble with the segregation laws.

In Alabama, Robinson and Louis failed to observe the 'whites only on the front benches' sign where they waited for a bus. In an argument with military policemen, Robinson grabbed one of the soldiers and wound up in the stockade. He was only released after Louis had protested to Washington.

Robinson often said things he later regretted. In 1946, while waiting to get a shot at the welterweight championship, he lashed

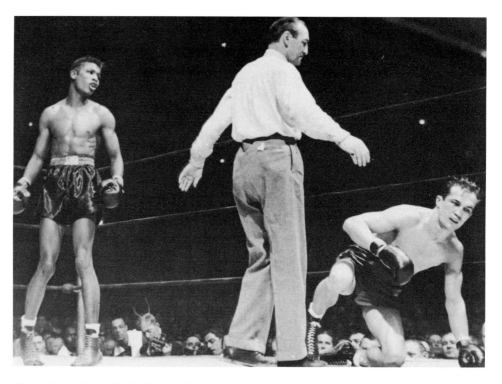

Sugar Ray stops Fritzie Zivic in the tenth round of their non-title fight in New York in 1942.

out at promoter Mike Jacobs, whom he believed was blocking the bout.

'Mike will manipulate anybody for a buck,' growled Robinson. 'He's always sore if I fight without his okay. If you don't do what he wants, he'll try to prevent you from getting fights anywhere. You don't earn the championship on merit any more, you buy it.'

Robinson was often accused of running out on fights but money was invariably at the root of the problem. 'If I was due a dollar, I felt I wanted that dollar,' he later told Peter Heller. 'If I could help a man make a dollar, I thought I deserved a part of it. And I took a stand to get that, and if they didn't pay me I didn't fight. And if something came up that could prevent me getting my end of the money, I would call off the fight.'

But Robinson could be generous, too. When he defended his

world welterweight title against Charley Fusari in August 1950 he gave his entire purse to the Damon Runyon Cancer Fund. He also gave Fusari the best boxing lesson of his life.

Many misunderstood Robinson because of his frankness. When Robinson knocked out Jimmy Doyle in defence of his welterweight title in June 1947 and Doyle died the next afternoon, they held an inquest.

'Why did you pick Doyle to fight?' the coroner asked him.

'Pick him!' said Ray, his voice rising. 'I didn't pick him. He picked me. I had something he wanted, my title.'

'Did you intend to get Doyle in trouble?'

'Mister,' said Robinson, trying hard to control his temper, 'it's my business to get him in trouble.'

Long before Muhammad Ali came on the scene, Robinson made the entourage fashionable in boxing. When he travelled to Europe in the 1950s, he was accompanied by an entourage that included a valet, a barber, a golf professional and a court jester. Ray drove a flamingo pink Cadillac and hotel porters were required to handle 53 suitcases.

Robinson looked upon the car as a symbol. 'When people think they recognize a celebrity, they hesitate a moment,' he said. 'But when they saw me in that car, they didn't have to hesitate. They knew. There was only one like it – Sugar Ray's pink Cadillac.'

And dare we say it? There was really only one Sugar Ray.

ROUNDS

The decision late in 1982 of the World Boxing Council to reduce the number of rounds in championship fights from 15 to 12 'to stop boxers from being pushed to the limits of human endurance' took both the World Boxing Association and the International Boxing Federation by surprise. And this despite the fact that the European Boxing Union had set the precedent four years earlier, following the ring death of Angelo Jacopucci in July 1978.

Gilberto Mendoza, president of the WBA, admitted at the time that the WBA had no plans to cut the number of championship rounds but added that he personally felt the final rounds of a fight could be shortened. Mendoza said that he was in favour of cutting a half-minute from each of the final three or four rounds, or lengthening the one-minute break between rounds.

According to a survey conducted early in 1988 by the IBF, 99.5 per cent of the people interviewed favoured 15-round world championship fights. 'We intend to keep the 15 rounds because we want to be the best and we want to do the very best for the fighters,' said IBF president Bobby Lee.

However, within months of that statement the IBF decided at their annual convention in Miami, Florida, to reduce their world title fights from 15 rounds to 12. And on 29 August 1988 Samut Sitnarupon successfully defended his IBF mini flyweight title against Hwang In-Kyo in Manila in the world's last 15-round title fight.

Although it took nearly five years for the other sanctioning bodies to follow the WBC example, the truth is that there never has been much conformity in relation to the length of fights. Back in the days when bareknuckle bruisers fought under London Prize Ring Rules, it was more important to record the length of a fight in hours and minutes than rounds.

This, because under London Prize Ring Rules the duration of a round varied, depending entirely upon how long it took for a man to fall to the turf. About the only fixed time in bareknuckle boxing was the 30 seconds permitted between rounds. Even so, some bareknuckle bouts went on for a very long time. The longest was between James Kelly and Jonathan Smith in Melbourne on 1 November 1855. The fight lasted for six hours and 15 minutes.

Not much shorter was the bareknuckle bout between Barney Malone and Jan Silberbauer which took place near the diamond fields of Kimberley, South Africa, in 1890. The fight lasted five hours and 30 minutes with Silberbauer unable to continue after 212 rounds.

The toll taken by the longest fight ever held under London Prize Ring Rules in Africa was shocking. As Chris Greyvenstein pointed out in his book *The Fighters*, Silberbauer did not fight again for three years, while it took Malone a full 12 months to recover from his injuries.

The amazing thing is that the longest fight ever recorded was not fought with bareknuckles – as one would expect – but with gloves. It took place on 6 April 1893 in New Orleans and after 110 rounds (or seven hours and 19 minutes) it was declared a draw. The contestants were Andy Bowen and Jack Burke.

Declaring finish fights 'no contest' or a draw was a cop-out used by many of the old-time referees. A case in point was the celebrated glove fight between heavyweights James J Corbett and Peter Jackson at the California Athletic Club on 21 May 1891. At the end of the 60th round, referee Hiram Cook left the ring to consult a group of gamblers as to how he should end the fight.

Jackson, on whom most had wagered, was weakening and was suffering agony from an ankle which he had hurt in training. Cook returned to the ring, waited one more round and then delivered his remarkable decision: 'I declare this bout no contest.' Most record books list the decision as a draw but no such verdict was rendered.

Strangely enough, the four longest recorded fights since 1887 all ended in draws. Besides the Bowen–Burke fight of 1893, Jake Kilrain and Jem Smith drew over 106 rounds in 1887, Patsy Kerrigan and Danny Needham drew over 100 rounds in 1890, and Tommy White and Dan Daly drew over 91 rounds in the same year.

Ah, you say, but surely things must have changed radically after the turn of the century?

Well, yes and no. In fact, there was even less conformity than before. Bareknuckle bouts and gloved boxing was illegal in the state of New York until 1896, when the Horton Law permitted contests without a limit to the number of rounds. The Lewis Law repealed the Horton Law and from 1900 to 1903 there was no legal boxing in the state. From 1903 to 1906 three-round exhibition bouts took place and six-round contests were permitted from 1906 to 1909.

Ten-round bouts were allowed in 1909 and the Frawley Law legalized 10-round no-decision bouts from 1911 to 15 November 1917. Club membership fights were sanctioned until 5 February 1918 when The People of the State of New York *vs* Packey O'Gatty made private fights illegal. The Walker Law brought boxing back to the state in 1920 with a maximum of 15 rounds per fight.

Boxing in other American states experienced the same kind of ping-pong treatment from lawmakers. Professional boxing was technically outlawed in the state of California from 1914 until 1924. A state bill, which took effect on 1 January 1925, legalized the sport but restricted fights to a maximum of ten rounds, or 12 rounds with no decision. Fifteen ten-round fights were only allowed from 11 January 1943. The same stop-start procedure was applied to the sport in most of the other states. Nevada was the one exception.

The lack of a uniform rule for rounds resulted in Jack Dempsey defending his world heavyweight title in fights scheduled for ten rounds, 12 rounds and 15 rounds back in the 1920s. When Dempsey knocked out Jess Willard to win the title in 1919 the fight was scheduled for 12 rounds. Dempsey ended it in the third. And when Dempsey defended the title against Georges Carpentier in 1921 the fight was also scheduled for 12 rounds. On the other hand, his title defence against Tommy Gibbons in 1923 was scheduled for 15, while his two fights with Gene Tunney in 1926 and 1927 were both restricted to ten rounds.

Some of the earlier heavyweight title fights fought with gloves were scheduled for 25 rounds, but when James J Jeffries attempted to regain the title from Jack Johnson in Reno, Nevada, in 1910 the fight was supposed to go 45 rounds.

Johnny Eckhardt, the old-time American referee and boxing writer, claimed just before his death in October 1934 that the game had lost something of its ancient barbaric thrill.

'Limiting bouts to ten and 15 rounds has completely altered the status of the fighter as a ring general,' he said. 'In the 25-round days a contestant planned his battle ahead as carefully as any marshal on the field of battle. He conserved his energies where necessary; he figured out ways of puzzling his opponent; he had to be as crafty as a serpent, as well as game as a bulldog.'

The last world heavyweight title fight scheduled for 45 rounds was between Jack Johnson and Jess Willard in Havana in 1915. Willard won on a knockout in the 26th round. Several major heavyweight fights were scheduled for 20 rounds in the 1930s but the last world

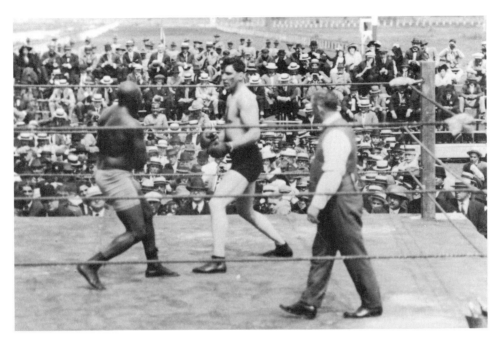

The heavyweight championship fight between Jack Johnson and Jess Willard in Havana, Cuba in 1915 was scheduled for 45 rounds. Willard knocked out Johnson in the 26th.

heavyweight title fight signed for this distance was between Joe Louis and Abe Simon in Detroit on 21 March 1941. Louis knocked out Simon in the 13th round.

As late as the 1970s, some fights were still being scheduled for 20 rounds. The last such recorded fight took place in Oklahoma City on 1 June 1971, when Kelly Burden knocked out Alonzo Harris in the tenth round.

An attempt to replace two-minute rounds with three-minute rounds in British boxing was heavily defeated when it went to the vote at the annual meeting of the British Boxing Board of Control in Cardiff in 1991. For the second year in succession the Welsh Area Council had sought to abolish the shorter rounds, arguing that well-trained professionals should be able to fight over the longer time span. But speaking on behalf of promoters, Johnny Griffin protested that the longer rounds would greatly increase the overhead costs and the proposal was defeated.

Scantily clad round-card girls have also been the subject of discussion. The question most often asked is, how much of a distraction are they? The Johannesburg *Sunday Express* once described a tournament as the 'boobs and bum' show after a round-card girl had kissed a boxer in his corner between rounds.

And yet, if you think the girls serve little purpose other than to show off their sexy figures, think again. The absence of round-card girls for the WBA lightweight title fight between Tony Lopez and Dingaan Thobela in the Arco Arena in Sacramento in February 1993 led to all kinds of confusion.

Both the Lopez and Thobela corners lost count of the number of rounds. Norman Hlabane, Thobela's trainer, admitted after the fight that when the 12th round came up he was under the impression it was the 11th, and when Lopez answered the bell for the 11th round his corner told him it was the 12th.

You could hardly blame the cornermen for the confusion. Without the round-card girls to remind them what round was coming up, it was difficult for them to keep count while also attending to the needs of their fighters.

Several times during the break between the tenth and 11th rounds, Lopez's cornermen told him, 'You've got to win this last round.' And as American television commentator Bob Spagnola pointed out, 'If Lopez shoots his wad during the next three minutes he may have nothing left.'

A year earlier, former heavyweight contender Scott LeDoux, the then chairman of the Minnesota State Boxing Commission, attempted to bar round-card girls from boxing.

'I initially tried to get rid of them,' LeDoux admitted. 'But I couldn't do it. As the father of a daughter, I don't like women to be exploited in that manner. Round-card girls are okay if they do their job. But some think they're the show. Freedom of expression is a sort of umbrella for that kind of behaviour.'

The San Diego Police Department evidently agreed. Four policemen arrived at a boxing show in 1991 and not only arrested promoter Bobby DePhilippis but also his four young girls. All five were charged with indecent exposure.

RULES

Tragedy has inspired many changes to the rules of boxing. In fact, the very first set of rules ever written in 1743 was the result of a tragedy. John Broughton, the then champion of England, wrote the rules with the assistance of several 'favoured gentlemen' at his Amphitheatre in Tottenham Court Road, London.

Two years earlier Broughton had badly beaten George Stevenson in 40 minutes of savage fighting and Stevenson died about a month later from his injuries – but not before he and Broughton had become good friends.

The distraught boxer vowed he would never fight again but Broughton was later persuaded to change his mind. Troubled by the tragedy, the boxer and his friends framed what later became known as Broughton's Rules. Entitled 'Rules to be observed in all Battles on the Stage', the seven simple rules were first published on 16 August 1743.

No mention was made of a referee but Rule 6 stipulated that two umpires be chosen before each fight to 'decide all disputes that may arise'. The fighters were to be given half a minute break between rounds and Rule 7 made it clear that 'no person is to hit his adversary when he is down'.

Broughton's Rules governed the prize ring until 1838 when the British Pugilists' Protective Association introduced the London Prize Ring Rules. Once again the new rules were largely a result of two ring deaths: James Burke died after a fight with Simon Byrne in 1833, and Bill Phelps (aka Brighton Bill) died after a battle with Owen Swift in 1838.

The London Prize Ring Rules were far more specific and among the many amendments was a requirement that a fighter 'toe the line unaided', that seconds be forbidden to carry their charge to the scratch at the start of a round, and that a referee be appointed to control the fight.

The London Prize Ring Rules were revised in 1853 and again in 1866 but were superseded by the Marquess of Queensberry Rules, published in 1867. The Queensberry Rules were originally intended for amateur boxing but were soon considered a good thing by the professionals. A Cambridge University graduate named John Graham Chambers framed the rules and then persuaded John Sholto Douglas, the eighth Marquess of Queensberry, to lend his name to them in order to give the rules credibility.

There were only 12 rules in all but their significance for the sport has seldom been fully appreciated. Prize-fighting was about to do a U-turn and become the sport of boxing – and all because of a new set of rules.

Among the important changes brought about by the new rules was the use of gloves, three-minute rounds with one minute's break, the introduction of the 'ten count' and the requirement that the fight be staged in a 24-foot ring 'or as near that size as practicable'.

The Marquess of Queensberry was himself an amateur boxer and loved the sport with a passion. Bill Doherty, the turn-of-the-century Australian middleweight, recalled meeting the Marquess in Melbourne in 1888.

'When I saw him he was in the prime of life – about 45 – and I was a thin, scraggy youngster in my teens, but with something of a reputation as a scrapper even then,' Doherty said in 1937. 'And I remember that his Lordship's eyes twinkled with amusement when I was jokingly introduced as a possible conqueror of John L Sullivan.'

The original Queensberry Rules have been amended countless times to bring them into line with modern practice and to make boxing a safer sport. Many of the changes were initiated by the so-called sanctioning bodies of boxing and in this respect the WBC is particularly proud of its record.

It was the World Boxing Council that did away with the practice of the bell saving a fallen fighter (1963), introduced the mandatory eight-count (1964), approved the thumb-attached glove (1979), reduced title fights from 15 rounds to 12 (1982), insisted on a minimum of eight-ounce gloves for all title fights (1984), and changed the weigh-in from the day of a fight to 24 hours before the bout (1990).

Not all the new rules are considered essential and few have been free of controversy. Both the standing eight-count and the three-knockdown rule are often excluded from championship fights at the request of the boxers or their backers.

'The standing eight-count is an abomination,' Dick Young declared in the *New York Post* in 1983. 'Few people who know anything at all about boxing support it, not in the professional game. It flies in the face of common sense. It is contrary to the object of the competition.'

The rule, which originated in the amateurs, allows a referee to halt a fight and give a standing count to a boxer who appears to be in trouble even though he has not been knocked down. Primarily a safety device, the unfairness of the rule is that it often favours one man at the expense of the other.

During the fight between José Baret and Floyd Mayweather in New York in 1983, referee Paul Venti twice gave Baret a standing count when he appeared to be in trouble, but when Baret staggered Mayweather in the eighth round and swarmed all over him, Venti

A genial man, the Marquess of Queensberry enjoyed doing the odd bit of boxing himself.

failed to give him a respite.

In 1984 California became the first state in America to give doctors the power, by law, to stop fights. But Dick Mastro, the then editor of *Official Boxing Record*, questioned whether the physicians appreciated their additional responsibility. 'No one can convince us that a physician, sitting ringside, is any more able to ascertain a fighter's condition than is the referee – or any other ringside spectator', Mastro wrote in the *Record*.

Despite a natural reluctance on the part of boxers to accept change, the boffins of boxing do sometimes get it right – as WBA junior lightweight champion Brian Mitchell discovered in 1989. All that stood between Mitchell and the loss of his title to Jackie Beard was a rule that was less than ten years old and which was roundly condemned when it was first introduced by the world sanctioning bodies.

Mind you, the first time the technical-decision rule was applied in a WBA title fight in June 1982 it did lead to confusion. Benedicto Villablanca was declared the winner over Sam Serrano when Serrano was unable to continue in his junior lightweight title fight because of a bad eye cut in the 11th round.

However, 20 days later, the WBA championships committee reversed the result and declared Serrano a winner on a technical decision because it was claimed that the cut had been caused by an accidental butt. Had it been determined that the butt was deliberate, Villablanca would have been disqualified ... and that goes for Jackie Beard, too.

Five years later the technical-decision rule was still subject to misinterpretation. Two key officials of the Nevada State Athletic Commission spoke out against the controversial rule when it led to Julio Cesar Chavez regaining his WBC super lightweight title from Frankie Randall in May 1994.

After Chavez suffered a cut on his right eye from an unintentional head butt in the eighth round, referee Mills Lane went to the scorecards and awarded Chavez the technical decision. What triggered the controversy was the WBC rule that the round in which the butt occurs is scored and one point is deducted from the score of the uncut boxer. The one-point penalty to Randall proved decisive in awarding the decision. Had a penalty not been assessed, Randall would have retained his title with a technical draw.

'This is a rule we don't like,' said Jim Nave, vice chairman of the Nevada State Athletic Commission. 'That's a rule we have argued about repeatedly. But that is the rule in a WBC title fight.'

'The rule is inherently unfair,' said Marc Ratner, executive director of the Nevada commission. 'That's what makes me feel bad. You cannot tell who initiated the butt. By the WBC rule, the man who is not bleeding has to have a point taken away from his score.'

SANCTIONING

There are so many titles up for grabs in boxing today that few know for sure who holds what – or even if it's worth holding. And if you thought that four world sanctioning bodies were four too many, you will be disappointed to learn that there may be twice as many by the time you read this.

One of the biggest misconceptions about the sanctioning bodies is that they control boxing. They do not. They control the titles held by the various champions. This has enabled them to demand exorbitant sanctioning fees from promoters and percentages of purse moneys from boxers. It has also given them the power to change the rules to suit themselves.

The effect on boxing has been devastating. Financially, boxers have never had it so good, but their prestige has suffered from too many champions and too many title fights. 'They have made boxing as big a joke as wrestling,' Lew Eskin, a top American referee and former editor of *Boxing Illustrated*, said in 1989. 'The only one I know who has benefited from this nonsense is my friend Phil Valentino, who makes the championship belts.'

Others have been just as cynical and when the World Boxing

Organization was established in the late 1980s, *The Ring* magazine described the new body as a 'bastard child born of the 1988 WBA convention'. Nigel Collins, the then editor of the magazine, claimed that the addition of the WBO to the ranks of the Alphabet Boys (the term used by the American media to describe the four major associations) was most unwelcome.

'To say we are at war to save boxing would not be overstating the case,' Collins declared in an editorial. 'The Alphabet disease is spreading like a plague, feeding on greed and corruption. Like society's life-and-death struggle against AIDS, lovers of the Sweet Science must prepare to fight the deadly acronyms ravaging the sport. It's a battle boxing can't afford to lose.'

Fred Blumstein, director of public relations for the WBO, told American boxing writer Robert Morales in 1994 that it was only a matter of time before the world noticed the organization. 'And we don't,' Blumstein said, 'have presidents for life.'

No matter. The WBO has proved to be no better than the World Boxing Association, the World Boxing Council or the International Boxing Federation. And some of the decisions taken by the Alphabet Boys over the years have been nothing less than scandalous. Mind you, whether we like it or not, these sanctioning bodies do have an influence on the sport. It is therefore essential that we get to know who they are and where they came from.

The oldest of the four major sanctioning bodies, the World Boxing Association, was established in 1921 under the name of the National Boxing Association following a meeting at the Flatiron Building in New York. The meeting was called by William A Gavin, an Englishman whose real interest at the time was a project to build an international sporting club in New York, to be run on similar lines to that of the National Sporting Club in London.

The NBA started with a membership of 13 American states, but did not begin naming its own world champions until 1927. The object of the exercise was to try to break the stranglehold the New York State Athletic Commission had on world championship boxing at the time.

In 1940, the NBA lobbied the US Congress to pass the Kennedy Bill which called for an investigation of boxing in the United States and the appointment of a National Commission of five men. Like all the other bills that have attempted to place American boxing under federal control, it failed to pass Congress.

In August 1962, the NBA changed its name to the World Boxing Association under the presidency of Emile Bruneau. At its inauguration the WBA had the support of 51 states and city boxing commissions.

The World Boxing Council was founded in February 1963 in response to the WBA's move to go international. It was the outcome of a World Boxing Committee formed by the British Boxing Board of Control and other interested controlling bodies anxious to invest the ownership of world titles in a single champion.

Today the WBC is unquestionably the most powerful boxing association in the world and under the presidency of José Sulaiman, the most politically motivated. Even the United Nations has acknowledged its achievements. Typical of the influence the WBC has on the sport was the decision to reduce the number of rounds for championship contests from 15 to 12 in December 1982. Reluctantly, the other boxing associations were all obliged eventually to follow suit.

Disgusted by the methods used to block his bid for the WBA presidency in 1982, Bobby Lee and his supporters broke away and formed the USBA/International, which later became known as the International Boxing Federation.

Lee, a black American, felt it was time that American interests were represented in the WBA, but largely due to South African support, Gilberto Mendoza beat him to the punch and won the presidency by the skin of his teeth.

The IBF at first had a troubled existence, and after a 'war' with the British Boxing Board of Control, called a truce. The IBF is still banned in Japan and several other countries because of its parochial constitution (only Americans are allowed to hold executive positions).

The World Boxing Organization was established late in 1988 when 27 members at the WBA's 67th convention in Margarita, Panama, broke away to form the new world body. Luis Batista Salas was named acting president but due to ill health was later replaced by Ramon Pina Acevedo of the Dominican Republic.

What caused Salas and his supporters to stage the walkout was the blatant double-dealing and violation of the WBA's constitution.

The new organization almost immediately ran into trouble and is still fighting for recognition in the United States. Several countries, including Britain, Japan and Korea, at first banned their boxers from competing for WBO titles.

SCANDALS

Few sports in the twentieth century have been able to escape scandal but boxing appears to have suffered more than most. At least five major scandals have rocked the sport to its very foundations since the turn of the century and yet somehow boxing has managed to survive.

The new century had hardly begun when a scandal surfaced in Chicago that led to the sport being banned in the state of Illinois for 20 years. At the heart of the scandal were allegations that the lightweight fight between Joe Gans and Terry McGovern on 13 December 1900 was fixed and that Gans would go down in an early round in order to collect wagers that his manager Al Hereford had discreetly placed on the result.

Almost from the day the fight was announced, rumours of a 'fake fight' had circulated throughout the city. Huge sums of money, both in Chicago and elsewhere, were being wagered on the outcome and as if to add fuel to the fire, a Chicago newspaper warned of possible race riots in the event that McGovern (a white man) lost to Gans (a black man).

Malachy Hogan, sports columnist for the Chicago *Times-Herald*, summed up the prevailing sentiment when he wrote: 'If Terry should go down before the Baltimore lightweight, I make a guess that there will be a scene at Tattersalls ... Not that I predict a disorderly time, but McGovern's defeat would cause a big howl of disappointment from the thousands who have reached the conclusion that he is invincible.'

A suspicious shift in the betting odds shortly before the bout added to the intrigue and when Gans failed to beat the count after being knocked down for the fifth time in the second round, all the pre-fight rumours seemed to have come true. Even the film of the fight could provide no logical explanation for Gans's pathetic performance.

Denials by Gans, Hereford and promoter Lou Houseman only served to infuriate public opinion. Writing in the *Chicago Tribune*, referee George Siler expressed his own doubts. 'I don't wish to accuse any fighter of faking,' Siler said, 'but if Gans was trying last night I don't know much about the game.' The Philadelphia *Evening Item* was even more outspoken: 'There is no manner of doubt ... that last night's fight ... between Terry McGovern and Joe Gans was a fake of the first water ... It outdid the most barefaced ring fraud that ever played in New York.'

The *Item* added that many politicians in Chicago had lost large bets on the fight and it was the politicians who carried the public's outrage against the sport into legislative action when Alderman Patterson introduced a resolution calling for boxing to be banned.

'If the game is too bad for the council, it certainly is too bad for me,' said Mayor Carter Harrison, and all permits for fights to be held in the city were revoked. By 1906 boxing was banned throughout the state of Illinois and remained illegal for the next 20 years.

In the early 1930s, a strong criminal influence began seeping into American boxing and although promoter Mike Jacobs was frequently accused of having some kind of relationship with the underworld, the scrupulously honest reign of heavyweight champion Joe Louis served to halt any serious spread of corruption.

However, when Jacobs and Louis left the scene in the late 1940s, the Mob – with frontmen like Frankie Carbo, Blinky Palermo, Felix Bocchicchio, Truman Gibson and Joe Sica – moved into the sport through a tie-up with the International Boxing Club (president: James D Norris).

Carbo had the classic background of a mobster. Born in New York in 1904, he was sent to reform school before he was 12 years old.

By the time he was 20 he faced the first of five murder charges. He regularly worked with such well-known assassins as Louis Lepke and Bugsy Siegel and he was implicated in four gangland killings between 1931 and 1939.

Carbo's presence in American boxing was first felt in the late 1940s when he held court in the Forest Hotel on West 49th Street in New York. With gangster pals like Palermo and others like Willie Ketchum and Bill Daly keen to act as his frontmen, Carbo played ping-pong with the lightweight, welterweight and middleweight titles.

Exactly how much Jim Norris knew of the unsavoury activities of his International Boxing Club has never been clear. In retrospect Norris appears to have been a wealthy playboy who never quite realized that his gangster buddies conducted a reign of terror with lead pipes wrapped in newspaper to impose their will on honest managers and promoters.

Norris eventually tried to salvage the situation when he offered J Edgar Hoover, the head of the Federal Bureau of Investigation, a

Jim Norris, the American boxing promoter, whose downfall was linked to the underworld.

salary in excess of $100,000 to run the IBC. Hoover, understandably, refused because by then the IBC had lost the confidence of both the public and the press.

It was US Senator Estes Kefauver, who had put together a sub-committee of the United States Congress to investigate the IBC's illegal monopoly, who eventually persuaded the Department of Justice and the FBI to act. A judgement handed down in March 1957 and confirmed by the Supreme Court of the United States on 12 January 1958 called for the IBC's 'divestment, dissolution and divorcement' from professional boxing.

Further charges were made against Carbo, Palermo, Sica, Louis Dragna and Truman Gibson and on 2 December 1961, the following sentences were handed down: Carbo – 25 years in prison and $10,000 fine; Palermo – 15 years in prison and $10,000 fine; Gibson – five years' suspended sentence and S10,000 fine; Sica – 20 years in prison and $10,000 fine and Dragna – five years in prison and $5,000 fine.

Norris then withdrew from boxing altogether and died only a few years later at the age of 59. And so the most determined and organized criminal stranglehold on boxing was finally broken.

What seemed like a good idea at the time went horribly wrong when American promoter Don King and the ABC television network launched the United States Boxing Championships in 1977. It soon transpired that only King-connected fighters were winning decisions and that ring records supplied for the purpose of making the matches were false.

'The stench gets stronger by the week,' Gary Deeb wrote in the *Chicago Tribune*. 'The outraged cries of injustice grow louder. And yet ABC, the undisputed worldwide champion of television sports, seems oblivious to the cruel charade being perpetrated.

'As things now stand, the US Boxing Championships may very well set prize-fighting back 20 years – to the days when the government stepped in and uncovered a series of scandals that nearly killed boxing.'

According to Deeb, most of the $1.5 million in ABC prize money was going to King, his pals and fighters under their control while Johnny Ort, an assistant editor of *The Ring* magazine, had allegedly falsified boxers' records in order to improve their rankings.

Adding to the suspicion was the locations chosen for the fights, all of which were outside the jurisdiction of the various US boxing commissions. The telecasts originated from such strange venues for boxing as the US Naval Academy in Annapolis, the aircraft carrier *Lexington* off the Florida coast and the Marion (Ohio) Correctional Facility.

The final straw came when heavyweight Scott LeDoux clearly outboxed Johnny Boudreaux, a member of the King stable, and the decision was awarded to Boudreaux. In front of millions of TV viewers, the enraged LeDoux first kicked Boudreaux and then accused King and company of putting in the fix while he was being interviewed by Howard Cosell, who lost his hairpiece in the fracas.

With pressure in the media mounting by the day, including the screening of a brilliant investigative television show on the rival CBS network, ABC Television eventually decided to throw in the towel and scrap the series.

Four years later American boxing was again rocked by scandal when Harold Smith, chairman of Muhammad Ali Professional Sports Inc (known as MAPS), was charged with embezzling $21.3 million from the Beverly Hills, California branch of the Wells Fargo National Bank.

For more than a year MAPS had doled out a seemingly endless supply of millions of dollars to promoters and fighters. Purses skyrocketed to astronomical levels and champions would not lace on their gloves for less than a million dollars. As more and more MAPS shows lost hundreds of thousands of dollars, rumours were rampant as to the source of the money supply.

Then the news broke that Smith was missing and the FBI was investigating a scam involving more than $21 million. 'Talks with law-enforcement officials, former Wells Fargo officers and rival bankers led to the conclusion that the fraud couldn't have continued as long as it did had it not been for flaws in the bank's internal auditing and operating controls,' the *Wall Street Journal* reported in January 1981.

The bank claimed that Smith and Ben Lewis, who in addition to his MAPS job was an employee of the Wells Fargo Bank, had embezzled the money by computer, funnelling it through 13 accounts. Most of the money was allegedly used to bankroll boxing

Promoter Don King and his lawyer Peter Fleming leave the New York Supreme Court after a mis-trial in the wire fraud case in 1995.

tournaments and Smith's lavish lifestyle, and while many boxers benefited by being handsomely paid for their fights, the spin-off once again hurt the sport.

Convicted, Smith served more than five years in federal prison. Now back in boxing as a promoter, Smith gained worldwide notoriety in 1993 by taking Muhammad Ali and about 120 other guests to Beijing for the first ever professional boxing tournament in China.

Just as disturbing, and more tragic, was the scandal of the cut gloves in the junior middleweight fight between Luis Resto and Billy Collins Jr at Madison Square Garden, New York, on 16 June 1983.

Resto, who had a reputation as a light hitter, badly banged up the face of Collins in their ten-round bout. 'Every time he hit me, it felt like I was getting hit by an ashtray,' Collins said the next day through bruised lips, a broken nose and eyes that were swollen shut.

Billy Collins Sr, who worked his son's corner, was the man who raised the alarm when he shook hands with Resto after the fight and felt 'no padding at all' in Resto's gloves. Over the protests of Resto's cornermen – Panama Lewis and Pedro Alvarado – the New York State Athletic Commission took possession of the gloves and turned them over to Everlast for examination.

At a hearing chaired by New York Commission chairman John Prenderville, Everlast vice-president John Towns and a police representative both stated that tests had shown the gloves had definitely been tampered with and that padding had been removed. Lewis and Alvarado denied any wrongdoing and termed the hearing a 'witchhunt'.

The New York Commission reacted swiftly. The result of the fight was changed to 'no contest'; Lewis and Alvarado were suspended for life and Resto for a period of not less than a year. Criminal charges were laid and Lewis was convicted in the New York Supreme Court in 1986 and sentenced to a term of imprisonment of three to six years. Resto also spent time behind bars.

Lewis, who returned to the fight game as a trainer after serving two years of his sentence, always insisted that he was innocent. 'I don't know where the tampering was done or who did it. I just know that I didn't do it,' he said.

Collins, who was 22 years of age at the time of the fight, suffered severe facial damage, including impaired vision. He never boxed again. Billy died in March 1984 when he drove his vehicle into a ditch while under the influence of alcohol. His father claimed his son was suffering from severe depression.

'Some other tricks might be called sly,' Michael Katz observed when writing about the incident for *The Ring* magazine in September 1983. 'This was slimy.'

SCORING

The beauty of boxing is that everyone considers himself an expert. Boxing is so basic that even those who can't tell a left hook from a right cross or have never heard of the ten-point must system are convinced they can find the winner.

Since scoring fights is not an exact science, the official judges are invariably on a sticky wicket in a closely contested bout. Personal perceptions – and the mass media – play an important part in shaping public opinion. Even so, it's surprising how many people allow their hearts to rule their heads in a boxing match.

You can start with the boxers themselves. Nowadays it's customary for both boxers to parade around the ring, their arms raised in token of victory, immediately after the final bell. Boxers do this even if they have been beaten by the proverbial mile, and yet there are some ringsiders and television viewers who still believe that it's an honest gesture.

It is also incredible how cornermen can tell exactly how many points their charge has won the fight by or how many rounds they scored in his favour. Are they *really* keeping a score? No matter, because the whole exercise is subjective.

Truth is, some judges prefer aggression to defence, fighters to boxers, blood and guts to skill and ringcraft. Some seemingly cannot make up their minds and score innumerable rounds as even. At the first fight between Sugar Ray Leonard and Roberto Duran in Montreal in June 1980, judges Raymond Baldeyrou, Harry Gibbs and Angelo Poletti between them scored 19 rounds even!

Admittedly, some rounds are impossible to divide, just as others often deserve more than a one-point margin. The trouble is, the ten-point must system does not allow for such variances. In fact, a colleague made a valid point the other day when he remarked that boxers do not score points, they lose them. 'After all, both boxers start the round with ten points,' he said, 'and the loser finishes with a lesser number.'

Nobody knows for sure when the practice of scoring fights first started – except that it began among the amateurs. According to British boxing historian Peter McInnes, bouts in the amateur Queensberry Cup (which began in 1867) and those in the Amateur Boxing Association championships (which commenced in 1881) were scored by points.

'They were certainly deciding contests on points before the formation of the National Sporting Club in 1891,' said John Morris, general secretary of the British Boxing Board of Control. 'And I believe contests were going to points decisions at establishments like the Pelican Club in the 1870s and 1880s.'

The earliest world championship fight to be decided on points was between Jack McAuliffe and Jack Hopper in New York on 27 February 1886. McAuliffe beat Hopper on points over 17 rounds for the lightweight title. And the first British championship fight to be won on points was between heavyweights Jem Smith and Jack Wannop in London on 30 September 1889. Smith was awarded the decision after ten rounds.

The first world heavyweight championship fight to be decided by decision was between James J Jeffries and Tom Sharkey at Coney Island, New York, on 3 November 1899. Referee George Siler declared Jeffries the winner after 25 rounds. However, the first world heavyweight title fight at which a referee and two judges officiated was between Jess Willard and Jack Dempsey at Bay View Park Arena, Toledo, Ohio, on 4 July 1919. Major Anthony J Drexel Biddle of Philadelphia and promoter Tex Rickard acted as the judges while Ollie Pecord was appointed to referee. Dempsey won on a technical knockout when Willard failed to answer the bell for the fourth round.

Although judges were regularly used in the 1920s and 1930s, often only a referee was appointed to officiate (this practice is still used for domestic boxing in Britain today). Moreover, the scoring systems used varied from state to state and from country to country.

Some American states – notably New York and New Jersey – required fights to be scored by rounds, others adopted a five-point must system and some even made the referee a non-scoring official. In both Britain and Australia, officials were permitted to score in fractions.

The New Jersey State Athletic Commission switched from scoring fights by the round to the ten-point must system in November 1986, and three years later the New York State Athletic Commission followed suit.

The practice of announcing the scorecards of the judges goes back to 9 February 1944 when Tippy Larkin beat Lulu Constantino on a unanimous points decision in Madison Square Garden, New York. Many now believe that the scores should be disclosed at the end of each round.

American promoter Don King raised the issue after the fights between Julio Cesar Chavez and Pernell Whitaker and between Azumah Nelson and Jesse Leija were both declared draws in San Antonio, Texas, in September 1993. 'We're demanding and requesting open scoring round-by-round. Every score should be posted round-by-round. Everything should be in public,' King told the Las Vegas *Review-Journal* in May 1994.

King also suggested that boxers should fight a 13th tie-breaker round when a fight is judged a draw, overlooking the fact that this experiment was first tried in 1987 and again in 1988. Doug DeWitt outpointed Tony Thornton over 13 rounds to win the vacant USBA middleweight title in Atlantic City on 6 November 1987 and Ron Essett outpointed Sanderline Williams over 13 rounds to win the vacant NABF middleweight title in Cleveland on 18 October 1988.

And while the Nevada State Athletic Commission chairman, Dr Elias Ghanem, had shown some interest in King's proposal, virtually everyone else associated with the commission considered the idea counterproductive. When the proposal was eventually brought before the commission, it was rejected. 'We brought it up, discussed it and voted it down,' said Marc Ratner, the commission's executive director.

The American television network NBC became the first to disclose the official scoring round-by-round in a fight during the world heavyweight title bout between Muhammad Ali and Earnie Shavers at Madison Square Garden in New York on 29 September 1977.

Nine years later scores were announced to the crowd after every round in a fight for the vacant USBA junior welterweight title between Frankie Warren and Ronnie Shields in Corpus Christi, Texas, on 11 May 1986. The crowd roared their approval as Warren stormed his way to a commanding lead over the last half of the fight, dropping Shields in the last round.

The most recent experiment in this regard took place in the Tulsa Convention Center in Oklahoma when Michael Bentt and Tommy Morrison contested the WBO heavyweight title in October 1993. During the undercard fights judges held up a blue or red card (representing the boxer's corner) at the end of each round, to keep the crowd informed as to who was winning the fight.

The last fight to be fought over 13 rounds was that between Ron Essett (left) and Sanderline Williams in Cleveland, Ohio in October 1988. Essett won on points.

'But the flaw in this system was that there is no way for the judges to communicate whether a round has been scored 10–9 or, in the event of a knockdown, 10–8,' said Glyn Leach, editor of *Boxing Monthly*. Leach witnessed the experiment from the ringside.

SOUTHPAWS

For perhaps a century or more, boxers who adopted a southpaw stance were either ostracized by boxing's establishment or turned around in the gym. 'Southpaw' was a dirty word in the world of boxing and men who fought with their right foot forward were often regarded as freaks.

William Thompson, the first southpaw to become a champion, was frequently criticized by experts for his unorthodox stance. Thompson, who was better known in the days of bareknuckle boxing as 'Bold Bendigo', was born a triplet, grew up to become a bit of a rascal, and ended his life as a preacher. He also won the heavyweight title from Deaf Burke in 1839.

'When it's nature's own way for a milling cove to put the last foot first, and lead off with the right mawley, 'tis best to let him toe the scratch as he sees best,' said John Jackson, a contemporary of Thompson, and a former bareknuckle heavyweight champion himself.

Others were less tolerant. 'High sounding words to the contrary, all men are *not* created equal,' Ben Sharav pointed out when he posed the question: 'Are left-handed boxers an endangered species?' in the May 1982 issue of *The Ring* magazine.

But by then there were almost as many lefties in boxing as there were orthodox fighters. Moreover, many – including Marvin Hagler, Pernell Whitaker and Hector Camacho – had become great world champions. But it would be another ten years before Michael Moorer became the first heavyweight champion of the world (WBO version)

Michael Moorer, the first southpaw to win the world heavyweight title, with trainer-manager Emanuel Steward.

to fight with his right foot forward, and two more years before Moorer won recognition as both WBA and IBF champion by beating Evander Holyfield in April 1994.

Mind you, there was a time back in the 1940s when Joe Louis declined to defend the world heavyweight title against Melio Bettina because Bettina 'fought the wrong way around' so progress had clearly been made.

There was also a time when the stigma of being a southpaw was so great that many of the world's best-known champions were men who had converted from lefties to righties. Among them were such legendary champions as the incomparable Sugar Ray Robinson, Carmen Basilio and Joe Frazier.

Prejudice dies hard, but perhaps the strangest case was that of Welcome Ncita, the young South African who became the IBF junior featherweight champion in March 1990. Until he challenged Fabrice Benichou for the title, Ncita had boxed his entire career as a southpaw.

So imagine Benichou's surprise when the leftie suddenly became a rightie on the night he defended his title against Ncita in the Hilton

Hotel ballroom in Tel Aviv. 'I did it to confuse him,' Ncita admitted. 'I try to frustrate all my opponents. I upset them any way that I can.'

Benichou was so angry he had harsh words with promoter Cedric Kushner after the fight, claiming the promoter had misled him by sending him videotapes of Ncita boxing as a southpaw. Benichou had evidently trained to fight a left-handed challenger and was bitterly disappointed when Ncita refused to oblige.

Mind you, even southpaws dislike fighting other southpaws, so perhaps it is not altogether surprising that the first modern southpaw champion – middleweight Al McCoy – only won the world title in 1914.

STAGE

Most boxers, it seems, have a secret desire to be actors. Why else have so many turned to the stage and screen, some even at the height of their boxing careers?

Before the golden age of cinema, one of the spin-offs of winning the world heavyweight title was for the champion to appear on the stage, often in a play especially written for him. John L Sullivan, James J Corbett, Bob Fitzsimmons and Jim Jeffries all became actors – well, sort of – while holders of the world championship.

Sullivan's popularity in the 1890s was evident everywhere, including the opening line of a popular Broadway play called *A Rag Baby*: 'Let me shake the hand that shook the hand of John L Sullivan.' And after he beat Jake Kilrain in the last bareknuckle fight for the championship in July 1889, John L spent the next year and a half touring America and Australia while playing the lead role in a melodrama called *Honest Hearts and Willing Hands*.

Written especially for Sullivan's limited talents as an actor by playwright Hal Reid, *Honest Hearts* was reasonably well received in the United States but flopped in Australia, where theatregoers were not mesmerized by Sullivan's larger-than-life personality or the way in which he bellowed his lines.

An interesting aside is that while Sullivan was appearing in *Honest Hearts* in San Francisco in June 1891 he was invited to spar on stage with James J Corbett, the young man who was destined to beat him for the championship. Sullivan accepted the invitation but stipulated that they both wear evening dress for their four-round exhibition.

Corbett's full, deep, rich voice and his poise on stage made him a far better actor than Sullivan, and theatrical impresario William A Brady asked him to do a fight scene in the British melodrama *After Dark*. Impressed, Brady arranged for Corbett to star in *Gentleman Jack* in cities all over the United States after he became world heavyweight champion in 1892. Corbett went into rehearsal for the play even while still training for the Sullivan fight.

James J Corbett, the first heavyweight champion of the world under Queensberry Rules, preferred acting on the stage to fighting in the ring.

Later Corbett appeared in a new play by Chas T Vincent called *A Naval Cadet* but was often heckled from the audience for avoiding a defence of his heavyweight title against Bob Fitzsimmons. The men eventually met in Carson City, Nevada, in March 1897 and Fitzsimmons won on a knockout in the 14th round.

Corbett continued to appear on stage even after he lost the championship and received high praise for an 18-minute skit entitled *The 18th Amendment* that he did with the famous comedian Billy B Van at the Moore Theater in Seattle, Washington, in March 1921. 'I feel that I was born to perform on a stage rather than in the boxing ring,' Corbett wrote in his autobiography *The Roar of the Crowd* in 1926.

Fitzsimmons was even less suited to acting than Sullivan, but the boxer and his wife both starred in a play especially written for him called *The Honest Blacksmith* after he became champion. Fitzsimmons was a qualified blacksmith and sometimes made horseshoes while on stage for his friends in the audience.

Jim Jeffries continued the tradition of the heavyweight champion appearing on stage after he knocked out Fitzsimmons in June 1899 to win the title. Brady put him in a play called *Eighty Minutes in New York* and then cast him in another play entitled *The Man from the West* after he beat Corbett in May 1900.

Having run out of challengers for his title, Jeffries began spending even more time on the stage and played the title role in *Davy Crockett*. The melodrama was given a touch of reality by use of live wolves, bloodhounds and deer on stage. The finale, with the champion embracing his 85-pound leading lady, invariably brought tears to the eyes of the audience.

With cinema taking over from the theatre as the world's leading form of entertainment, most of the successors to Sullivan, Corbett, Fitzsimmons and Jeffries turned their attention to the silver screen. A rare exception was Jack Dempsey, who won the world title by beating Jess Willard in 1919.

After successfully defending the title against Luis Firpo in 1923, Dempsey had his nose reshaped by surgery, married actress Estelle Taylor and honeymooned in Europe. Upon his return to the United States, Dempsey agreed to star in a Broadway play called *The Big*

Fight. Unfortunately, Dempsey never learned how to project his voice and the play lasted only six weeks before it folded. It was directed by David Belasco.

Arguably the most successful Broadway play with a boxing background was *Golden Boy*, which opened at the Belasco Theater on 4 November 1937 and ran for 250 performances. Written by Clifford Odets, it was made into a movie in 1939 starring William Holden and Barbara Stanwyck. British boxer Eric Boon played the title role in a Johannesburg production in 1947.

Muhammad Ali made his acting debut on Broadway in December 1969 in a black power musical called *Buck White*. The former world heavyweight champion wore an Afro-style beard and wig for the part. Twenty-three years later, the boxer himself was the subject of an off-Broadway play entitled *Ali*.

The one-man play was written by actor Geoffrey C Ewing and Graydon Royce. Ewing researched his subject for eight months and opened the play as an ageing Ali shaking hands with the audience. 'I'm gonna get to y'all in a minute,' he said slowly. 'I'm talking about my life so much, I'm starting to believe it.'

'The ultimate compliment you can pay him is that he looks the part – he has the body of a heavyweight fighter, and he moves with Ali's grace,' wrote Harry Mullan, editor of *Boxing News* in his review of the play after it opened at the Mermaid Theatre in London in June 1993.

The one-man production was a smash hit in New York, where Ewing won the award for the Most Outstanding Single Performance.

Other plays with a boxing background to catch the eye were *Lippe*, which opened at New York's Quaigh Theater on 18 December 1985 and ran for 12 performances. Written, directed and produced by Ron Scott Stevens, the play was based on the life of veteran fight manager Lippe Breidbart. Earlier in the same year the Sydney Dance Company of Australia presented an offbeat boxing ballet called *Black and Blue* at the City Center in New York. The ballet featured the music of Harry Nilsson and Randy Newman.

A new play about boxers called *Blade to the Heat* opened at the Public Theater in New York in 1994. Loosely based on the rivalry between Benny 'Kid' Paret and Emile Griffith, the play was written

Wearing an Afro-style beard and wig, Muhammad Ali makes his acting debut in the Broadway black power musical *Buck White*.

by Oliver Mayer. *The New Yorker* theatre critic John Lahr claimed that Mayer's writing was mediocre but conceded that the direction by George C Wolfe and the fight choreography by former middleweight contender Michael Olajide was outstanding.

STATISTICS

Boxing as a sport has been well served by its historians, and the chances are it will be even better served by its statisticians if the work of Bob Cannobio and Logan Hobson is a foretaste of what the future holds.

Between them these two men produce the most amazing statistics.

Sitting at the ringside with a couple of computers, Cannobio and Hobson can tell how many punches were thrown in a fight and by whom. When they first began by supplying statistics to the Madison Square Garden television network in 1984, the two Americans called their service Fiststat. Now working under the name of CompuBox Incorporated, their service is widely known as Punchstats.

Some of the stats they have supplied to the media are worth repeating, if only to highlight the ingenuity of the service.

Examples: Zack Padilla holds the record for the most punches thrown in a fight. In a 12-round bout with Ray Oliveira in December 1993, Padilla threw a total of 1,596 blows, an average of 133 per round or 0.74 per second. Padilla also holds the record for the most punches thrown in a round: 207 blows in the 12th round of his fight with Oliveira.

The record for the fewest number of punches thrown in a round belongs to heavyweight Trevor Berbick, who unloaded only four blows during the first round of his fight with Carl Williams in June 1988.

The record for the most punches connected in a round is held by Mike McCallum, who landed 93 blows (or 73 per cent of the punches he threw) in the fifth round of his fight with Nicky Walker in October 1991.

Statistics of a different kind came from Australian writer Reg Walker in 1987 when he pointed out that John Siriotis could claim to have had the shortest ever reign of any champion anywhere in the world. Thirty seconds after Siriotis had been incorrectly announced as the new Australian junior middleweight champion for outboxing Steve Renwick in Darwin, the decision was reversed.

'It was like the 1942 bombing of Darwin all over again,' Walker reported in *Fighter* magazine. 'John Siriotis fought his heart out. It was the best performance of his career – an amazing feat when it is considered that he not only fought but promoted the programme, made all the matches, wrote the printed programme, obtained ads to go in that programme, sold tickets, did interviews, gave stories to the papers, trained himself and fought the 12 rounds for no payment!'

Other record keepers and statisticians who have done sterling work for the sport are Bob Yalen (USA), Julio Ernesto Vila (Argentina), John Hogg (Australia), Bob Mee (England), Ron Jackson (South Africa), Joe Koizumi (Japan), Barry Hugman (England) and Herb Goldman (USA).

Goldman, who was appointed editor of *Boxing Illustrated* magazine in 1995, looks like taking over the mantle of the late Nat Fleischer as the world's greatest boxing historian.

STYLES

Technically, boxing today is at its zenith and the 'manly art of self-defence' has reached the point where it is unlikely to improve further. But to claim, as some historians and archaeologists do, that the ancient Greeks did not know how to throw a straight punch is to suggest that fist-fighting only originated in the twentieth century.

While all available evidence confirms the suspicion that the Greeks were largely headhunters and the Romans first to appreciate the value of body blows, boxing is such a basic sport that it would be foolish to assume that only modern fighters were capable of throwing hooks, uppercuts and crosses.

So to claim that John Jackson was the first exponent of the straight left, that James J Corbett was the first to make use of a feint, that Ben Brain fathered the straight right, that Jack Dempsey invented the left hook or Jack Johnson the right uppercut is wishful thinking. They may have popularized the blows but they hardly invented them.

What has changed radically over the years is physical conditioning and the selection of punches. And yet, as far back as 1747 when Captain John Godfrey wrote the first book on boxing, theory had already outstripped practice. 'Boxing is a combat depending more on strength than the sword,' Godfrey wrote. 'But art will make up for strength in it also.'

A couple of hundred years later men like Willie Pep, Sugar Ray Robinson, Pernell Whitaker, Billy Conn and a host of others were putting Godfrey's theory into practice ... and discovered that it paid handsome dividends. We are yet to see the perfect fighter, although many will argue that Robinson came closest to the description. And if and when we do the chances are he will be more skilful than anyone who has so far climbed into a ring.

When boxing was revived in England in the seventeenth century prize-fights involved a fair amount of wrestling. Most men boxed from an upright stance and made much use of the straight left. And since boxing men still insist that everything should happen off the jab, the British obviously got it right from the start.

However, the greatest advance in ring technique was made not by the British but by the Americans, when they began to dominate the sport after the turn of the century. American boxers were prepared to experiment until they found a style that suited them best. Fluidity of movement was channelled into naked aggression or masterly exhibitions of what A J Liebling called 'the sweet science'.

John L Sullivan smashed the Jem Mace tradition of boxing by rushing into his opponents and terrifying them into submission with a barrage of blows. James J Corbett fine-tuned the feint and suckered one opponent after another into falling for his tricks. Bob Fitzsimmons proved that body blows could be match-winners. Jack Johnson perfected the right uppercut and tore the teeth out of his opponent's mouths. Jack Dempsey plunged headlong out of his corner, and fighting from a crouch, sacrificed defence for sheer aggression.

Despite his poor footwork and suspect defence, Joe Louis used his great handspeed and awesome punching power to turn counter punching into a fine art. Sugar Ray Robinson rolled all these attributes into one to become the greatest fighter, pound for pound, of his time. And Muhammad Ali, although clearly hopeless at infighting, made full use of his remarkable reflexes and amazing mobility to turn the sport into a dazzling spectacle.

'Styles in boxing have changed more than in any other sport,' Nat Fleischer said in 1938. It was the understatement of the century.

The fact that 'finish fights' were a thing of the past had greatly

Jackie 'Kid' Berg and Laurie Stevens exchange blows during their Empire lightweight title fight in Johannesburg in 1936. The punches came so fast and furious that ringsiders could hardly count the blows.

helped. Boxers were able to pick up the pace early, without fear of punching themselves out. And since they were infinitely better conditioned than their predecessors, they were able to maintain a higher work rate for longer periods. The end result was flashier styles and more exciting matches, with many of the greatest fights of all time taking place this century.

Harry Greb was perpetual motion in the ring, and so too were Henry Armstrong and Jackie 'Kid' Berg. Exotic blows like the bolo punch were invented by men like Ceferino Garcia and the hook off the jab became almost commonplace in rings around the world.

State-of-the-art style had made the sport an ideal subject for television in an age when image was everything, and hi-tech training methods had turned most modern boxers into marvellous physical specimens who would have been the envy of the old bareknuckle bruisers.

Eat your heart out, Pierce Egan.

TELEVISION

It is hard to believe that boxing promoters once thought that radio broadcasts of fights would hurt their gates. And having entered the era of pay-per-view television, it's hard to believe that some promoters actually consider this latest development in technology to be the salvation of the sport.

In the forefront of those who were anxious to take advantage of America's pay-per-view networks was US promoter Bob Arum, who joined forces with Time Warner in 1991 in an attempt to milk the medium to the maximum.

'This hasn't been the easiest thing to put together,' Arum said after a meeting with the TV moguls in New York. 'This is historical in that it aligns a sport that's been much maligned with one of the biggest, most powerful companies in the world. It's taken boxing out of the sweaty, smoke-filled back rooms and given it instant respectability.'

Arum seemed to have forgotten that it really all began back in Britain in the 1930s. On 22 August 1933 to be exact. That was the date on which two British middleweights, Archie Sexton and Lauri Raiteri, boxed a six-round exhibition in front of BBC-TV cameras at Broadcasting House, London.

Five years later, the BBC took their cameras to Harringay Arena in London to televise the fight between Len Harvey and Jock McAvoy for the British light heavyweight title. The transmission was shown on closed circuit.

But the big breakthrough for boxing came on 23 February 1939 when the fight between Eric Boon and Arthur Danahar at Harringay

Arena was televised live on to three cinema screens in London – the Marble Arch Pavilion, the Monseigneur and the Tatler. The Gaumont-British Corporation made use of Britain's only TV transmitter at the time (at Alexandra Palace) to beam the fight on to screens measuring approximately 16 feet by 12 feet.

'The story of the fight is not half so interesting and thrilling as the story of the television of the contest,' Johnny Sharpe reported in *The Ring* magazine.

John Baird, the television pioneer, sat in one of the London cinemas watching the fight on the screen, and was overcome with emotion. 'Little did I think when I first made television an accomplished fact in 1924 that I would attend a fight in a cinema house and see before my eyes everything that was going on in the arena where the fight was being staged,' he said. 'I never dreamed of a night like this when I would sit, one of thousands, looking-in on a big fight.'

A critic in the *Listener*, the journal of the BBC, was quick to point out that TV boxing would require a new approach from sports commentators.

'Boxing on television provides the commentator with a rather unusual task because it is no use for him simply to tell us, as he would in an ordinary sound commentary, that boxer A has just succeeded in hitting boxer B on the jaw,' the critic wrote. 'We can see that perfectly well for ourselves.

'Neither can he confine himself to saying that he thinks boxer A is getting the best of the round. Most of us who take an intelligent interest in boxing prefer to work that out without being told.'

Meanwhile, across the Atlantic, fights were being televised on an experimental basis from the Ridgewood Grove, St Nicholas Arena and Jamaica Arena in New York. But the first major fight to be seen live on TV screens in the United States was the heavyweight bout between Max Baer and Lou Nova, which took place at Yankee Stadium in New York on 1 June 1939.

The Ring magazine had predicted in 1939 that television would revolutionize the promotion of boxing but it was not until September 1944 that the first contract for the regular screening of fights was signed. Mike Jacobs, head of the Twentieth Century Sporting Club,

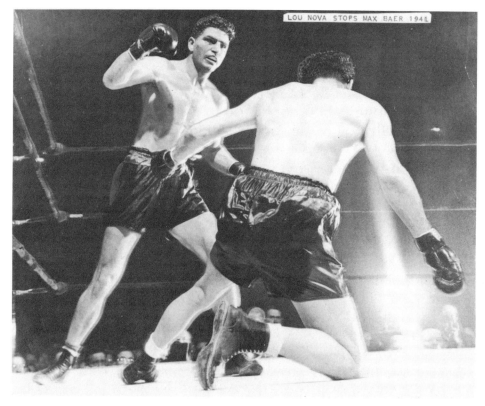

LOU NOVA STOPS MAX BAER 1941

Lou Nova stops former world heavyweight champion Max Baer in their second fight in 1941. Their first fight, two years earlier, was the first major fight to be seen live on TV screens in America.

completed arrangements with the Gillette Safety Razor Company for 50 boxing shows to be televised on a regular basis by NBC, an American TV network.

Ten years later, TV had made such an impact on the sport that Arthur Daley, the veteran American sportswriter, was moved to ask in the *New York Times* whether boxing was on the ropes. Daley blamed TV for the sport's decline.

'The television revolution has dislocated all sports in one way or another,' Daley declared. 'But boxing has become its prize captive. No form of athletics reproduces on the video screen with the faithful exactness of boxing – unless you insist on including wrestling, which isn't a sport but a dramatic burlesque of consummate fakery.

'The TV camera can't begin to cover all the fringe happenings in baseball or football or basketball or hockey or any other sport. But boxing has no fringes. The ring is small enough to be always in focus. The contestants are the absolute minimum of two. It's the ideal arrangement because every seat in front of a video screen is a ringside seat. And the price is perfect – free.'

At the time there were five network boxing shows a week in the United States: two on Monday night (DuMont *vs* ABC), one on Wednesday (CBS), Gillette's *Fight of the Week* on Fridays (NBC), then the *Saturday Night Fights* (ABC).

'The situation started to reverse itself in 1955, when CBS dropped boxing after the first sixteen weeks and ABC, which had stopped its Monday telecasts, switched its remaining fight series from Saturdays to Wednesdays,' Herb Goldman recalled in the November 1985 issue of *The Ring* magazine. 'DuMont, which had been on shaky wheels since 1955, went out of business in 1958, leaving the fight game with "only" two network TV shows a week.'

In 1960, NBC dropped out and when the Gillette *Fight of the Week* breathed its last on 11 September 1964 after screening the middleweight fight between Dick Tiger and Don Fullmer from Cleveland, Ohio, it marked the end of boxing's first television age.

Arthur Daley had suggested in his piece for the *New York Times* that pay-as-you-go television might prove to be boxing's salvation. And, sure enough, in March 1971 approximately 1.3 million people bought seats to watch the first fight between Muhammad Ali and Joe Frazier live on closed-circuit television.

But that was the biggest closed-circuit fight in the history of TV boxing, and since then the market has declined dramatically. Dan Duva, the American promoter, explained why in 1984. 'Before, a closed-circuit fight was in every movie house; now they put them on only in the big arenas,' he said. 'The fact is that the closed-circuit money just isn't there like it used to be any more. The closed-circuit people are folding rapidly and are close to being out of business.'

Pay-per-view and the subscription television networks around the world have since taken over where closed-circuit TV left off.

Showing uncanny foresight, Johnny Sharpe had pinpointed the problem in his report on the Boon–Danahar fight in the May 1939 issue of *The Ring* magazine. 'If what I saw in the vicinity of the cinema house and within its walls is any criterion, I predict that the million dollar gate is a thing of the past once television is introduced in America for fights.'

TRAINING

Training and trainers are an essential part of modern boxing but there was a time when both were considered relatively unimportant. Incredibly, when boxing was revived in England in the seventeenth century, training was badly neglected and virtually ignored for nearly a hundred years.

And yet, training and trainers go way back in boxing history, with Menander of Athens gaining a reputation as a trainer of Olympic champions as long ago as 48 BC. Menander was followed by Pythagoras of Samos, who after winning the Olympic boxing championship in 500 BC, became the greatest trainer of fighters in antiquity.

First to make a name for himself as a scientific trainer in modern boxing was Barclay Allardyce, or Captain Barclay, as he was known. Barclay trained Tom Cribb for his second fight with Tom Molineaux in 1811 and did such a splendid job of slimming him down that Molineaux barely recognized Cribb as the man he had fought only ten months before.

William Muldoon was Barclay's counterpart in the US. A strict disciplinarian, Muldoon wasn't averse to enforcing his dictates with a baseball bat and he was the only man alive who earned the respect of John L Sullivan.

Sullivan trained at Muldoon's house in Belfast, New York, in 1889 for his fight with Jake Kilrain in Richburg, Miss. Called 'Champion Rest', Muldoon's house was surrounded by two graveyards, a church, the home of a priest and a little cottage which housed two old maids.

Alexis Arguello, the former three-time world champion, has returned to the ring at the age of 42 and is training daily at Barry's Boxing Gym in Las Vegas.

Nellie Bly, a woman reporter for the New York *World*, visited Sullivan six weeks before the fight. Sullivan was surprisingly courteous but evidently did not think much of his surroundings.

'I couldn't sleep after five o'clock this morning on account of Mr Muldoon's cow,' he told Miss Bly. 'It kept up a hymn all the morning and the birds joined in the chorus. It's no use trying to sleep here after daybreak.'

Training in a country retreat became fashionable at the turn of the century and largely because of a recommendation made by Professor Mike Donovan, ex-middleweight champion, boxing instructor at the New York Athletic Club, and the man who made punching a ball in training a popular exercise.

'Choose your training quarters in a mountainous or hilly part of the country, where you can be sure of pure air and be free from dust,' Donovan advised all boxers.

Donovan devoted a lifetime to the study of boxing and his knowledge of the sport showed in the work of his pupils. Others who carried on the tradition included Ray Arcel, Whitey Bimstein, Jack Blackburn, Freddie Brown, Charley Goldman, Angelo Dundee, Eddie Futch, Emanuel Steward and over in Britain men like the Gutteridge twins, Dick and Jack, Nat Sellar, Jack Goodwin, Ted Broadribb and a host of others.

When Ray Arcel died in New York City at the age of 90 on 7 March 1994, sports columnist Jerry Izenberg of the Newark *Star-Ledger* spoke at his service. 'You did not simply know Ray Arcel,' he said, 'you experienced him. We came here not to say goodbye to an old friend, but to celebrate the joy, the love, and the example he gave to all of us.'

While boxing is among the oldest of sports, training techniques have seldom varied. Until Evander Holyfield became a champion in the 1980s, most boxers trained no differently from boxers of a hundred years before. They did roadwork, shadow-boxed, punched the bag and sparred. Holyfield went a step further and experimented with high-tech training methods.

We got our first glimpse of it when Holyfield beat Muhammad Qawi for the WBA junior heavyweight title. Before the fight Evander went through his paces on a variety of machines and looked very impressive, but it was only when he stripped for action that many were convinced of the benefits of his training programme.

Perseverance and dedication are essential requisites for the modern boxer. I once watched American trainer Victor Valle spend 15 minutes putting Glenwood Brown through his paces on the pearball in Gleason's Gym in New York. All Brown did was throw the left hook.

'Throw it again,' Valle insisted. 'Throw it again.'

And it was not until Valle was satisfied Brown had got it right that he allowed the New Yorker to do something else. Valle, the man who guided Gerry Cooney to a shot at the world heavyweight title, was looking for perfection.

I saw something similar in a downtown gym in Sacramento, California, when Dingaan Thobela was training for his first WBA lightweight title fight with Tony Lopez in February 1993. American trainer Jesse Reid was working on Thobela's combination punching.

'Give me four!' Reid instructed Thobela as he kept changing the angle of the handpads. 'Give me six! Give me five!'

At first Thobela looked bored and lethargic but as the sweat began to pour from his body Dingaan picked up the pace and soon his punches were sizzling through the air – three, four, five, six at a time.

TWINS

Twin brothers in boxing are not nearly as rare as many might suspect but few have been outstanding fighters and it was not until 1988 that twin brothers both became world champions.

That happy event was recorded in Thailand when Kaokor Galaxy

Kaosai Galaxy won the WBA junior bantamweight title in 1984. His twin brother, Kaokor Galaxy, won the WBA bantamweight title in 1988.

joined his identical twin brother Khaosai as a world champion when he outpointed Wilfredo Vasquez of Puerto Rico over 12 rounds to win the WBA bantamweight title on 8 May 1988 in Bangkok. Brother Kaosai had earlier won the WBA junior bantamweight title by knocking out Eusebio Espinal in six rounds in Bangkok on 21 November 1984.

The first twin to win a world title was Mike Sullivan, who outpointed Honey Mellody over 20 rounds in Los Angeles on 23 April 1907 to win the world welterweight title. Mike, who was knocked out by Stanley Ketchel in one round early in 1908, gave up the title later in the year because of eye trouble.

Jack Sullivan, Mike's twin, was not nearly as good with his fists as his brother. Even so, after Mike had been knocked out in one round by Ketchel, Jack challenged the 'Michigan Assassin' in order to restore the family honour but was defeated in 20 rounds.

Arguably the most famous twin brothers in British boxing were George and Henry Cooper. George, who later boxed as a professional as Jim Cooper, could not match Henry for ability and

Guess which of the Cooper twins is Henry? If you choose the man on the right of this wedding photograph you are correct. George Cooper is on the left, and manager Jim Wicks is standing next to George's new wife Barbara.

had an abbreviated career. Henry won the European, British and Commonwealth heavyweight titles and challenged Muhammad Ali unsuccessfully for the world title in 1966, after having dropped Ali in a non-title fight in 1963.

A couple of French twin brothers made boxing history on 24 January 1987 when both won national titles while boxing on the same bill in Calais. Thierry Jacob won the French bantamweight title by stopping Alain Limarola in the fifth round and twin brother Bruno won the French featherweight title with a points win over Marc Amand.

MIKE TYSON

To understand the contempt Mike Tyson had for his challengers when he was undisputed heavyweight champion of the world, you need to know that until he was knocked out by Buster Douglas in the tenth round in Tokyo in 1990, 'Iron Mike' had been rocked by only four punches in his entire ring career.

A right hand from Frank Bruno that momentarily wobbled him, a right uppercut from Tony Tucker, a right from James 'Bonecrusher' Smith in the final round of their title fight, and a blurred memory of a punch thrown by James 'Quick' Tillis when Tyson was still a teenager.

None of these men was able to take advantage of his brief moment of glory. No wonder Tyson held them in such contempt. 'How dare they challenge me with their primitive skills?' he asked. 'They're as good as dead.'

Well, just about. After Tyson had finished with them, men like Trevor Berbick, Bonecrusher Smith, Pinklon Thomas, Tyrell Biggs, Larry Holmes, Tony Tubbs and Michael Spinks were literally finished as fighters. Only Tony Tucker gave the impression that he was good enough to fight another day, but mentally Tucker became so screwed up he turned to cocaine and became a drug addict.

Mike Tyson smashes a right to the head of Frank Bruno during their world heavyweight title fight in 1989.

'Mike Tyson can be beaten,' said Bruno after Tyson had stopped him in five rounds in their first fight. 'He's a human being, a very young human being. He's got legs, he bleeds and I'd love to fight him again.'

They all said that, of course. Not only because a Tyson fight meant a boxer had finally found his pot of gold at the end of the rainbow, but because all boxers have their pride.

Few were prepared to argue when Tyson claimed in 1989 that he was the best heavyweight in boxing. 'I'm the best,' he said after beating Bruno. 'I may not be the greatest, but I'm the best.'

That was something even Larry Holmes was prepared to concede after Tyson annihilated him in less than four rounds. Ferdie Pacheco, the well-known American television commentator and boxing analyst, described Holmes's defeat as the 'kind of beating that makes guys walk funny when they're fifty'.

Holmes had claimed before the fight that he was not challenging Tyson for the money. 'Everybody knows I'm rich,' he said. But afterwards he reluctantly admitted that he had been trying to get

Tyson is the youngest man ever to win the world heavyweight championship.

back his dignity. 'I found out that Mike Tyson is better than I thought,' Holmes said.

That's something Tony Tucker refused to come to terms with when Tyson outboxed him in 1987. 'The guy actually thought he'd won the fight,' Cedric Kushner told me afterwards. 'He walked around as though he was the winner, as though he was the world champion.' Tucker gave Tyson one of his hardest fights as champion but only Tucker believed he had done enough to win.

Another Tyson challenger who retired immediately after Tyson beat him was Michael Spinks, who until Tyson knocked him out in 90 seconds, was undefeated as a professional. Ringsiders claim that Spinks froze in the corner before the first punch of the fight was thrown. At least he had the good sense to hang up his gloves before anyone else hurt him, and with $12 million in the bank he could afford to live in style.

Trevor Berbick's life was never the same after Tyson destroyed him in two one-sided rounds. After turning to the church he adopted an African name, calling himself Obim Tedechi, and as his money started to run out he got into trouble with the law.

Tyrell Biggs was so savagely beaten by Tyson and cut up in a subsequent fight with Francesco Damiani that his handlers gave him back his contract and advised him to hang up his gloves. Tyson took a personal dislike to Biggs. 'He talked so much, he didn't show any class or respect,' Mike said. 'I wanted to make him pay with his health.'

Many felt that Tyson won more than half his fights because of a fear factor. As champion he came to the ring wearing only the barest necessities: no gown, no socks – and if he had had his way – no gloves. But it takes only ten seconds to remove the aura of invincibility in boxing and for Tyson those soul-destroying ten seconds were tolled in Tokyo in February 1990.

Buster Douglas, considered by many as one of the biggest no-hopers in boxing, turned the trick in the tenth round. A right uppercut set Tyson up for the four-punch combination that ended his championship reign.

To many, Tyson had already become a riddle wrapped in an enigma. What he was saying was beginning to make less and less sense, and what he was doing – both in the ring and out – was causing consternation among the critics.

Things started to go wrong when Tyson's sex life went public in 1989. Thanks largely to three books – *Fire and Fear, Bad Intentions* and *Blood Season* – Tyson's inner thoughts and sexual prowess had become public knowledge. But while all three books revealed Tyson's insatiable appetite for sex, the most damning was written by a former friend and confidant – José Torres.

Torres told me that everything he had written about Tyson was true. And when I suggested that he might have taken advantage of his friendship with the boxer, he insisted that this was not the case. 'It was Mike Tyson who asked me to write the book,' he said. 'I didn't approach him; he approached me.'

'But Tyson did call you a traitor on US national television,' I reminded him.

'Yes, Tyson called me a traitor, but he never called me a liar,' Torres said.

According to Torres, Tyson and a friend once bedded 24 women in one night. Tyson also allegedly told Torres that the best punch he had ever thrown was at his TV actress wife, Robin Givens. Torres claimed that Tyson once told him: 'I like to hurt women when I make love to them. I like to hear them scream with pain, to see them bleed. It gives me pleasure.'

Tyson denied making the remarks. 'Perhaps there are some people who want to believe it,' he said, 'but it's absurd.'

Little did Tyson know that when Douglas knocked him out in Tokyo, the long, dark night of his life had already begun. A year later he was to meet Desiree Washington in an Indianapolis hotel room – and his life would be changed for ever.

Sentenced to ten years' imprisonment by Judge Patricia Gifford after being convicted of rape and 'criminal deviate conduct', Tyson was thrown a lifeline less than four years after being indicted when he was released from prison in March 1995. Inevitably, Tyson decided to return to the ring.

However, stoppage victories over Peter McNeeley and Buster Mathis did little to convince the critics. It was only when he battered Frank Bruno (by then the WBC heavyweight champion) into defeat in three rounds, a year after he had regained his freedom, that the cynics were prepared to admit that Tyson was back with a bang.

UNIONS

Professional boxing is not easily unionized – there have been many failed attempts in the past – so the success of the Professional Boxers Association in Britain must be a source of satisfaction for Barry McGuigan, the former WBA featherweight champion, who was largely responsible for turning the dream into reality in February 1993.

Unlike many other boxing unions that have been established elsewhere in the world, the PBA appears to be going from strength to strength. The Association's infrastructure not only includes the patrons, officers and management committee, but also highly motivated individuals to represent boxers on an area basis.

The objects of the PBA, as outlined in their draft constitution in 1992, are:

1 To promote and protect the interests of members and former members.
2 To protect the rights including contractual and (where applicable) employment rights of members connected with professional boxing.
3 To provide assistance, including legal assistance, where the PBA in its absolute discretion deems appropriate in any matters arising out of a member's involvement in professional boxing.
4 To establish and/or administer funds for the benefit of members and former members or for such other purposes as the PBA in its absolute discretion deems appropriate.

McGuigan made sure he brought out all the big guns of British boxing for the first meeting of the association. Among those present at the Whitbread Brewery in the City of London were Lennox Lewis,

Chris Eubank, Steve Collins, Dave McAuley, Lloyd Honeyghan and Colin McMillan, as well as former fighters Henry Cooper, John Conteh, Billy Walker, Jim McDonnell and Mark Kaylor. Over 60 fighters, past and present, attended the inaugural meeting.

A formal meeting with senior members of the British Boxing Board of Control is held on a quarterly basis, and the PBA is also working towards developing closer links with the associations of other professional sports people.

One of the earliest boxing unions was established in South Africa. The South African Professional Boxers Union came into being after the First World War and was only dissolved when boxing in South Africa was legalized by an act of parliament in 1923.

Several attempts have been made to establish boxers' unions in the United States. On 29 May 1937 a letter from former world heavyweight champion Jack Dempsey appeared in the *New York Times* pleading for the formation of a union to assist the hundreds of 'half-blind, mentally-deficient former ringmen who stalk about in the city'.

'Surely, there can be no opposition to such a plan,' Dempsey

Ike Williams, the former world lightweight champion, attempted to form a boxers' union in the United States in 1946.

wrote. In an editor's note, the *Times* called the letter a good idea and claimed that Dempsey had the prestige to get the plan off the drawing board. They were wrong, of course, and nine years later it was world lightweight champion Ike Williams who called for the formation of a union to counter the powerful International Boxing Managers Guild.

In 1986, a strike by more than 250 fighters led to the creation of a boxers' union in Mexico. The boxers refused to accept the meagre payments offered to them by promoter Hilario Flores for fights at Mexico City's La Arena Colisseo. The labour action forced the cancellation of a dozen boxing tournaments, including those broadcast by Mexico's huge communication conglomerate, Televisa. Flores eventually agreed to meet the boxers' demands.

UNTOUCHABLES

Of the hundreds – possibly even thousands – of men who have held world titles, only five have retired from the ring without suffering a single defeat throughout their career. Two were champions before the turn of the century, one had a total of only 16 professional fights, one was a heavyweight and the other had his career cut short when he fell foul of the law.

Rocky Marciano, who boxed as a professional from 1947 until he announced his retirement as undefeated heavyweight champion of the world on 27 April 1956, remains the only heavyweight champion to have retired with an unblemished record (49 fights, 49 wins).

James J Jeffries and Muhammad Ali, both of whom retired as undefeated champions (although under different circumstances), were beaten in comeback fights. And Larry Holmes was within one fight of matching Marciano's record of 49–0 when he was beaten by Michael Spinks in fight No 48 in April 1986.

Jack McAuliffe and Jimmy Barry both boxed during the transitional period from bareknuckles to gloves. McAuliffe, who was world lightweight champion from 1887 until 1897, boxed under both the London Prize Ring Rules and the Queensberry Rules.

McAuliffe came close to suffering his first defeat when he was matched with Jem Carney, the English champion, late in 1887. Carney was evidently getting on top in the fight when the American's supporters broke into the ring in the 74th round and the referee was obliged to call the fight a draw. McAuliffe retired unbeaten in 1897, having won 41 of his 52 fights, drawn nine and boxed two no decisions.

Barry is listed in the record books as having been the world bantamweight champion from 1894 until he retired undefeated in 1899. After knocking out Jack Levy in 17 rounds in 1893 for the

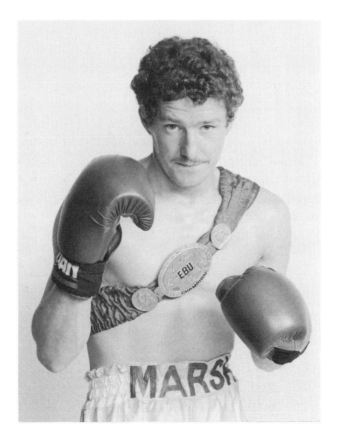

Terry Marsh, the former IBF world junior welterweight champion, was unbeaten as a professional.

world's 100-pound title, he travelled to England to fight Walter Croot for the bantamweight title in 1897. The fight took place at the National Sporting Club in London and three days after he was knocked out in the 20th round, Croot died from his injuries. Of the nine fights Barry had after this tragedy, only one was recorded as a victory while the other eight all ended in draws.

The other two men to have remained unbeaten throughout their professional careers were little known as world champions, both because they were early IBF titleholders and one because his career was cut short when he was imprisoned for attempted murder.

Ji-Won Kim of Korea won the IBF junior featherweight title in his 14th fight, knocking out Seung-Il Suh in the tenth round in Seoul in January 1985. Kim made four successful title defences before retiring from the ring in 1986. His total ring record reads: 16 fights, 15 wins, one draw.

Terry Marsh of England became the IBF junior welterweight champion in March 1987 when he stopped Joe Manley in ten rounds in Basildon. Marsh defended the title only once, stopping Akio Kameda in six rounds in London later in the same year, before he became involved in an attempted murder charge. When the British boxer's career was cut short he was undefeated in 26 fights (25 wins, one draw). Marsh was later acquitted of the charge.

Many other boxers have missed joining the list of boxing's untouchables because of a single setback. Julio Cesar Chavez was hoping to achieve 100 victories and then retire when he lost fight No 91 to Frankie Randall on 29 January 1994. Chavez boxed for 13 years, 11 months and 24 days without a loss on his record.

VENUES

Marlon Brando put it into words in that famous film, *On the Waterfront.* 'I could've been a contender,' he told his brother

Charlie. 'I could've been somebody. I could've fought in the Garden.'

There was a time when almost everyone in boxing wanted to fight in the Garden. That was back in the 1930s, 1940s and 1950s when New York's legendary Madison Square Garden was unquestionably the mecca of boxing. Even *The Ring* magazine had its offices in the building.

However, the advent of television and the growth of the gambling casinos in Las Vegas and Atlantic City changed all that. Today the Garden is better known for its past rather than its future. And besides, they closed the boxing department in the summer of 1993, only to reopen the main arena for fights late in 1995.

There were four Gardens altogether. The original, built in 1871, stood on Madison Square. Destroyed in 1889, the second Garden was built a year later on Madison Avenue. This became the house of boxing until 1925. The third Garden stood between Eighth and Ninth Avenues and between 49th and 50th Streets and served boxing until 1968. The fourth Garden played host to the heavyweight fight between Joe Frazier and Buster Mathis on 4 March 1968 and was also the venue used for the first fight between Frazier and Muhammad Ali on 8 March 1971.

Many world championship fights were staged in the four Gardens, and it's worth noting that no fewer than 20 world heavyweight title fights took place there between 1916 and 1979. Joe Louis defended his title in the Garden more often than any other champion. Only Joe Frazier, with five championship fights, came close to equalling the eight of Louis.

Muhammad Ali defended his title there three times and had his second comeback fight in the Garden in 1970 against Oscar Bonavena. Even Larry Holmes managed to squeeze in at least one title fight at the Garden, knocking out Mike Weaver in 12 rounds in 1979. After that most of the heavyweight title fights went to Las Vegas.

But while Madison Square Garden was the mecca of boxing for more than half a century, other famous venues also made their mark on the sport. Among the earliest was the National Sporting Club of London, which opened in King Street, Covent Garden, in 1891. Later the club moved to Holborn, then to Soho, and finally to the Café Royal in Regent Street.

Arguably the most popular boxing venue between the wars was The Ring at Blackfriars, an octagonal building that hosted two or three shows a week until it was destroyed during an air raid in the Second World War.

The Madison Square Garden of the American West Coast was Mechanics Pavilion, which was a popular venue in San Francisco until it was destroyed in the earthquake and fire of 1906.

When boxing followed the gambling casinos to Nevada, Caesar's Palace became the premier venue. The hotel held its first boxing tournament on 21 January 1978 when Roberto Duran retained his world lightweight title in a fight against Esteban DeJesus in the Caesar's Palace Sports Pavilion. The heavyweight title fight between Evander Holyfield and Michael Moorer on 22 April 1994 became the 100th championship fight to be held in the 'Home of Champions'.

WEIGH-INS

In an age when pre-fight rituals are designed primarily to meet the demands of the media, the weigh-in ceremony still remains the most important. And the most famous weigh-in ceremony of all time was for a fight that never took place.

It happened in June 1937, when Max Schmeling stepped on the scales of the New York State Athletic Commission for his 'phantom fight' with James J Braddock, the then heavyweight champion of the world. Schmeling had done everything that had been asked of him after signing to fight Braddock six months earlier, and all that remained for him to fulfil his contract was to weigh-in and fight.

On the morning of 3 June 1937 the German jauntily stepped on the scales in the commission office and was told he weighed 196 pounds. To nobody's great surprise, Braddock was nowhere to be seen. In fact, the champion was in Chicago preparing to defend his world title against Joe Louis.

'This body,' declared commission chairman John J Phelan, 'after due and lengthy consideration of the matter, finds James J Braddock and his manager, Joe Gould, in violation of the commission's orders and hereby imposes a civil fine of $1,000 apiece on Braddock and his manager.

'In addition, this board suspends Braddock from fighting in this State, or in any State affiliated with the New York commission, for an indefinite period.'

'The ruling is a joke,' said Schmeling, visibly stunned. 'It practically legalizes the fight in Chicago and leaves me out in the cold. What does it mean to suspend Braddock? He's going to fight Louis anyway, and certainly the title will pass to Louis if he wins.'

As usual, Schmeling had called the shots correctly. Louis beat Braddock for the title and Schmeling had to wait another 12 months before he got his title shot.

Schmeling's strange ritual once again underlined the fact that there is often more drama at a weigh-in than in a fight. Moreover, the battle of the bulge invariably has a strong influence on the outcome of a fight.

'A fighter's weight for any particular bout tells much about his performance,' said Dick Mastro, the then editor of the *Official Boxing Record*. 'If he comes in much lower than his customary weight he may be over-trained or weak. If he is several pounds heavier than usual he may be sluggish and slow.'

The weigh-in also gives observers an opportunity to judge the mental condition of the contestants. Muhammad Ali (then still known as Cassius Clay) deliberately acted like a wild man at the weigh-in for his first fight with Sonny Liston, and fooled everyone into believing that he was afraid of the champion.

So convincing was Clay's performance that rumours swept Miami Beach's Convention Hall that Cassius was not going to show up for the fight and that the thin line of hysteria he had trod during the morning weigh-in had become full-scale fear.

When Clay's pulse rate was checked at the morning weigh-in it

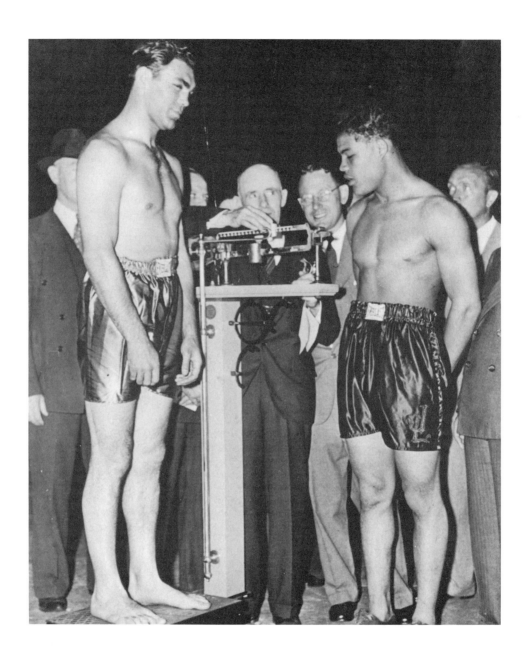

Max Schmeling and Joe Louis weigh-in for their first fight in New York in 1936.

was said to be around 120, more than double his norm of 54. But 45 minutes before the fight, Clay's pulse was 64, the same as Liston's.

Nowadays most weigh-ins take place 24 hours before the fight, but there was a time when weigh-ins took place at the ringside.

Jimmy Wilde, the then world flyweight champion, insisted on two weigh-ins for his fight with Pete Herman in London in 1921.

The first was to be held at midday as usual, and the second at the ringside immediately prior to the start of the contest. Wilde believed this would deprive the American of eating a big steak after coming off the scales the first time. But while the clause was duly written into Wilde's contract, it was omitted from that of the American.

When Herman refused to weigh-in again at the ringside, Wilde dug in his heels and refused to go on with the fight. Only the arrival of the Prince of Wales, a great admirer of Jimmy, persuaded Wilde to change his mind. Not that it mattered in the end: Wilde was knocked out in the 17th round.

While Clay may have fooled Liston and Herman may unwittingly have tricked Wilde, the weigh-in ceremony often serves as a tip-off as to a boxer's physical and mental condition. It is also one of the oldest rituals of the prize ring.

WOMEN

It seems that in boxing, the best man for the job is often a woman. The 'weaker sex' have proved surprisingly adept at assuming a variety of roles in a sport that was once a bastion of male chauvinism. Not only are women now recognized by the boxing establishment, they are respected for their contribution to the sport.

The day was won, I fancy, in the late 1940s when Miss Baby Bear James was issued a referee's licence in Kansas City, Miss Sussie Reece began announcing fights in Philadelphia and Mrs Eva Shain

became the first woman to judge a world heavyweight championship fight.

Such milestones have gone largely unheralded in the world of
boxing, probably because the fight game is still essentially a man's
world. But the days when women were barred from the ringside are
long gone. Women are now even welcome to box as amateurs,
following the decision of the 13th IABA congress in Beijing, in
November 1993 to sanction women boxing in international IABA
competitions.

And yet, although the first woman to gain distinction in the ring
was Elizabeth Wilkinson in 1722 (her fight with Hannah Hyfield was
reported by a London newspaper), and the *Police Gazette*
recognized Hattie Leslie of Buffalo as world champion in the 1880s,
it is largely as promoters, administrators, managers and publicists
that women have made their mark.

In the forefront of the female revolution in boxing was Mrs Bella
Burge, who succeeded her husband Dick as the promoter at The
Ring, Blackfriars, London, after his death during the First World War.
Bella promoted at The Ring until it was destroyed by German
bombers during the Second World War.

Eileen Eaton took over control of the Olympic Auditorium in Los
Angeles under similar circumstances when her husband Cal died
towards the end of the Second World War. Mrs Eaton promoted
boxing uninterrupted at the Olympic for almost 40 years and only
tossed in the towel when she lost her lease on the old stadium.

On this side of the Atlantic, Mrs Beryl Gibbons of Bermondsey
became the first woman promoter to be granted a licence by the
British Boxing Board of Control in December 1969.

By the 1980s, women boxing managers had become almost
commonplace. One of the most colourful was KO Becky O'Neill,
who handled the affairs of WBA bantamweight champion Jeff
Chandler. Becky, a former vaudeville performer and jitterbug
champion, hardly stood higher than a dwarf and yet she spoke in a
foghorn voice that always got everyone's attention.

Chandler was 19 when he first wandered into the O'Neill gym in
Philadelphia and soon the O'Neills became like a second set of
parents for him. Becky once told a reporter that the first fight she

went to was in 1962. 'I saw a lot of blood that night and that made me say I wasn't coming back any more,' she recalled. 'Then one night Willie put on his coat. I asked him where he was going and he said, "The fights." I said, "Wait, I'm coming with you." I've been addicted ever since.'

A Jewish grandmother who lives in New Jersey in the United States has influenced the career of almost every famous fighter since the 1970s. What Eva Peron is to Argentina, Eva Shain is to boxing. Today she is regarded as the most celebrated woman judge in the sport, having officiated in fights that featured such legendary greats as Muhammad Ali, Larry Holmes, Thomas Hearns, Marvin Hagler, Roberto Duran, Leon Spinks, Mike Weaver and a host of others.

But her biggest thrill came in 1977 when she became the only woman to judge a Muhammad Ali world title fight. Ali was defending his title against Earnie Shavers at Madison Square Garden and Floyd Patterson, who was then with the New York State Athletic Commission, appointed Mrs Shain as one of the officials.

At the press conference after the fight, Ali was asked if he had

Eva Shain was the first woman to judge a world heavyweight title fight.

been aware that one of the judges was a woman.

'No,' he replied.

'What did you think of this lady judge?' he was asked.

'How did she score the fight?' Ali shot back.

'She scored it 9–6 in your favour,' he was told.

The heavyweight champion of the world smiled. 'She's a mighty fine judge,' Ali said.

In 1985 Mrs Shain was inducted into New Jersey's Boxing Hall of Fame. Ali was a guest at the function. Turning to the lady judge, he asked in confidential tones: 'Doesn't all that blood bother you?'

'No,' Eva replied.

'Why not?' Ali asked.

'Because it's not mine.'

Women are now accepted as officials almost everywhere the sport is practised and when Riddick Bowe defended his WBA and IBF heavyweight title against Jesse Ferguson in Washington, DC, in May 1993 three women were appointed to judge the fight.

They were Patricia Jarman, Sheila Hormon-Martin and Eugenie Williams. Jarman, who became interested in the sport after doing a boxing interview in 1980 as a TV reporter for KTNV-TV, admits that 'most people look at me and can't believe I'm a boxing judge'.

'I always wonder if I'm seeing the same match as my colleagues,' she says. 'You dread being out of line in the scoring, but you must have the confidence to call it as you see it. And you must be able to justify your scoring.'

It is not widely known that women boxed exhibitions during the Olympic Games in St Louis in 1904 and as recently as 1975 even the *Wall Street Journal* recorded the fact that one Caroline Svendsen had knocked out a Jean Lange in the Bucket of Blood Saloon in Reno, Nevada. Presumably the fact that Svendsen was a grandmother attracted the wide media interest.

In 1981, female boxer Robin Haukaas lost on a TKO to Angie Lopez in an exhibition bout held in the aptly named Liberal (Kansas) National Guard Armory. It seems that the fight was stopped by a red-faced referee after he was informed by Robin's corner that she could not continue on account of a broken bra.

American promoter Don King has shown an interest in woman

Anissa Zamarron (left) *en route* to beating Andra Gorman in New York State's first professional female fight, staged in Melville NY on 21 April 1995. Zamarron was San Antonio's 1994 and 1995 Golden Gloves Champion, while Gorman was a Maryland nursery school teacher and mother of three.

boxer Christy Martin ('The woman who fights like a man,' said *World Boxing* in its August 1994 issue), and the Women's International Boxing Federation staged the first ever women's pro boxing tournament in Britain at the York Hall, Bethnal Green, on 19 February 1994.

Among the many other remarkable women in boxing is Sister Liz Smith, a member of the Dominican Order of Catholic nuns in Dublin. Smith qualified as an amateur boxing coach with the Cabra Club in 1995. And most people still cannot understand how Jackie Kallen has made a success of managing top professionals like James Toney.

'My family understands that what Mom does is a little different, the people she works with are a little different, but that's OK,' Kallen said by way of an explanation.

And on the American West Coast, Lorraine Chargin has been her husband Don's right-hand man for years. The Chargins are one of the most successful promotional teams in California. Lorraine is known in the business as the Dragon Lady for her no-nonsense attitude.

Mrs Chargin added to the Dragon Lady legend when she disclosed how, on a visit to South Africa, a number of VIPs were invited on safari to a local game park. While they were in the park a rhinoceros came charging up to their vehicle. 'It took one look at me and stopped dead in its tracks,' Lorraine said.

Mind you, it's not only rhino who are afraid of the Dragon Lady. I recall how Mrs Chargin insisted that half the people at the Molefyane–Lopez fight in Sacramento leave the official weigh-in 'because the room was over-crowded'. And it was Lorraine who ordered several newspapermen to leave the Arco Arena and stand outside in the cold because they had arrived 'fifteen minutes too early'.

I once asked Mrs Chargin if she minded being called the Dragon Lady of boxing. 'If that's what it takes to earn the respect of boxing men, I can live with it,' she said.

YOUNGEST

Age has always been a factor in the fight game and the age restriction placed on young men turning professional by boxing boards, commissions and federations around the world has made it virtually impossible for anyone younger than 17 to win a world championship.

Wilfred Benitez, who won the world junior welterweight title by outboxing Antonio Cervantes over 15 rounds in San Juan in March 1976 at the age of 17 years five months and 24 days, actually turned

Wilfred Benitez became the youngest man ever to win a world title when he beat
Antonio Cervantes at the age of 17 years, five months and 24 days.

professional in Puerto Rico at the age of 15. In the majority of countries around the world Benitez would have been barred.

Next youngest to win a world title was Hiroki Ioka, who became the WBC strawweight champion on 18 October 1987 by outpointing Mai Thornburifarm over 12 rounds in Osaka. The little Japanese

Pipino Cuevas won the world welterweight title at the age of 19.

boxer was only 18 years nine months old, having turned professional at the age of 17 a year earlier. It was Ioka's eighth professional fight.

Several boxers won world titles at the age of 19. These include Pipino Cuevas of Mexico, Netrnoi Vorasingh of Thailand, Lionel Rose of Australia, Fighting Harada of Japan, Wilfredo Gomez of Puerto Rico and Chul-Ho Kim of Korea.

Youngest man to win the world heavyweight championship was Mike Tyson, who turned the trick at the age of 20 years four months and 22 days, by stopping Trevor Berbick in two rounds for the WBC title in Las Vegas on 22 November 1986.

Next youngest heavyweight to win the world championship was Floyd Patterson, who was only 21 years ten months and 26 days when he knocked out Archie Moore in five rounds for the vacant title in Chicago on 30 November 1956.

The claim that heavyweights invariably mature later than lighter-weight boxers is not confirmed by the record books, with many of boxing's greatest champions winning the title before the age of 25. Among them were Muhammad Ali (22 years one month), Joe Louis (23 years one month and nine days), John L Sullivan (23 years three months and 22 days), Jack Dempsey (24 years), Joe Frazier (24 years one month), James J Jeffries (24 years two months and 24 days), Max Schmeling (24 years eight months and 14 days) and George Foreman (25 years).

ZODIAC

Can the stars *really* foretell? And do the signs of the zodiac really have an influence on our lives?

According to a survey conducted a few years ago by a British employment agency, out of 10,000 temps on their books, an astonishing 75 per cent were born under just two signs – Capricorn and Gemini. The fact that Capricorn is the sign of business, while Gemini is the sign of communication gave the study of astrology a new boost, so to speak.

In any event, to put the theory to the test, it was decided to check the signs of the men who have laid claim to the heavyweight championship of the world since 1889.

Perhaps the most amazing revelation is that not one of them was born under Sagittarius 22 November to 21 December and that Jimmy Ellis alone was born under Pisces. With the possible exception of Marvin Hart (Virgo), Ellis is arguably the most forgettable of all the heavyweight champions.

Capricorn may be the sign of business, but the seven champions born between 22 December to 19 January make strange bedfellows. What on earth did Jess Willard (a cowboy who was more at home on the range) have in common with Floyd Patterson (who often took to wearing disguises), Muhammad Ali (who claimed that he could float like a butterfly and sting like a bee), George Foreman (that walking advertisement for cheeseburgers), Joe Frazier (who once fancied himself as a singer) and Tim Witherspoon and Tony Tucker (both of whom wasted their talent)?

It is far easier to find a correlation between the five men born under Cancer – Jack Dempsey, Ezzard Charles, Leon Spinks, Michael Spinks and Mike Tyson. All were physically small for heavyweights but while Dempsey and Tyson will be remembered for their killer instinct and savage punching power, mild-mannered Charles and nice guy Leon Spinks, who enjoyed the shortest reign of any heavyweight champion, remains a basket case.

Only two heavyweights were born under Taurus the Bull. At first, both were regarded as sullen and anti-social. Only later did we discover why Joe Louis rarely spoke in public and never smiled in the ring (he was told to keep his mouth shut and to show no pleasure in beating white men), and why Sonny Liston scowled a lot and sulked for days on end (he was illiterate and unschooled in social graces).

On the other hand, both boxers could hit like a mule's kick and struck such fear into the hearts of their opponents that many of their fights were won long before they climbed into the ring.

It is believed that Taureans prefer a smooth rise to the top and it is much more important to them (according to astrologers) to do the job well than finish it quickly. Well, Louis and Liston both had a relatively smooth ride to the top, but neither believed in working overtime in the ring. Most of their fights ended in knockouts.

Boxers born under Aries need to be boss and the five heavyweights born under this sign – James J Jeffries, Jack Johnson, Ernie Terrell, Bonecrusher Smith and Buster Douglas – certainly enjoyed lording it over their contemporaries. None, however, had very long championship reigns and Johnson was arguably the most unpopular heavyweight champion of all time.

An interesting trio, born under Virgo, are James J Corbett, Marvin Hart and Rocky Marciano. Lennox Lewis is also a Virgo but he was given the title on a plate and many still question his right to have been called 'world champion'.

Virgos are often bureaucrats who keep the wheels of society ticking over, and once their boxing days were finished Corbett, Hart and Marciano did exactly that. Corbett was nicknamed 'Gentleman' (which should tell you a lot), while Marciano was in great demand as a public speaker. Marciano remains the only heavyweight champion to retire undefeated with an unblemished record, even though Larry Holmes later claimed Rocky was not good enough to carry his jockstrap.

If and when Lewis regains the title he lost to Oliver McCall, the chances are he will also become a diplomat for the sport of boxing. His laid-back personality and carefully chosen words when speaking make him an ideal candidate.

Five champions were born under the sign of Leo, and according to astrologers they should make excellent politicians, generals and teachers. All I know is that at least four of them did not make good heavyweight champions. Mind you, Ken Norton, Michael Dokes, Gerrie Coetzee and Trevor Berbick still have time in which to show their other talents.

Actually it's doubtful whether anyone would make a better politician than Riddick Bowe, who literally turned Pierre Coetzer's South African connection into a crusade of sorts when they fought in Las Vegas in July 1992. Bowe also has ambitions to continue his education.

Speaking to students at Thomas Jefferson High School in East New York in 1993, Bowe told the youngsters: 'I'm going back to school. Y'all would make me happy if y'all would go to college, too. If I can do it, I know you guys can.'

Five of the men who won the world title were born under Gemini – the sign of knowledge – and Bob Fitzsimmons, Tommy Burns, Gene Tunney, James J Braddock and Mike Weaver all knew a thing or two about making money. Tunney became the first boxer to earn a million-dollar purse (against Dempsey in 1927) and then married an heiress, while Braddock did a deal with the Louis camp that entitled him to a percentage of Joe's ring earnings for ten years.

STAR SIGNS OF THE HEAVYWEIGHT CHAMPIONS

Capricorn Jess Willard, Floyd Patterson, Muhammad Ali, Joe Frazier, George Foreman, Tim Witherspoon, Tony Tucker

Aquarius Max Baer, Jersey Joe Walcott, John Tate, Pinklon Thomas, Tony Tubbs

Aries James J Jeffries, Jack Johnson, Ernie Terrell, Bonecrusher Smith, Buster Douglas

Gemini Bob Fitzsimmons, Tommy Burns, Gene Tunney, James J Braddock, Mike Weaver

Cancer Jack Dempsey, Ezzard Charles, Leon Spinks, Michael Spinks, Mike Tyson

Leo Ken Norton, Michael Dokes, Gerrie Coetzee, Trevor Berbick, Riddick Bowe

Libra John L Sullivan, Max Schmeling, Ingemar Johansson, Evander Holyfield

Scorpio Jack Sharkey, Primo Carnera, Larry Holmes, Greg Page

Virgo James J Corbett, Marvin Hart, Rocky Marciano, Lennox Lewis

Taurus Joe Louis, Sonny Liston

Pisces Jimmy Ellis

Sagittarius None

ACKNOWLEDGEMENTS

Property people claim the key to successful selling is 'Position! Position! Position!' and if I were asked to list the most essential requirement for a book like this, I'd have to say 'Research! Research! Research!'

I once asked the late Jim Jacobs, the famous American collector and one-time manager of Mike Tyson, whether he had referred to old copies of *The Ring* magazine when preparing a script for his film series *Greatest Fights of the Century*. We were surrounded by thousands of feet of old fight films in the New York offices of Big Fight, Inc at the time. 'Oh, no,' Jacobs said. 'We go directly to the best available source – the newspapers of the day.'

While I appreciated what Jacobs was saying, I found it strange that he and his partner Bill Cayton should ignore boxing's trade press, which is surely one of the best mirrors of the sport available at any given time.

In researching and writing the *A–Z of World Boxing*, I have made frequent reference to publications like *The Ring, Boxing News, KO Magazine, Boxing World, Police Gazette, Flash, Boxing Monthly, Boxing Illustrated, World Boxing* and *Boxe Ring* because I believe that these are a valuable source of information that no writer should ever overlook. And besides, I also think that it is time boxing's trade press was recognized for the sterling service it provides.

Reference has also been made to *The Ring Record Book, Pugilato*, Phill Marder's *The Boxing Record Book* and Bob Mee's *British Boxing Records*. The sport is fortunate that it has men like Marder, Mee and Bob Yalen to carry on a tradition that started in 1841.

A great many boxing men around the world assisted in the gathering of information for this book, either directly or indirectly, and in particular I would like to thank Bernard Hart, the boss of Lonsdale Sports Equipment in London, for the advice, encouragement and guidance he gave me so freely over the last two years.

Others who were a great source of inspiration and at times assisted materially with photographs and information were the late Chris Greyvenstein, Jim Houlihan, Lew Eskin, Michael Marley, Linda Platt, Teddy Blackburn, Jan Hamman, Ron Jackson, Harry Mullan, Nigel Collins, Dick Mastro, Peter McInnes, John Morris, Reg Gutteridge, Mitch Levine, George Luckman, Don Marks, Jerry Fitch, Mike Mortimer, Robert Mladinich, Beau Williford, Stanley Weston, Herb Goldman, Rinze van de Meer, Terry Gallagher, Mykel Nicolaou and Kenny Wade.

I owe them all a great debt of gratitude.

INDEX